Timeless

TYROLEAN

KNITWEAR

Recreating the vintage style

Linda Ivell

Timeless TYROLEAN KNITWEAR

Recreating the vintage style

THE CROWOOD PRESS

First published in 2022 by
The Crowood Press Ltd
Ramsbury, Marlborough
Wiltshire SN8 2HR

enquiries@crowood.com

www.crowood.com

British Library Cataloguing-in-Publication Data
A catalogue record for this book is available from the British Library.

ISBN 978 0 71984 114 9

Cover design: Sergey Tsvetkov

Photography: Clio Potter
Model: Annie Cullen

Typeset by Chennai Publishing Services
Printed and bound in India by Parksons Graphics

CONTENTS

ABBREVIATIONS

alt.: alternate
beg.: beginning
ch.: (*see* crochet st. guide, Appendix 1)
dc.: double chain (*see* crochet st. guide, Appendix 1)
dec.: decrease (by working 2 sts. tog)
foll: following
inc.: increase (by working twice into same st.)
K: knit
MB: make a bobble (instructions as in each pattern)
P: purl
patt.: pattern
psso: pass the slipped st. over
rep fr.: repeat from
sc.: single chain (*see* crochet st. guide, Appendix 1)
sl.: slip
st.: stitch
st.st: stocking stitch (1 row K, 1 row P)
T2B: twist 2 sts. (*see* explanation under 'Stitch Grids', Chapter 3)
T2F: twist to sts. (*see* explanation under 'Stitch Grids', Chapter 3)
tbs: through back of stitch
tog.: together
trb: treble stitch (*see* crochet st. guide, Appendix 1)
wl. fwd. / w.f.: wool forward
w.r.n.: wool round needle
yf: yarn forward
yo: yarn over needle

ACKNOWLEDGEMENTS

My gratitude extends across the globe, and to so many whose support has been infinite.

There are three incredible women I want to thank very especially, from the heart, for the part they have played and their talent, patience and love:

- Annie, I can never thank you enough for being the perfect vintage model, for your warm friendship and for the very special magic you bring with you.
- Clio, my lifelong friend and talented photographer, for bringing your remarkable flair and understanding of my vision in creating these stunning images.
- My Laura, my daughter, my angel, you have watched, encouraged, believed in me, kept me focused and inspired me with your sensitive creative insight. I am blessed to have your love all around me.

Huge thanks to Cygnet Yarns of Bradford for their incredibly generous support of the book, providing such beautiful wool and encouraging my endeavours.

Very special thanks to the wonderful staff at Gloucestershire Warwickshire Steam Railway, who were so welcoming and accommodating to us at Broadway Station in Worcestershire, for providing the perfect vintage setting and for arranging the glorious sunshine.

To the many friends and supporters who have helped me put together the collection of patterns and originals:

- Karen Creed and Rosie Gleave for the beautiful treasures of original vintage knitwear, and to Gabriella's LilyMothVintage for some fabulous Austrian buttons.
- Teresa Young, Chris Gough, Judy Dodson, Sue West The Vintage Knitting Lady, Deb of Juandah Patterns and Carole Tidy of Blackwater Vintage Knits, for drawing on their collections of original patterns.

My thanks also to:

- Heidi Cartmell for her expert post-production of the images.
- The Knitting and Crochet Guild, and especially Barbara Smith for help with copyright and sources.
- The Millicent Rogers Museum in El Prado, New Mexico for their dedicated help in finding the perfect photograph of the great lady in her Tyrolean home.

Very special thanks and heartfelt appreciation to The Crowood Press, who first lit the fire for this book and fuelled it with encouragement through one of the most difficult years our world has known.

I would like to dedicate this book to my knitting angels, the one who taught me long ago, and the one who has encouraged my passion all her life.

WE MUST Have a TYROLEAN TOUCH
A Jumper Embroidered with the Gayest of Little Flowers—Scarlet Daisies with Bright Green Leaves
for the Spring
MAGAZINE
6d
MARCH 1937
PICTUREGOER Weekly
June Clyde Sets a Fashion
BELOW we give full instructions for knitting a Tyrolean coat jumper pictured here, which was especially designed for the charming American star. It strikes an up-to-the-minute note and is exclusive to our readers.
Materials Required
Measurements
Tension
ORIGINAL TYROLEAN COSTUMES
Österreichs Trachtenbüchlein
afternoon.

CHAPTER 1

THE ORIGINS OF THE KNITTED TYROLEAN STYLE

The Face that Launched a Thousand Tyrolean Hats

When Elsa Schiaparelli revealed her first knitted Tyrolean hat in 1933, the innovative and lovable *enfant terrible* of the fashion world caused quite a stir. Even as a renowned fashion designer to the highest society ladies, she could never have predicted then that the style she launched would continue to influence distinctive knitwear into the next century; yet here we are, with every successive decade contributing its own contemporary interpretation of Tyrolean style.

By the 1930s knitted garments were becoming accessible to everyone who could knit or was now learning the skills, and were no longer the sole preserve of the privileged elite buying from exclusive couturiers. New and experienced knitters were encouraged by a growing variety of publications aimed at promoting the craft as one which was available to all, and from these we can learn about the timeline celebrating the new Tyrolean craze that swept through fashion and especially knitwear.

Fashion advertising and promotion in the 1930s focused on famous people and titled aristocratic ladies to endorse products and styles. The illustrious names associated with the first interpretations of Tyrolean style include film stars, society belles, vanguard couture designers, even royalty, all attracting public attention through the press and fuelling the desire to imitate their style (something still so familiar to us today).

The earliest 'Tyrolean' pieces – mostly hats – date as far back as 1897, appearing in drawn illustrations in the most influential magazines, including *Vogue* on both sides of the Atlantic. This reflects the growing interest in Alpine fashions, and notably with skiing for the wealthy at their elite winter sports playgrounds. In 1924 *Vogue* illustrated a charming felt cloche by Reboux[1] designated as Tyrolean, and by the early 1930s they regularly included features such as 'Going Tyrolian'[2], which celebrated the popularity of Tyrolean themes in theatre and light opera. The delightful yodelling headline 'Oh lee lay ee oh' appears in the 1933 article for actress 'Miss Whitney Bourne in the shadow of the Tyrol'.[3]

By then, followers of high fashion were familiar with millinery Tyrolean chic, but it did not appear in knitted form until later that year, created by Elsa Schiaparelli.

In collaboration with her powerful patroness and muse, American heiress Millicent Rogers, Schiaparelli started a fashion that still captivates us today. Photographed in November 1933 by Horst P. Horst, famed photographer with *Vogue*, Millicent Rogers (then Mme Artur Ramos, who was her third husband) wears a knitted Tyrolean style hat, which in true Schiaparelli style is embellished with a novelty woollen feather. That was it! A style was born.

It was the hat that everyone wanted to copy and make for themselves. The first to appear were patterns for crochet rather than knitting, most probably because of the better suited nature of a crocheted fabric, first released in America in early 1934 in quick response to the new trend.

Millicent Rogers, Schiaparelli's muse

Millicent Rogers was a firm friend and patroness to Schiaparelli, and they often worked collaboratively to create many innovative designs that always took the fashion world by storm. She was a wealthy American heiress, revered as a leading fashion icon and Industrial Royalty with a highly individual style, always with the spotlight on her wherever she went. As soon as she embraced Tyrolean style – and her own distinct interpretation of it – it was endorsed the world over.[4]

Millicent had a close relationship with Austria and the Tirol, having eloped to Vienna in 1924 with her first husband, Austrian Count Ludwig von Salm-Hoogstraeten (though their marriage and residence in Austria were short-lived). She returned to St Anton in 1934 with her third husband Arturo Peralta-Ramos, where they built their own home, Villa Shulla, in the Arlberg mountains at the heart of the skiing elite.

A serious student of true traditional Tyrolean style, Millicent reportedly made sketches from the costume collections in the museum at Innsbruck, and had her designs made up by local tailors, closely based on original traditional costume 'Trachten und Dirndl'. Local seamstresses made jackets, dresses, peasant blouses, quilted skirts and hats for her, all based on their expertise in traditional costume. Though it was unusual for society belles to dress in this way to say the least, she was committed to being authentic in her inspiration and to dress in harmony with her adopted surroundings. She wore these as her everyday dress when not in full ski clothes, and when her friend Diana Vreeland (writer for *Harper's Bazaar* and later Editor in Chief of *Vogue*) visited in 1936, she noted a particular Tyrolean jacket of hers:

Millicent Rogers in her customary Tyrolean dress at home in the Tirol in 1936.

> Millicent's style was her own, but its lasting impact was made through her friends, advocates, and admirers in the fashion world.[5]

Never without the attention of the press in general and the fashion press in particular, her influential friends – Diana Vreeland and Louise Dahl from *Harper's Bazaar* and *Vogue* – ran articles in 1939 on her Tyrolean lifestyle and commitment to maintaining traditional dress, following her return to America in 1938. Holding such sway in the world of haute couture, it was automatic for her style to become a main inspiration for the fashions of the day.

Even Wallis Simpson was inspired by her fellow American and followed her lead. For her wedding in June 1937 the Duchess of Windsor commissioned Millicent Rogers' own favourite designers – Schiaparelli and Mainbocher – to create the trousseau for her honeymoon (taken in Austria, naturally) in the Tyrolean style. The Windsors had their own undeniable influence on fashion and played their part in drawing elite social circles to Austria.

The continuous English attraction to the Tyrol is delightfully related in the preface to a book of illustrations taken from eighteenth-century styles. *Original Tyrolean Costumes*[6] was published in 1937, the year of the notorious Windsor wedding. This expresses Austria's attributes '...the peasant dances and yodelling in which English people take so much delight...and that it has become almost a second home to so many English people.' This brief but enlightening preface confirms that 'Austrian peasant dress has in the last few years so markedly influenced styles in the international fashion world' and prophetically 'The Tyrolean vogue has achieved universal success; it is the fashion of to-morrow *[sic]* as well as to-day'.

Even more significantly from the point of view of Tyrolean-inspired fashions, we are encouraged to be inspired by the traditional dress: 'If you want to make an interesting test of your personal taste, let these classic designs work on your imagination, then pick out something out of the ordinary and use it for a (design) of your own'. This welcome advice has been followed, using such details as inspiration in designing the Flowers for Laura cardigan in Chapter 5.

The 1937 book of Original Tyrolean Costumes *charmingly illustrates traditional dress from the Tirol and neighbouring Austrian states, taken from historical sources. This page illustrates costumes of Kitzbühel from the Tiroler Volkskunstmuseum in Innsbruck.*

'Schiaparelli's newest little knitted hat, extremely reminiscent of that which the Tyrolese [sic] *mountaineer wears.'* Stitchcraft, *November 1933.*

Britain's Response: The *Stitchcraft* Story

As to the rise in popularity of the Tyrolean style in Britain, we have an invaluable resource in the editorial reviews featured in *Stitchcraft* magazine, which was published each month by Patons and Baldwins from October 1932. Anne Talbot was their designated Paris correspondent with her finger on the pulse not only of fashion trends in general, but of knitwear in particular. Her monthly reviews are most informative, and sometimes surprising from our perspective, making many assumptions which history was indeed to prove were incorrect, but nonetheless are revealing of how the Tyrolean style came to make its mark in our knitting history.

Anne Talbot wrote for *Stitchcraft* from the first ever issue through to November 1937. We can make the most of what she tells us in that five-year time span, which turn out to be the pivotal years in the arrival and ever-growing popularity of knitwear in the Tyrolean style. She first makes mention in October 1933 of a knitted hat '...decidedly Tyrolean with a flat brim...and a stiff knitted "feather" up the side back of the crown', which must be the same knitted Tyrolean hat by Schiaparelli that was causing such a stir in the fashion world in general. In November she mentions it again more specifically and credits Schiaparelli's original design.

Anne Talbot would undoubtedly have had privileged insight into the emerging fashions from her vantage point in Paris. It was not until April 1936 that she began to include references in *Stitchcraft* to knitted jackets in the Tyrolean style, citing 'The Tyrolean feeling has crept in bit by bit, starting with the hats of a year ago [even though she herself had mentioned them three years previously] and is a definite 1936 feature.'

Studying her reviews, it seems we can attribute the first examples of knitted jackets in the Tyrolean style to a fascinating designer who was new to the Paris scene in 1935: Kostio de War: 'To Mlle De War, alone, goes the credit for all this chic originality...'

Lyska Kostio de Warkoffska was born in Baku, Azerbaijan in 1896. Also known as Lyska Kostio and from 1935 onward as

Kostio de War, she was a French actress and fashion designer. In 1935, she founded the fashion house Kostio de War in Paris, specializing in high quality knitwear, which made her especially famous. She is credited with creating the first knitted plaid jacket, which also became an iconic piece of 1930s knitwear. During the war years she moved to Argentina, but her Paris fashion house remained open until 1953. In 2017, the Maison de War was reopened by her great-granddaughter, Sayana Gonzalez de War.

The design by Kostio de War which Anne Talbot describes shows every sign of being the first incarnation of what we now automatically think of as a Tyrolean cardigan, described in May 1936 as 'a delightful little jumper of white knitted wool embroidered all over in a Tyrolean pattern of small wool flowers in gay colours'. Sadly any image of this has been lost in time but we have the description to fuel our retrospective imagination. Over the following months Anne Talbot gives us more tantalizing descriptions, as other designers pick up on the style, with occasional illustrations to whet our appetite further.

'Early Autumn in Paris' featuring a selection of illustrated Tyrolean-style cardigans (called 'jumpers') from Stitchcraft, *September 1937.*

The August 1936 issue of *Stitchcraft* features a two-page article with the title 'Let's go Tyrolean!' (curious that so many similar titles for 'Tyrolean' felt the need for exclamation – there was evidently something inherently exciting about featuring this style). Even in this dedicated article there is a conspicuous absence of any knitted pattern in *Stitchcraft*, even though it acknowledges 'the prevailing craze' and encourages readers that 'these inspirations from the Tyrol are good for other things besides clothes'.

In February 1937 Anne Talbot reports that 'The Tyrolean influence in knitted wear has gradually waned in Paris, but has left a definite stamp in that its colourfulness is still evident. The gay Alpine flowers are gone, withered by the frost of Parisian satiety, but their vividness...lingers on.' On and on, Ms Talbot, for almost ninety years and still going strong...

It seems curious that there are no Tyrolean patterns for knitted garments in the *Stitchcraft* magazines at this time when their own reporter was heralding the style (the only design which appeared in November 1937 has none of the characteristic colour work or embroidery). Nevertheless we owe Ms Talbot a debt of gratitude for her chronicles of the rise of the Tyrolean style in knitwear in the mid-1930s, month by month.

It isn't until the later 1940s that we begin to see Tyrolean patterns featured in *Stitchcraft* magazine, when they then become *de rigueur* throughout the 1950s as front covers. Two of these patterns are included in the Pattern Collection (Chapter 4) as Knitted for Best from 1949 and Cosy for Cold Days from 1951.

'We must have a Tyrolean Touch!'

Meanwhile, other contemporary British publications – *Needlewoman* and *Good Needlework Magazine* to name but two – were doing less talking about the style and more in the way of practical responses with actual patterns. There are superb examples which typify what we now think of as Tyrolean cardigans or jackets, with delightful variations to tempt knitters of all abilities. The earliest that research has so far revealed is from *Needlewoman* magazine of February 1937, with the superb example 'The Needlewoman Cardigan', which is offered as a full pattern, recreated in modern yarn, in the Pattern Collection (Chapter 4). Earlier patterns exist from 1936 as featured in American publications, notably Minerva's superb collection 'Minerva Styles the Future'. The Edelweiss Jacket from this is also included in the Pattern Collection as a fine example of colour work and embroidery.

STITCHCRAFT

STITCHCRAFT shows you here the inexpensive—and amusing—way to follow the prevailing craze. Look out all your most vivid odds and ends of wool, send for the special transfer, and set to work to brighten your sartorial scheme with these gay little flowers and hearts and so forth.

A PLAIN, fitted bodice of heavy white or cream linen (you can get the right sort of thing ready-made) becomes fetching to a degree under this treatment. Cut the square neck rather dashingly low, then tuck a modest frill inside. You'll like the result!

Let's go Tyrolean

14

August 1936

● Transfer No. 85, price 4½d., post free, from STITCHCRAFT, Halifax, England, brings you the collar and belt set ready to iron off and embroider, and a variety of little separate motifs as well.

THIS collar and belt set is guaranteed to rejuvenate an old black frock! The transfer brings you both items, plus a quantity of odd hearts and flowers to use for other things. Choose heavy linen again, and to be really peasant, add a lining of checked gingham. Bright red cord ties in a bow to fasten the collar, and is laced through six curtain rings to do up the belt.

LINEN hats are cool and comfortable, but apt to be ordinary. Here's the way to add that certain something! Scatter these enchanting little fripperies over the crown, and add a few wee flowers along the hat-band—it's all on the transfer.

INCIDENTALLY, these inspirations from the Tyrol are good for other things besides clothes—whimsical cushions, for example, or early-morning tea sets, or anything else that takes kindly to a dash of colour.

15

'Let's go Tyrolean' embroidery projects for 'an amusing way to follow the prevailing craze', Stitchcraft, *August 1936.*

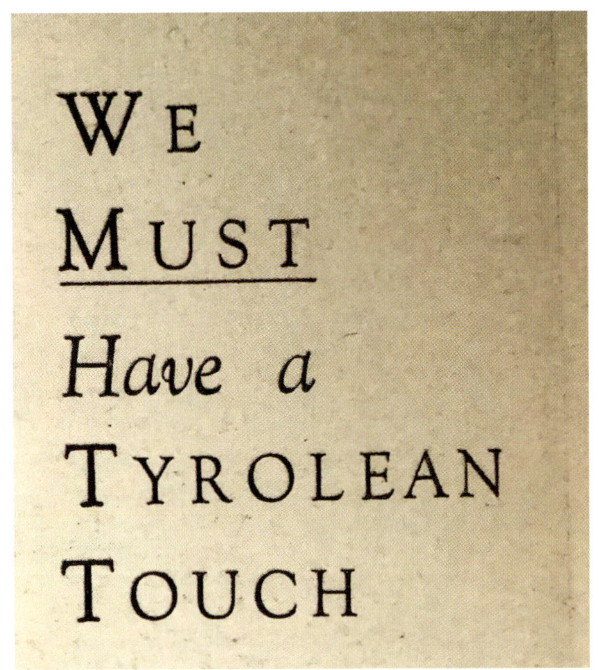

'We must have a Tyrolean Touch!', featured in Good Needlework Magazine, *April 1937.*

Good Needlework Magazine *for April 1937: 'A Jumper Embroidered with the Gayest of Little flowers – Scarlet Daisies with Bright Green Leaves'.*

'June Clyde Sets a Fashion'

Probably the very first pattern bearing the name of Tyrolean was published in Britain as early as 1936, designed by Copley's and endorsed by the charming American film star June Clyde, who was living and working in England at the time. First published in *Picturegoer* magazine, the story behind this pattern and its significance is given with the full instructions in the Pattern Collection in Chapter 4.

Popular Influence

Imagine the influence of the society beauties who adopted the Tyrolean style and their enviable lifestyles travelling to the elitist ski resorts of the Austrian Tirol, and add this to the rise of knitwear and the craft itself of knitting. Combined with the glamour of Hollywood and its celebrities endorsing the style, and the compelling coverage in the fashion press, the result is a formidable wave of powerful influence for a style which everyone wanted to share. Even popular songs about Tyrolean hats were the hits of 1937, recorded by no less than Gracie Fields and Billy Cotton and his Band (complete with yodelled introductions!) and promoted by the ever-popular Henry Hall.

Suddenly, every publication which included knitting and patterns began to feature something Tyrolean, with engaging headlines to convince their readers that their pattern was the genuine article, and even making it imperative to make something in the style. It was a compelling message.

'June Clyde Sets a Fashion', featured in Picturegoer, *Saturday 17 October 1936.*

Star quality

1936 was certainly the pivotal year for the meteoric rise of the Tyrolean style and many film stars of the day followed the fashion and were captured on camera wearing fashionable outfits and notably knitted jackets. Marlene Dietrich herself wore hats and jackets alike, and was seen in Salzburg accompanied by her daughter and friend wearing classic 1930s Tyrolean-style cardigans. The following year, Claudette Colbert was featured on the front cover of *Picturegoer* on 17 July 1937 as part of a photo shoot where she wears a distinctive Tyrolean-style knitted cardigan.

The Influence from Austria

It is worth noting here the part played in spreading the style by Austrian companies, including Lanz and Geiger. In Salzburg in 1922 Josef Lanz founded what was to become an international empire around traditional Tyrolean designs, still going strong today. He maximized the momentum that popularized the recently launched Salzburg Festival, which was firmly placed as a highlight of the season for international high society. No doubt looking to escape the horrors of the Anschluss, the Nazi annexation of Austria, and on the strength of the popularity of his brand of traditionally inspired Tyrolean designs, Lanz emigrated to the States in the later 1930s. In 1936 he opened his first shop in Manhattan as purveyor of fine Tyrolean-style garments for the winter sports elite. In 1940 he set up in Los Angeles, enjoying a roaring trade feeding that insatiable appetite for all things Tyrolean which was still evolving in the 1940s and onwards.[7]

'A Feather in her Tyrolean Hat', by Annette Mills, song sheet from around 1937, recorded by Gracie Fields.

Lanz designed two knitted cardigans in Tyrolean style which were illustrated in the *New York Times* in July 1936, featured in an article by Fashion Editor Virginia Pope:

> HIGH-STYLE KNITTING: Yarn and Needles Produce Latest Trends – Flower Patterns for Dress and Sports. All over the country needles continue to click, and justifiably so, for styles in knitting become better looking all the time. More distinguished designers are taking a hand in planning and working out beautiful garments for women who knit. Lanz of Salzburg is the author of the two sweaters shown [in the article], or rather their prototypes, for these were produced in this country. They are typical of the enchanting things worn in the Tyrol, with their snug collar bands and their attractive buttons. The patterns in typically gay peasant color schemes are embroidered after the knitting is completed.[8]

It may well be that these were the earliest designs for Tyrolean cardigans to be brought to the attention of America. Josef Lanz assuredly deserves credit as one of the first creators of the style, for after all he had extensive knowledge of the traditions on which to base his designs. No reference is given in the article to the Minerva pattern collection of the same year, 'Minerva Styles the Future', where both patterns appear, and similarly the patterns make no mention of their apparent designer. The Edelweiss Jacket is included in the Pattern Collection in Chapter 4 of this book, as one of the defining designs from the early days.

'Minerva Styles the Future', collection of patterns from 1936/7 with a focus on Tyrolean designs.

The darling of Lanz was fellow Austrian and beautiful Viennese-born film star Hedy Lamarr, who wore dresses created by him in *Ziegfeld Girl* (MGM, 1941), amongst other films, and who helped fuel the fire for Tyrolean fashion, as witnessed by the stellar list of customers who became Lanz followers as a result, including Marlene Dietrich. Knitted Tyrolean garments are still created by Lanz, and continue to be highly collectible, nearly 100 years on.

The Genuine Article: 'Trachten und Dirndl'

But what was the genuine article...and were any of these new knitting patterns even close to the original Tyrolean costumes which they claim inspired them?

The traditional style of Tyrolean dress and all its glorious variety from community to community is known as 'Trachten und Dirndl': *Tracht* refers to national dress and *Dirndl* means a folk or rustic style (though the meaning evolved to mean young girls and their style of dress). This translated into English fashion as dirndl skirts, which are deeply gathered at the waist. Each region of the Tyrol has its own distinctive Trachten, which is proudly preserved by their community, headed by their own Heimatwerk or association, guarding its heritage and perpetuating traditional crafts and costumes. Tyrolean costume must be one of the rare examples of a traditional national dress which still has an eager market and is still in demand to be recreated in detail – the list of thriving makers and shops is impressive.

Comparing historical illustrations and old photographs, including 1930s contemporary costume, evidence that shows where the familiar formula for knitted Tyrolean jackets originated remains elusive. The key garment was the 'Janker' or Loden jacket, but very few original images show this or any type of winter attire for ladies, who are usually captured in summer clothing. In a climate which plummets with annual reliability to snowy sub-zero temperatures, this does seem perplexing. The Janker jackets are recorded as being made of boiled wool for insulation and hard-wearing, with the typical leg-of-mutton sleeves and tailored shape, and often embroidered, but crucially none of them is knitted.

An original postcard of traditional Tyrolean dress, 'Tiroler Trachten', dated 4 November 1908.

Tyrolean buttoned-top pattern by Weldons 585.

The familiar embroidered flowers were featured on the corset-style bodices called 'Lieberl', but very few knitting patterns feature a bodice effect and this does not seem to have caught on in knitwear designs at the time. It is not a knitted style that has survived the decades in the same way as the fitted jacket or cardigan which has embroidered 'panels', but the 1940s pattern by Weldons captures this perfectly.

The Costume Museum of Innsbruck holds a collection of samples of knitting stitches, but an original version of what we consider a Tyrolean cardigan with added embroidery and coloured edgings remains undiscovered. It may not even matter how historically accurate the first designs were, but rather that we should just enjoy how the style evolved and how it has given us a glorious legacy of knitted treasures which still lives on today. It is rather like trying to identify the real King Arthur… Tyrolean style may use the name, some of the traditional stylistic details, and yet be far removed from the original costumes. Like Arthurian literature through the ages, what counts is that it has inspired such a wealth of wonderful creativity!

A political undercurrent

Tyrolean-style knitwear was beginning its long and happy journey in the later 1930s, but this was a time when European politics was taking a very sinister direction, and the background of historical events cannot be overlooked. As the Nazis appropriated traditional costume 'Trachten und Dirndl' as a nationalistic emblem, it is even more surprising that any related style, such as the knitwear, was able to rise above this and not be rejected by association.

Hitler attempted to enforce 'Trachten und Dirndl' as the only acceptable mode of dress for women but not surprisingly this was ultimately unsuccessful. In his insightful chapter in *Forties Fashion: From Siren Suits to the New Look*[9], Jonathan Walford explains in detail the way in which Naziism attempted to take hold of German fashions by prescribing the Dirndl as the ideal for German women.

Austria was subjected to enforced annexation in the Anschluss of 1938 when it lost its independence to Germany. Many Austrians fled while they still could, leaving for America or Britain to escape the terrors of the Nazi regime. Those who came to Britain did not always find the refuge they sought, believed to be German and being interned soon after as enemy aliens. Trudi Kanter, an established and talented Viennese hat designer, escaped to London in 1938 and the published diary of her experiences, *Some Girls, Some Hats and Hitler*[10], is a most moving account of the perception of Austrians in Britain during the war years.

In spite of the fear and rejection of Austrian culture, the fashionable Tyrolean style which came from the same country was never subject to the same suspicious discrimination, and continued to thrive throughout the war years. It is heartening for all knitters that this was the case, and whether from blissful ignorance or conscious choice, it ensured the survival and continued celebration of the Tyrolean style in all its glory.

Tyrolean Style in the Twenty-first Century

The legacy of Tyrolean style continued right through the twentieth century and can be seen in fashions of the 1970s, 1980s and 1990s, especially in knitwear designs. Even in the 1960s when fashion styles made some highly questionable detours, there are a few knitting patterns related to the style, mostly in patchworks of primary colours, but nonetheless claiming their Tyrolean inspiration. The huge impact of the Rogers and Hammerstein film *The Sound of Music* in 1965 should not be forgotten. Set in Salzburg, the Tirol's neighbouring state, the iconography is generally perceived, rightly or wrongly, as Tyrolean in style. A new revival of the 'Peasant Look' in the late 1960s and early 1970s, reminiscent of the 1930s trend, also drew on Tyrolean patterns for fashionable styles.

The 1980s saw a huge revival of hand knitting and Tyrolean patterns were reliably found in collections by all leading designers throughout the decade, such as the splendid colour work 'Tyrolean Cardigan' by leading designer Edina Ronay in her collection of 1988[11] and the wonderfully textured 'Tyrolean Jacket' by Debbie Bliss in the *Country Knits* collection of 1990[12], both still so relevant and wearable today.

The links in the Tyrolean style chain continued unbroken at the turn of the century, and under the revered banner of Rowan Yarns many of their leading designers brought out a new generation of Tyrolean-style knitwear. With the excessive volume favoured in the 1990s now tamed, designs of the first decade of the twenty-first century relate even more closely to the styles of the 1930s and 1940s, following a huge wave of revival for vintage styles in knitwear. Leading knitwear designers featured beautiful patterns in Rowan publications. *Vintage Style*[13] includes the 'Tyrolean' pattern by Sarah Dallas; an intricately bobbled and embroidered cardigan, also featured on the cover of this 2004 collection. Martin Storey's *Alpine* collection of designs for Rowan Classic in 2008[14] includes a number of superb patterns directly inspired by Tyrolean knitwear, such as the chunky wool jacket 'Tyrol'. Contemporary knitting magazines also continue to feature new patterns on the theme of Tyrolean knitwear, such is the everlasting enjoyment and interest.

Tyrolean style in haute couture

Far from losing its appeal after so many years, Tyrolean style has continued to inspire fashion designers of knitwear and haute couture clothing into the twenty-first century. The very height of international fashion focused on Tyrolean and Alpine style once again in 2014–15, seen most notably in the new season's collections by Karl Lagerfeld for Chanel[15] and Riccardo Tisci for

Cotton Tyrolean-style cardigan by Zara, Autumn/Winter Collection 2020.

Givenchy[16,17]. Tyrolean style continues to inspire, from haute couture to the high street.

As recently as Autumn 2019, high street fashion leaders ran collections of knitwear entirely Tyrolean in style, attracting huge popularity with hand-embroidered flowers adorning vintage-inspired shapes and great attention to detail.

The universal passion for Tyrolean style is as alive today as it was ninety years ago, and will continue to be celebrated for many more generations to come.

The Pattern Collection in This Book

The collection of vintage Tyrolean knitting patterns in Chapter 4 has been carefully chosen from the ones that stand out, not just as statements of the style, but also as opportunities for the knitter to recreate vintage treasures from a pattern that works. This does not include every single pattern that might qualify for the title as there are many (and not all of them would be worthy!), but it endeavours to be a refined collection of key designs focusing on the golden era of the 1930s, 1940s and early 1950s.

Some of the more familiar patterns have been omitted in order to make way for some rarer discoveries. There will be some presented here for the very first time to modern knitters, with original patterns offered alongside adapted versions. Techniques, colours, materials and finishing touches are explained to achieve an authentic vintage garment, along with new interpretations capturing that unmistakable vintage Tyrolean style.

The Tyrolean hat button symbol at the beginning of each pattern indicates the level of skill required to knit the garment. Patterns are graded from one to four buttons.

The Smartest Knitted
Good
AND
BESTWAY
LEAFLET
No. 826
3d
P&B
PURPLE
400 QUALITY
BESTWAY
LEAFLET
1640
3d
TYROLEAN JUMPER
EMBROIDERED WITH FLOWERS
6 ozs. of 3-ply; 1 oz. of Contrast; and Oddments
TYROLEAN JUMPER
6 ozs. of 3-ply, Main,
Oddments of Contrast for Fair Isle
BESTWAY
LEAFLET
1511
3d
7273

CHAPTER 2

MASTERING VINTAGE YARNS AND PATTERNS

A Practical Guide to Vintage Yarns

For the lover of vintage knitwear eager to knit from an original pattern, one of the first challenges is to know which wool to use to create the closest match. New and experienced knitters alike often take a chance when buying a modern yarn to use with vintage pattern instructions. There is much generalized recommendation for substituting yarn weights, but this chapter gives exact comparisons using actual vintage yarns as the starting point, comparing like-for-like with modern yarns and their own variations.

A vintage 3 ply or 4 ply is not the same as a modern yarn of the same name. Vintage yarns in these weights are slightly thicker than their modern name-sakes, which can be misleading 'faux amis'. The following guidance will help to decode vintage yarn weights and how to substitute these successfully with modern counterparts.

A note on tension

Modern yarn very helpfully includes an expected average tension on the ball band, but this does not appear anywhere on vintage yarn labels. Individual vintage patterns designate a yarn type, usually by brand, and sometimes by delightfully poetic names – Glengarry, Cryscelle, Totem – which do not give any clue as to ply or weight. The only indicator is to check the suggested tension given in the pattern, and match this to a modern yarn with a compatible tension. Note that vintage patterns usually give their tension as the number of stitches per 1″ or sometimes 2″ (2.5 cm and 5 cm respectively), where modern yarn states tension per 4″/10 cm.

If the pattern states a completely different size needle from that given for the modern yarn, go with the modern needle size recommended for your chosen yarn to achieve the same tension as in the pattern (but always adapting the needle size as necessary to accommodate your own tension results). The size of needles used is not the governing factor in this situation: what you are aiming for is a *stitch count* that is equivalent to that in the pattern.

The secret is always, always in the tension. Seen by many as an irritating side step and delay to starting a new exciting project, it is of crucial importance. It is the surest way of matching your work to the intended size of a vintage pattern with a modern yarn equivalent. The advantage of doing this is that once you have verified your own individual tension with a particular yarn and needle size, you will not need to run it again, and can assess other vintage patterns accordingly. It will also help to find the modern yarn that works best for you. Keep a note of your tension for future reference, knowing how to adapt this to the vintage patterns you will be knitting.

Some vintage patterns do not give a tension at all, or only give a tension size based on a complete repeat of the specific stitch pattern, which is of no immediate help in ascertaining which modern wool to substitute. There are still clues!

Vintage Patons Beehive 'white' wool in original packaging.

Vintage 3 ply yarn with original labelling.

The number of stitches cast with the recommended needle size suggests which weight or ply has been used (even if there are anomalies such as 2 ply knitted with 3.75 mm/9 needles, which is not unusual in the 1940s in particular, when less wool needed to go so much further). The direct comparisons of yarn given here offer a general guide to help with matching equivalents.

Vintage 3 ply

The majority of patterns from the 1940s use 3 ply yarn, a fine yarn which produced around 30–32 sts. to 10 cm/4″ tension knitted on size 3.25 mm needles. Many patterns also knitted with this on size 3.75 mm needles (old imperial size 9) in order to make more with the wool available. It is thicker than modern 3 ply, which is generally used today for babies' knitwear, and using modern 3 ply in its place will give results which are too small for knitters with an average tension, unless the needle gauge is adjusted accordingly to a larger size, which in turn will create a very open stitch and loose fabric.

Vintage 3 ply is not as thick as most of our modern 4 ply yarn, but this is the closest match available and there are some which come very close in fineness and the resulting fabric they achieve. Modern 4 ply has the added advantage of giving very slightly bigger results, which are often welcome in comparison with the small measurements that so many vintage patterns work to.

3 ply was usually sold in skeins or balls of 1 oz, equivalent to 28 g, and as a rule, *you will need as many balls of 50 g in modern 4 ply* as are given in the materials specifying 3 ply – surprisingly this is almost double the weight specified in a vintage pattern, but taking into account the slightly finer ply, and longer length as a consequence within the ball or skein, it seems to work out with fairly fail-safe results.

Modern labels also usually state the length of the ball of wool, but vintage labels do not, so this is not a readily useful measure of comparison.

Matching modern 4 ply to vintage 3 ply

Modern 4 ply has an average tension of 28 sts. to 10 cm/4″ knitted with 3.25 mm/10 needles. However, the real results can vary widely according to different brands. Shown here are a few of the popular brands and how they compare to original vintage 3 ply. This is not exhaustive, but gives a range of examples and their different results.

In order to compare yarns as closely as possible, each of the samples of 3 and 4 ply given here has been knitted in the same way: 30 rows knitted on 30 stitches using 3.25 mm/10 needles. The standard recommended tension for modern 4 ply is for 28 sts. to 10 cm/4″.

Vintage 4 ply

Thicker than our modern 4 ply, this yarn weight is not as thick as our modern Double Knitting (DK). There are some lighter weight DK yarns available today which come closer, and some of our 4 ply yarns that knit up more densely are also a good substitute. The tension given in the pattern will be your guide as to which type of yarn to choose. Some vintage patterns that specify 4 ply (of the vintage variety) use 10/3.25 mm needles, which if used with most of our DK yarns would result in a very dense, stiff fabric. If smaller sizes of needles like these are specified in the pattern, this would indicate that a finer yarn would work better than a DK.

One of the Patons annual Woolcraft booklets with the original 3 ply yarn illustrated on the cover.

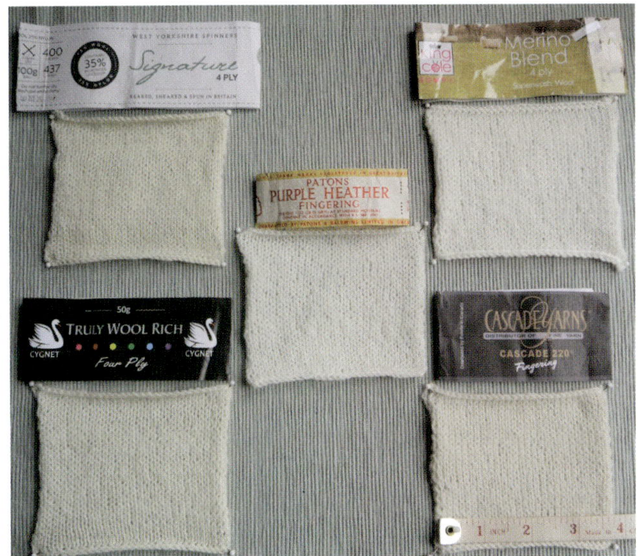

Original vintage 3 ply (centre) achieves an average tension of 30–32 sts. to 10 cm/4" knitted on 3.25 mm/10 needles. These like-for-like samples are each of 30 sts. and 30 rows and the four knitted in modern 4 ply yarns show which offer closest matches: Cygnet, Cascade 220, West Yorkshire Spinners and King Cole Merino.

If the pattern's tension states 6 sts. to 1" (equivalent to 24 sts. to 10 cm) then a DK would work well, using the needle size recommended on the modern ball band to achieve this tension, or adjusted to your own tension, irrespective of the needle size stipulated in the pattern. As with 3 ply substitutes above, the key is to match the stitch count to that of the pattern with the appropriate size of needles and a compatible yarn type.

Original vintage 4 ply (centre top) achieves an average tension of 26 sts. to 10 cm/4" and is thicker than modern 4 ply, but finer than modern double knitting, which has an average tension of 22 sts. to 10 cm/4" on 4 mm/8 needles. These like-for-like samples of modern DK are each of 30 sts. and 30 rows, showing the additional width this achieves.

Sizing up

Most vintage patterns work to a size 34" bust – often as a given, without even specifying this – and an easy way to size up to a 36" bust is to use a modern 4 ply with no alterations to the pattern or numbers of stitches. Use this with larger needles – 3.75 mm/9 – and it will work out to a size 38–40" bust. Similarly, if you are working with modern 4 ply and want to keep the size to a 34" or less, use smaller needles – 3 mm/11 – to achieve this. It can be that easy! In all cases, check your tension before starting, to make sure your work will achieve the size required.

Vintage Patons Purple Heather 4 ply.

As before, in order to compare yarns as closely as possible, each of the following samples of vintage 4 ply and modern Double Knitting (DK) given here has been knitted in the same way: 30 rows knitted on 30 stitches using 4 mm/8 needles. The recommended average tension for DK is 22 sts. to 10 cm/4″ on 4 mm/8 needles.

Comparison sample of vintage Patons Double Quick yarn with Sirdar Country Classic Worsted (used in June Clyde's Jacket in Chapter 4), which is thicker than modern DK and closer to vintage 'Double Knit'.

Vintage 'Double Knitting' or Quick Knit

After the war, towards the end of the 1940s, thicker yarns were produced again that are comparable to modern DK but, again, slightly thicker than our modern yarn. The names given to these appealed to the desire for speedier knitting, and were variations on the theme of 'Quick Knitting', 'Speediknit', and even 'Kwiknit'. These were often closer to our modern (UK) Worsted weight, which is between DK and Aran (usually worked at a tension of 20 sts./10 cm on 4.5 mm needles). This new weight of post-war wool is easier to match today, as we have such a wide range of DK and thicker yarns available in varied fibres.

The first Quick Knit yarns would still have been in pure wool until the early 1950s, when nylon started to be added. Many modern-day yarns include some synthetic fibres, most often acrylic, but our modern pure wools have a great advantage over their vintage relatives by being fully washable. Modern synthetics are welcome not only for their ease of care, but also for avoiding allergic reactions, even with wool content. Some modern brands of pure wool are specifically marketed as 'anti tickle', usually using Merino wool which is softer.

Thicker vintage yarns

These were very popular in the 1930s, before the war impacted wool supply. They are rarely given a name or ply (like our Aran, Chunky etc., which are more modern terms) and are identified by the tension, size of needles and number of stitches specified in the pattern. These were very rarely used in patterns during the 1940s, and only started slowly to reappear after wool rationing ended in 1949.

Vintage Patons Double Quick yarn.

Vintage 2 ply

Popular from the 1930s into the 1940s, and even more so in the post-war years when coupon saving continued to be a necessity, this very fine yarn was less commonly used from the 1960s onwards. Even if knitted with larger needles (which gives a very open fabric), it requires much work to produce a whole garment. It has had a resurgence in the last ten to fifteen years as Lace Weight, mostly for delicate pieces such as lace shawls. Our modern 2 ply is once again much finer than its vintage counterpart, and does not achieve the same finished size unless adjustments are made to compensate for the finer stitches.

As none of the Tyrolean patterns sourced are worked in 2 ply yarn, and this is not applicable for the Pattern Collection in this book, this weight of yarn is not compared here for modern substitution. Only Shetland 2 ply has retained its original application, favoured for traditional Fair Isle knitting, and indeed is compatible with modern 4 ply yarn.

Buying Vintage Yarn

There is something infinitely satisfying about knitting from a vintage pattern in original vintage yarn, especially if you have the good fortune to chance upon the very yarn specified in the pattern. It is hard to find, but there is still some out there and it surfaces in often unexpected places.

The greatest enemy of vintage yarn is moth, the dreaded tiny destruction machine. To be precise, it is moth larvae that are the culprits, devouring their way through any yarn once they have hatched, and the softer it is the more appetizing to them! Before buying vintage yarn, check if it has been invaded by moth – this is more difficult to see in balls and easier in loose skeins. The tell-tale signs are breaks in the wool which look like frays, or holes in the paper of the ball-bands. Breaks do not necessarily go all the way through the ball or skein but if they have, then it is a hopeless case. You could end up with a bundle of very short sections, sometimes too short to use, even if knotted together in any practical way. These are more useful for embroidery or colour work, if you are lucky, but unusable for larger main pieces.

Even if you cannot see any evidence of moths having gorged themselves, it is advisable to put the yarn in a plastic bag and consign to the freezer for a minimum of three days, ideally ten days or more. This puts paid to any eggs hatching and doing further damage. Alternatively – and even additionally – washing is the best remedy for dormant moth larvae. If you have acquired vintage wool skeins, it is easy to wash these before you start your work, and this also helps to address any potential shrinkage or colour running prior to making. If the wool is in balls, you can wash the garment once completed.

Caring for Vintage Yarns

Washing vintage skeins

To freshen skeins of vintage wool that will have been stored for many years, a gentle wash will revive them and have the added bonus of eradicating any traces of dreaded moth. Before washing, untwist the skein without cutting or unwinding the yarn. It will naturally fall into a large loop which will have the ends tied together. It is a good idea to tie additional scraps of wool around the yarn in two or three places along the skein to hold it together and avoid any tangling during washing.

Some vintage wools will give off a very strong smell of mothballs (naphthalene) when they hit the water, which was not previously noticeable. Though this can seem overpowering while the wool is wet, it fades away again as soon as the wool is thoroughly dried out, and we should be thankful to notice the distinctive smell as it is reassurance that the wool has been protected, at least a little, so far.

1. Use a little amount of gentle handwashing liquid or flakes, and dilute in warm water – never use hot or very cold water with the wool.
2. Swirl the wool skeins gently through and immerse for no longer than fifteen minutes in the water.
3. Remove from the water, gently squeezing out the suds but never twisting or wringing the skein.
4. Change the water for clear warm water and gently swirl the soapy skein in the clear water to rinse – repeat this at least three times until the water runs completely clear of suds.
5. Gently squeeze out as much excess water as you can without twisting, then lay the skein on a dry towel and roll up.
6. Leave for about an hour to soak up the excess water and then remove from the wet towel. You can now spread the skeins flat on a dry towel or drying rack to leave to dry naturally. This takes about one day to dry through.
7. Never dry wool directly on a radiator or other heat source as it will shrink and felt.
8. Don't wind the skeins into balls if there is the slightest remaining dampness. Wait until the wool is thoroughly dry before winding with your favourite method.

Proper wool winding equipment is a most useful investment. An expanding 'umbrella' holds the unwound skein and the yarn is attached to a separate secured winding mechanism, which spins the yarn from the skein into a wound and readily usable flat-sided ball. If you hand-wind the wool from the skein, the disadvantage is that the ball of wool scoots around the floor as you work the yarn. The answer to this is to use a wool holder,

A collection of vintage early celluloid and Bakelite wool holders with needle gauges in the base.

Collecting wool

If you have space to store vintage wool, collecting odd balls of colour can be very rewarding when you come to knit from a pattern using varied colours of one ball each. You will have a ready-made selection for Fair Isle knitting or so many of the 'Make Do and Mend' patterns, which deliberately aim at using up odd colours effectively.

which allows the yarn to be pulled through but keeps it contained. These were very popular for transporting your knitting, keeping the wool clean and dry. Vintage wool holders can still be found, in an array of glorious vintage colours, and are very collectable in their own right.

Storing vintage yarn

Storing unknitted yarn is a favourite with many vintage knitters and the 'stash' is a universally recognized phenomenon. Vintage wool needs a little additional care compared to modern wool, which is generally treated to repel moths. It is best to avoid plastic bags to keep your vintage yarnin, both for the wool and for ecological reasons. Plastic retains moisture and acids, which are present in some colour dyes (such as black dye) and which if 'trapped' will start to destroy any natural fibres, including wool and silk especially. Also, if any stray moth larvae are hiding, they will be delighted to find themselves in an undisturbed and enclosed space with their favourite lunch.

Wool and knitted garments alike should be stored clean – at least aired – after wearing and before storing. There are many proprietary products available to keep with your woollens wherever they are stored, to treat drawers and cupboards, and which have pleasant smells, unlike the familiar smell of old-fashioned mothballs. A time-honoured helper is lavender, which moths detest, and which is very pleasant as well as effective. Regularly shaking out wool and knitwear also helps to deter moth from settling. Remember to renew any moth repellents regularly to maintain their beneficial effects.

Dating Vintage Yarn

Different brands of wool have logos and labels which reveal their age, at least to within a decade. The graphics usually help identify when they were manufactured, and ball bands tell a wonderful story. Modern ball bands share a wealth of information, not just the weight of the ball of wool as on older yarn. You will have washing instructions, tension and needle recommendation, and yardage or length of wool in the ball. If only vintage labels had half of this to help modern knitters working from vintage patterns!

Here are some pointers on dating vintage yarns:

1. The pure wool mark was first adopted in 1964, and its presence on a ball band confirms that it would not have been made earlier.
2. Nylon content: until the later 1940s there were no synthetic knitting yarns produced in quantities available to the public. With the advent of nylon in 1939, yarns with nylon-based content only began to appear in the later 1940s after the war, which again helps to date them. By the early 1950s, nylon became a fashion aspiration, and was just beginning to become available as a knitting yarn.
3. Surprisingly, acrylic was first manufactured as early as 1893, but only began to make an appearance as knitting yarn from the 1950s. It was originally introduced as orlon in the early 1940s, used in manufactured garments and not readily available through the war years, but very popular from the 1950s for its lightness and softness, likened to cashmere.
4. Once synthetic fibres were introduced in the late 1940s and early 1950s, manufacturers ensured that 'pure wool' was branded to distinguish it from any synthetic mixes, so a ball band mentioning that it is pure wool is likely to be from after this time, rather than from before when it was the norm.
5. Before 1965 and the gradual adoption of the metric system in Britain, wool was sold in 1 oz skeins or balls. Once metric measures were introduced, wool producers were also expected to show the equivalent weight of 28.35 g on the ball band. Though this wasn't formalized, its presence nevertheless gives an indication of wool that dates after 1965. In addition, this impacted on the weight sold, which reduced down to 25 g, in line with metric standards. Wool labelled as 1 oz only is therefore going to pre-date metrication.

Wool manufacturers Patons and Baldwins are a most helpful reference in dating yarns. In the patterns appearing in their monthly publication *Stitchcraft* from 1932 to 1982, they proudly herald new yarns and new colours, as well as featuring their range of yarns in the patterns included in each issue. Some of the names they were given have even survived until today but have sneakily changed their weight and ply, so be aware of these false friends (e.g. Totem, Diana, Coral).

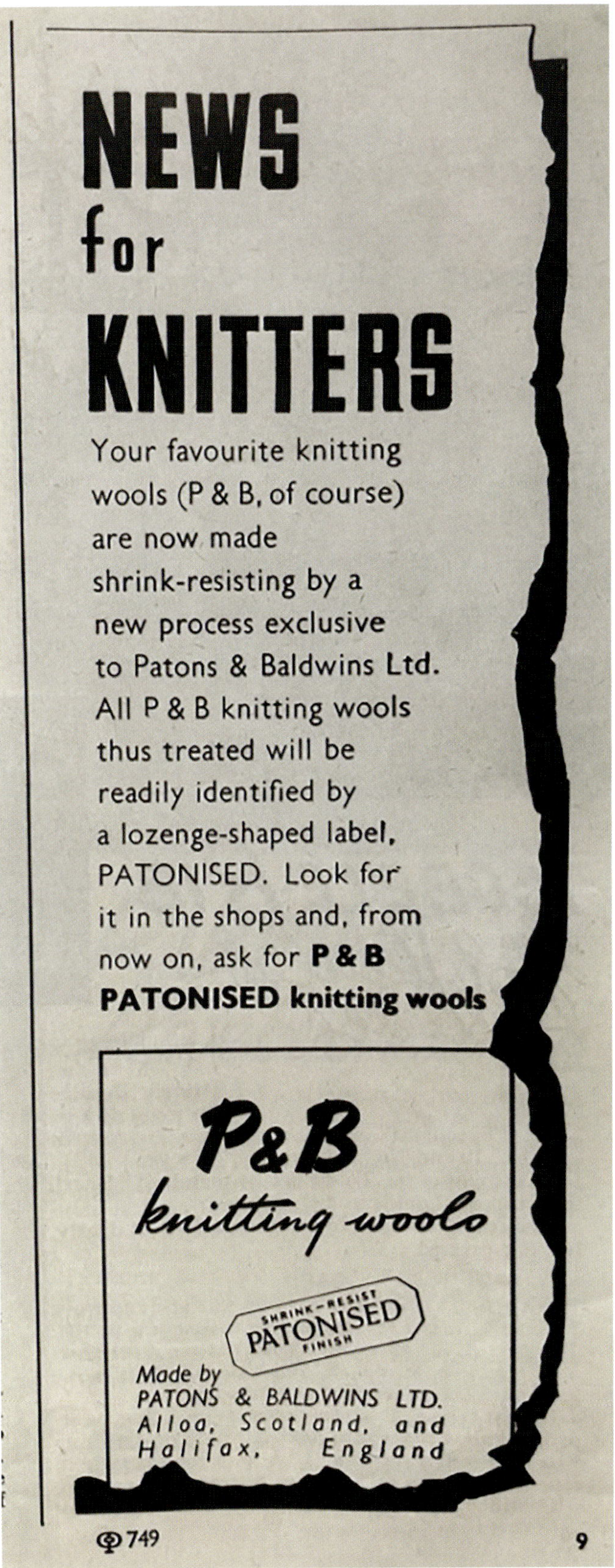

Advertisement by Patons of the launch of their new shrink-proof 'Patonised' wools in Stitchcraft, *September 1944.*

In 1944 Patons launched a new shrink-resistant finish to their most popular Beehive ranges of yarn – a process they called 'Patonised'. Once patented, this became included on their labels, so any ball band or skein label emblazoned with this can only be from 1944 onwards. For Patons' most popular Beehive and Purple Heather yarns, any ball band which doesn't have this printed on its label would pre-date 1944. They were rightfully proud of this innovation and you have to admire any manufacturer who achieves this in the middle of a war. This was largely pioneered to assist in the war effort for producing warm protective clothing and benefitted knitters all the more.

Calculating Quantities

If you find vintage wool you would like to use, Table 2.1 is an indication of quantities needed, so that you can gauge if there is sufficient of any one colour for a whole garment or just contrasts.

If substituting modern 4 ply to replace vintage 3 ply, then on average you will need 1 x 50 g ball for each vintage 28 g (1 oz) ball. This does mean almost double the weight is needed, and some of the modern finer 4 ply yarns will use less quantity, but to ensure sufficient supply this rule of thumb is reliable.

If you purchase 25 g balls of yarn for a vintage pattern, remember you will need more balls of yarn to compensate for the smaller weight than vintage 28 g balls.

Stitchcraft magazine of January 1944 very usefully gives quantities of vintage 3 ply yarn needed for the separate

Table 2.1 Typical quantities of yarn for average vintage knitting patterns sized at 34–36".

3 ply (vintage weight)	Short-sleeved jumper	5 x 1 oz (28 g) balls
	Long-sleeved jumper or cardigan	8 x 1 oz (28 g) balls
	Sleeveless top	3–4 x 1 oz (28 g) balls
4 ply (vintage weight)	Short-sleeved jumper	7 x 1 oz (28 g) balls
	Long-sleeved jumper or cardigan	12 x 1 oz (28 g) balls
	Sleeveless top	6 x 1 oz (28 g) balls

One of the jumpers from Stitchcraft, *January 1944, which featured a selection of patterns recommending quantities needed for 'Make Do and Mend' knitwear.*

elements of the jumper as pictured here. Although this isn't a Tyrolean pattern, the all-over cabling gives a very good indication of quantities, which would translate for a Tyrolean design that uses a textured pattern and contrast colours for edgings. The quantities given in the pattern are for vintage 3 ply yarn knitted with 12/2.75 mm needles (for ribbing) and 9/3.75 mm (for the patterned bodice), to fit a size 32–34″ bust. They recommend using size 8/4 mm needles for a size 36″ bust.

The tension given is 10 sts. to 1″ (2.5 cm) over the unstretched pattern = 40 sts. to 4″/10 cm (which will be smaller than stocking stitch due to the cabling pattern, but for the purposes of quantities is still a useful indicator). *(If substituting modern 4 ply you will achieve a larger size, also taking into account your individual tension.)*

Of vintage 3 ply yarn:

- The bodice takes 5 oz (142 g) for front and back
- Contrast colour for ribbing (welts, cuffs and neckband) 2 oz (57 g)
- Short sleeves 2 oz (57 g)
- Long sleeves 3 oz (85 g)

(Please note that you will need to buy ***double*** *the quantities in grams of modern 4 ply.)*

The Dye-lot Dilemma

Dye lot numbers appear on vintage labels in the same way as modern yarn. Most often the colour variations between dye lots are imperceptible, though sometimes they are very obvious, in which case it is more difficult to get away with combining them. Vintage yarn often turns up in the same colour but from different dye lots, and it does not have to be a disappointing deterrent to using the vintage yarn for a project.

If the differences are only subtle, and as long as there is sufficient quantity altogether (as indicated above) or combined with other colours, then it is perfectly possible to achieve satisfying results – and is very much in the 1940s spirit of 'make do and mend'!

If using different dye-lot batches for a main colour, work the ribbing or welts in one batch, leaving the greater quantity for the main parts and body. If you start with the fronts, then work the sleeves and lastly the back, any inevitable variations will be less noticeable. Working sleeves both at the same time, and fronts in the same way, ensures that if one batch runs out then changes are symmetrical and less noticeable. 1940s ingenuity teaches us that if you make a feature of such challenges, they become a stylish design statement and will even look intentional.

Adding separating stripes, yokes or panels of different textures (or colours) will all detract from any changes of tone. The eye is very forgiving when moving across changes in textures and stitches, and with carefully planned placement of the different batches, and incorporating clever patterns of colour or texture, only the knitter will know.

Working with Vintage Knitting Patterns

Vintage patterns have survived extraordinarily well over the decades and are also available in abundance as PDF files to download from numerous sellers online. There is great pleasure in working from an original, though these may have become fragile, having added charm if they have been written on by

Original Tyrolean knitting patterns and knitters' collectibles from the 1930s, 1940s and 1950s.

previous knitters keeping their own notes. (The curator instinct prefers to keep the original intact and photocopy or download and print patterns from which to work, so that notes can be added or accidental tea spillage isn't a tragedy!)

Working from vintage patterns is not so different from working with modern, though the standard of instructions can vary greatly in their comprehensiveness and clarity, and many processes were often taken for granted, such as how to assemble the finished garment. The biggest challenge is usually in matching the yarn used to achieve the same results as the original – and this is described in detail earlier in this chapter in the section 'A practical guide to vintage yarns'.

Some patterns list every single row to be knitted in the instructions, which at first glance can appear daunting, but this is usually a much easier method than patterns which refer backwards and forwards to previous rows and workings, requiring constant cross-referencing (and greater potential for accidental mistakes). It is also encouraging to be able to mark off each row as it is completed as a benchmark to the progress of the knitting.

Vintage knitting patterns for colour work or Fair Isle designs often do not have charts of the counted stitch and row patterns or colours, but will list each row line by line, colour by colour. In these cases it can be helpful to translate these onto squared paper so that you can see the shape of the pattern and coloured areas more easily (as with the chart taken from the Bestway 1511 line-by-line pattern, offered in the Pattern Collection in this book as 'Forties Favourite').

Vintage patterns in English will work in imperial measures and not in metric, so all instructions will be given in inches and not centimetres. It is worth investing in a tape measure which shows both together to save constant calculations, where 1" (inch) is equal to 2.5 cm. Similarly, knitting needles and crochet hooks will be given in old sizes and not modern metric. A conversion chart is given at the back of this book for reference (Appendix 2).

In the patterns offered in the Pattern Collection in Chapter 4, all instructions to work the knitted garments give both sets of measures for ease of conversion.

Vintage Tyrolean patterns

The first of these from the mid-1930s were all eager to boast of their Tyrolean pedigree and so are easy to identify. The 'peasant style' of fashion was already popular before Tyrolean earned its own distinguishing label, and some patterns which have all the marks of being Tyrolean were sometimes called 'Peasant' or 'Hungarian' (Austria's neighbour and historical cousin). These tend to have more all-over colour patterns and less textured stitching than a more typical Tyrolean design, but are worth a second look for any obvious traits of Tyrolean style.

From the 1930s onwards, right through to the 1990s, many patterns with just a few coloured details claimed the label 'Tyrolean', but bear little or no resemblance to the style. It had quickly become a desirable label and a marketing tag in its own right, such was its success (for example, the vast jumpers fashionable in the late 1980s to early 1990s with no textures or edged front opening, but with coloured patterns of stylized flowers, more like a sampler).

It is also possible to overlook some patterns which don't always bear the title 'Tyrolean' on the front, but then refer to it inside, such as the 1940s Heartfelt Waistcoat in the Pattern Collection. It is all too easy to be drawn to the word Tyrolean in a pattern title to find that it bears little or no relation to the true style.

So many knitted pieces that are evidently and gloriously Tyrolean in every aspect are from patterns created in the 1970s and early 1980s, in the heyday of the knitting revival of the decade. The majority of heavily bobble-textured, extravagantly embroidered and deeply ribbed pieces that are heralded as the ultimate Tyrolean style are indeed from a much later time than the 1930s or 1940s. Such attributes began to be popular in 1950s designs (such as the *Stitchcraft* December 1949 design included in the Pattern Collection in this book as 'Knitted for Best') but only became more extreme in the 1970s through to the 1990s – when more was indeed more, much more.

These patterns have their own special charm and produce beautiful knitwear, but are apparently not in the style of the 1930s or 1940s patterns that were available to the English-speaking knitter at the time (though they may have closer connections to patterns available to German knitters not included in this present study).

All the leading pattern producers of the 1930s and 1940s – initially Copley's, Weldons, Bestway, followed by Patons, Sirdar, Lavenda and others – published Tyrolean-style knitting patterns, so it is worth looking out for their brand when looking for Tyrolean patterns in particular.

Dating patterns

In addition to the guidelines given earlier regarding yarn specifications, there are ways of dating vintage patterns which may be useful for knitters seeking historical authenticity. There are more than enough easily found dated patterns if seeking historical accuracy for a specific purpose or just for personal aspirations to authenticity.

Women's magazines are the best reference point for dating styles, with specific patterns featured in their pages. *Woman's Weekly* and *Home Notes*, to name but two, always included a pattern in each issue (often amusingly assuming that the previous week's pattern had already been completed), and always with a date on the front. *Woman's Weekly* in particular often reproduced patterns which were also printed as separate leaflets by their designing brands – notably Bestway, Weldons or Copley's – and offer precise dating for these to be matched. Alongside the patterns given in magazines, these also have advertisements by the various wool and pattern brands which show specifically numbered patterns and act as reference points for dating leaflet designs.

Copley's patterns were not usually dated, though some of the earlier 1930s leaflets that were endorsed by aristocratic ladies offering their style advice and notes occasionally give dates as very welcome benchmarks – and of course the 'June Clyde' pattern in the Pattern Collection (Chapter 4), though not dated itself, can be related to a precise day pinpointed in the *Picturegoer* magazine to which it refers. During the war years, Copley's little 'mascot' bellboy, James, very endearingly and helpfully donned a tin hat, so that we can at least scope the dates of these to 1939–1945 (though some were reprinted from earlier pre-war patterns).

The Copley's mascot, James, who featured on all their knitting patterns until the 1950s, and sensibly wore a tin hat during the war years.

The numerous needlecraft and knitting publications that thrived from the 1930s (many of them through to the 1970s or even later) are mostly dated, but not all. Many of these focused more on embroidery and sewing projects than on knitting but featured knitting patterns in tune with major fashion trends, such as the 'Tyrolean Jumper' from *Needlewoman* of 1937 included in the Pattern Collection in Chapter 4 (even though it is a cardigan).

Stitchcraft was published by Patons and Baldwins from October 1932 with at least three knitting patterns in each issue and with precise month and year dating. However, they only featured one specifically named Tyrolean knitting pattern in 1937 (and which itself wasn't typical of the style) until the later 1940s.

The *Needlewoman* magazine was first published in 1919, issued monthly and dated until January 1940, when it merged with *Needlecraft* (published since 1907) to become *Needlewoman and Needlecraft*, later becoming part of *Stitchcraft* in the 1970s. Most such publications downsized and reduced the number of issues to save paper during wartime, and *Needlewoman and Needlecraft* frustratingly stopped dating issues at this time. Their editorial notes and frequent articles featuring needlework patterns in support of wartime events give significant clues on dating, as well as working out the issue number sequence. Published by W.M. Briggs, they also issued their patterns as separate leaflets under their own brand name 'Penelope', and these leaflets can be dated from the magazines in which they had featured, which thankfully started to include their dates once more within the magazines during 1944/5.

The leading magazines for knitting patterns all reduced their sizes quite early in the war, in an endeavour to save paper and some, like *Stitchcraft*, cut down twice, and also reduced the number of issues per year. Whilst *Stitchcraft* magazines were all clearly dated, others, like *Needlewoman and Needlecraft*, were not, and the smaller size which appears from issue 9 to issue 10 is a further clue to dating from around 1941–42.

The series of knitting collections in book form by Margaret Murray and Jane Koster, published by Odhams from the 1930s onwards, can also be dated from the publishing code, where the last two digits represent the date. Some of their books were reprinted later but the photographs were not updated and these can sometimes look confusing. They illustrate knitwear styles which are obviously from the early 1950s, identifiable by hair styles, rounder shoulders, volumes of skirts, and often just by being photographed in colour rather than black and white. These appear side by side with 1940s designs, marked by their squarer shoulders, shorter cropped knitted garments

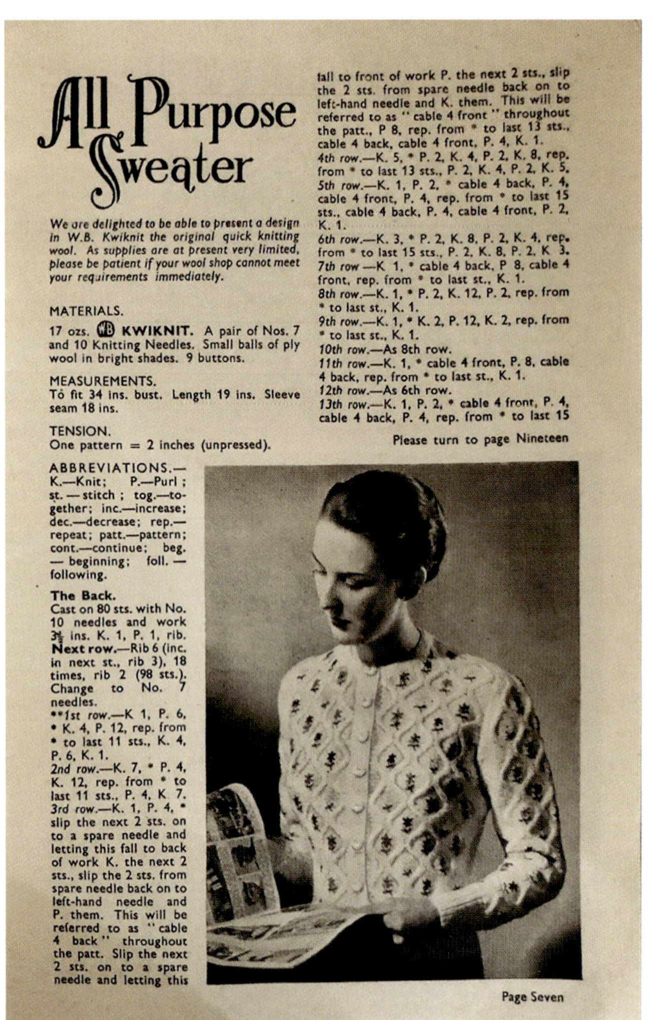

All Purpose Sweater

We are delighted to be able to present a design in W.B. Kwiknit the original quick knitting wool. As supplies are at present very limited, please be patient if your wool shop cannot meet your requirements immediately.

MATERIALS.
17 ozs. WB **KWIKNIT.** A pair of Nos. 7 and 10 Knitting Needles. Small balls of ply wool in bright shades. 9 buttons.

MEASUREMENTS.
To fit 34 ins. bust. Length 19 ins. Sleeve seam 18 ins.

TENSION.
One pattern = 2 inches (unpressed).

ABBREVIATIONS.—K.—Knit; P.—Purl; st.—stitch; tog.—together; inc.—increase; dec.—decrease; rep.—repeat; patt.—pattern; cont.—continue; beg.—beginning; foll.—following.

The Back.
Cast on 80 sts. with No. 10 needles and work 3½ ins. K. 1, P. 1, rib.
Next row.—Rib 6 (inc. in next st., rib 3), 18 times, rib 2 (98 sts.). Change to No. 7 needles.
**1st row.*—K 1, P. 6, * K. 4, P. 12, rep. from * to last 11 sts., K. 4, P. 6, K. 1.
2nd row.—K. 7, * P. 4, K. 12, rep. from * to last 11 sts., P. 4, K 7.
3rd row.—K. 1, P. 4, * slip the next 2 sts. on to a spare needle and letting this fall to back of work K. the next 2 sts., slip the 2 sts. from spare needle back on to left-hand needle and P. them. This will be referred to as "cable 4 back" throughout the patt. Slip the next 2 sts. on to a spare needle and letting this fall to front of work P. the next 2 sts., slip the 2 sts. from spare needle back on to left-hand needle and K. them. This will be referred to as "cable 4 front" throughout the patt., P 8, rep. from * to last 13 sts., cable 4 back, cable 4 front, P. 4, K. 1.
4th row.—K. 5, * P. 2, K. 4, P. 2, K. 8, rep. from * to last 13 sts., P. 2, K. 4, P. 2, K. 5.
5th row.—K. 1, P. 2, * cable 4 back, P. 4, cable 4 front, P. 4, rep. from * to last 15 sts., cable 4 back, P. 4, cable 4 front, P. 2, K. 1.
6th row.—K. 3, * P. 2, K. 8, P. 2, K. 4, rep. from * to last 15 sts., P. 2, K. 8, P. 2, K 3.
7th row—K 1, * cable 4 back, P 8, cable 4 front, rep. from * to last st., K. 1.
8th row.—K. 1, * P. 2, K. 12, P. 2, rep. from * to last st., K. 1.
9th row.—K. 1, * K. 2, P. 12, K. 2, rep. from * to last st., K. 1.
10th row.—As 8th row.
11th row.—K. 1, * cable 4 front, P. 8, cable 4 back, rep. from * to last st., K. 1.
12th row.—As 6th row.
13th row.—K. 1, P. 2, * cable 4 front, P. 4, cable 4 back, P. 4, rep. from * to last 15

Please turn to page Nineteen

Page Seven

Tyrolean cardigan pattern from Needlewoman *and* Needlecraft, *April 1949.*

Tyrolean cardigan pattern leaflet by Penelope 1381, as featured in Needlewoman *and* Needlecraft, *1949.*

and distinctive hair styles. Nevertheless these are treasure troves of vintage patterns. The 1940s 'Warm Red Cardigan' featured in the Pattern Collection in this book is adapted from one of these publications, *Practical Family Knitting Illustrated*, printed in 1946.

Vintage Haberdashery and Trimmings

It is the attention to added details which gives a vintage garment the convincing hallmark of style and era. Carefully chosen trimmings and embellishments can make all the difference to the finished look of a knitted garment. These can be buttons, braids, felt appliqués, metal zips, metal press-studs, and generally avoiding anything too obviously plastic, with the exception of original jewellery of the time (and many modern plastic buttons can be very good substitutes).

Buttons

Original vintage buttons can add the perfect finishing touch to a garment, giving it a convincingly authentic look. These are still easily available in a vast range of sizes, colours and styles from every era, and well worth hunting down to achieve the best finish, especially after the dedicated hours of knitting. An accurate effect is best achieved from finding buttons as close to those on the pattern's photographed model as possible. With these usually being in black and white, the shape can be matched if not the colour, which is sometimes given precisely in the materials listed.

The downside of sourcing vintage buttons is that it is a matter of luck finding the exact number required. If there

Haberdashery, patterns and inspiration for vintage Tyrolean knitting.

Typically Tyrolean vintage glass buttons decorated with edelweiss flowers.

Tip

It's a good idea to obtain the buttons before making the buttonholes to avoid mishaps...especially if the buttonholes are integral to the knitting and not on separately made bands.

Tyrolean hats in all their varied shapes and sizes, from felt hats to plastic buttons, postcards and souvenir brooches.

is only one too few, it is usually possible to adjust the number of buttonholes so that the buttons can be used just as well (this is explained in the buttonhole band section of the 'Flowers for Laura' pattern in Chapter 5) and this should not be a deterrent if you have found the perfect vintage match.

Modern buttons can provide an ideal substitute in most cases, and will be easier to find in larger numbers when needed.

From the 1930s onwards 'novelty' buttons have been hugely popular, and floral details are found in various designs and colours, moulded or painted, which fit especially appropriately with Tyrolean knitwear. Favourites for Tyrolean style are the endearing little Tyrolean hats which come in many cheery colours. These would most probably have appeared in the late 1940s or early 1950s, but if they suit the garment knitted, they can add a light-hearted touch to any era. Once plastic was widely available, it tended to replace the earlier glass, metal or leather buttons, and allowed for infinite variety of shapes.

Appliquéd felt hearts and flowers on the yoke of the Heartfelt Waistcoat from the Pattern Collection of this book.

Braid

Decorative jacquard cotton braids are traditionally Tyrolean, and can add a colourful touch to a knitted garment, especially if you would prefer not to work embroidery. These work well to embellish the edges, but if placing across larger areas of knitting remember they will not have any elasticity and may cause puckering where stretch is needed.

Wider braid can also be backed with stiffening and a decorative buckle or fastening added to make a vintage style belt, along the lines of original pieces made at the time.

Felt appliqués

Felted and boiled wool are very much in keeping with Tyrolean style, as seen in the traditional boiled wool 'Loden' jackets which are still a hallmark of regional dress. Adding cut shapes of coloured felt to knitted garments is simple and very effective, and these are an ideal way to add decoration as an alternative to embroidering. Decorating with felt was hugely popular in the war years especially, recommended accordingly in many vintage Tyrolean patterns, as with the 'Heartfelt Waistcoat' design by Bestway included in the Pattern Collection (Chapter 4).

Cotton jacquard braid, including vintage belts with decorative buckles.

Appliquéd felt motifs on knitted belt and braces from the 'Straight from the Tyrol' pattern in the Bestway Booklet of Tyrolean Designs *of the 1940s.*

Souvenir jewellery was very popular, originally carved from antlers or bone and later in plastic, mostly representing alpine flowers and hand-painted. These offer wonderful inspiration for embroidery and choices of colours, and add a delightful finishing touch to knitted garments.

Jewellery

With the Alps a favourite destination for tourists since the nineteenth century, all manner of souvenirs from the region have always been very popular. Once winter sports became firmly associated with the elite social season from the 1920s onwards, the associated souvenir industry boomed. The popularity of small pieces of jewellery rose with the newly available early plastics, or celluloid, alongside the traditional craft of bone carving. Beautiful little floral pieces were made based on the native flowers of edelweiss, blue gentian and pink rhododendron amongst others, and add an extra charming touch of vintage authenticity when worn with Tyrolean-style knitwear.

JUMPER

CHAPTER 3

TECHNIQUES FOR WORKING IN THE TYROLEAN STYLE

The hallmarks of Tyrolean style have not altered much since the mid-1930s when the first patterns became more widely available. The three defining attributes that have evolved to give Tyrolean knitwear its distinctive style are: texture of stitches of varied complexity; touches of colour with edgings and added decoration; and a front fastening for a cardigan, waistcoat or jacket. Additional features also became part of the Tyrolean-style vocabulary, such as neck or waist ties, seen in some form in many designs. With each decade, Tyrolean knitwear has been influenced by fashionable shapes, the yarns available, and trends in knitting styles. The characteristics have adapted to their own times while retaining the essential features that still define the style today.

The key techniques for creating the look are explained in this chapter, from simple coloured edgings to more complicated stitches and additional detailing.

Textured stitches of cables, twisted grids and double moss stitch used in the Flowers for Laura design.

The Knitted Foundation

Colours

From the early patterns of the 1930s, Tyrolean knitting has typically used a cream background as the perfect canvas for adding coloured detail. Though other colours have become part of the

Details of the diamond grid worked in the Annie's Jacket pattern.

palette, from pastel through to strong vibrant colours, cream has remained the time-honoured favourite.

Pattern designers of Tyrolean garments have always encouraged knitters to explore a wide range of colours, as varied as blush pink, scarlet, navy, powder blue to dark green. As long as there is a contrast between the background colour to set off the added details, the choice is as wide as the colours available (as like all fashions, wool manufacturers change their colours in tune with the times). There is no doubt that the most popular choice is cream, but this is not exclusively prescribed.

Most vintage patterns will specify the main colour which they will have used in their photographed garment (which will most likely be shown in black and white only) and this is usually 'natural' or 'white'. A cautionary word here: a vintage 'natural' is not the cream colour we would refer to today. It is closer to a light beige, even a fawn colour in our modern vocabulary. What vintage patterns called 'white' is what we would call 'cream'.

To qualify fully as a Tyrolean garment, there needs to be added colour. A plain coloured garment with textured stitches alone is not entirely in true vintage Tyrolean style. A garment with no texture but with characteristically coloured motifs and/or edgings passes the Tyrolean test! Red is unrivalled through the decades as the favourite colour to add in, along with green, then yellow and often blue. These touches of colour appear in edgings, yokes and collars, embroidered details, coloured drawstring cords (with or without pompoms or tassels to finish), and co-ordinated buttons.

Knitwear shapes

In homage to its origins in traditional costume, Tyrolean knitwear typically fastens at the front as a jacket, cardigan or waistcoat. Vintage patterns often call these designs 'jumpers', although this is not the description we use today for garments which have a front opening. Necklines are fastened high at the neck and V-necks generally only appear in waistcoat designs. No 'closed' jumpers or sweaters appeared adopting the title until the mid to late 1950s, and though they usually have the characteristic embroidery and textured stitches, they are a close relation, rather than the classic garment. Many vintage patterns from the 1930s and 1940s refer to garments which open at the front as 'jumpers', unlike our modern use of the term to define closed garments.

The front fastening allows for highly creative and striking touches of colour, with decorative edgings of knitted or crochet stitches and feature buttons or clasps. These are the touches that enable the modern knitter to add authentic vintage Tyrolean style to newly knitted pieces by sourcing original or reproduction haberdashery, which is explored later in the chapter.

The most noticeable changes to shape over the decades have been in waistline placement (if any), length of bodice, and profile of shoulders and sleeve tops. Tighter or looser fit is also indicative of the era of a pattern, altering with the trends and influences of the time.

1930s shape

The bodice was short to the waist, or longer but tailored with a defined waist, such as a belt or drawstring creating a 'skirt' or peplum effect. Shoulders were gently rounded or gathered sleeves accentuated the shoulder line – sometimes dramatically. This was a new era of knitting for all, with wide varieties of wool thicknesses, textures and colours available to meet the growing number of keen knitters.

1940s shape

The extended shoulder line and exaggerated sleeve heads made a strong style statement, and are now firmly associated with the decade. The body was close fitting and short to the waist, typically with 3.5–4" (10 cm) ribbing. Sleeves were most often

The Edelweiss Jacket from the Minerva 1936 collection, illustrating a typical 1930s shape.

short, and the popularity of waistcoats had grown. These elements were all influenced by the shortages of wool until the end of the 1940s, and the need to use this precious commodity sparingly. With rationing continuing until 1949 there were fewer options of thicknesses of wool and most garments were made in finer 3 or 2 ply yarns.

1950s shape

Defined by the return to softer shoulder lines and smooth sleeve heads without gathers, longer bodice but still with accentuated waistbands. New synthetic yarns start to become available with the wider range of colours these allow, and thicker yarns are increasingly favoured for their speed of knitting.

The popular peplum

The peplum appears in Tyrolean design throughout its history. Different patterns offer varied versions of this attractive feature, adding extra length to a garment as well as flair. This is achieved

A 1940s silhouette with strong shoulder lines illustrated by the Forties Favourite design.

Copley's pattern 1928 for 'Lady's Tyrolean Jumper Coat' from the early 1950s, included as Clio's Cardigan in the Pattern Collection (Chapter 4).

One of the Stitchcraft *designs from the early 1950s with the rounder shoulders, longer line and defined waist.*

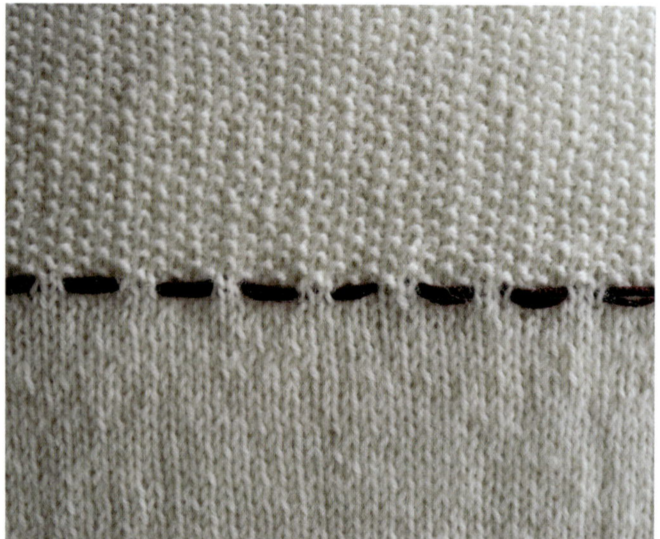

The Forties Favourite design, a 1940s Tyrolean design by Bestway, uses minimal texture with a single moss stitch yoke to economize on wool.

by gathering additional length and any volume with a cord tied at the waist, such as in the 1930s-style Evergreen Jacket in the Pattern Collection of Chapter 4, or with shaped godets, as in the Flowers for Laura Cardigan of Chapter 5. For less volume, longer panels create a most effective peplum in patterns such as the 1930s Copley's design 870 for a Lady's Tyrolean Coat, which offers long or short sleeves.

Texture through Stitches

Elaborate textured stitches, usually worked in the background or main colour, are a key part of the Tyrolean style vocabulary and act as a foil to the essential areas of coloured embellishment. It is perfectly possible to create a vintage Tyrolean garment with no texture, as long as it has colour work which identifies the style. Indeed, some patterns – notably of the 1940s when wool was a precious commodity and wool-devouring stitches were an extravagance – achieve the look magnificently with little or no heavily textured stitches.

The Lilli Bolero design, originally by Bestway, only uses small areas of texture but achieves a distinctive Tyrolean style.

The 1940s patterns pictured keep the textures to a minimum in an endeavour to save wool, using basic knit and purl combinations to create the effect with moss stitch, garter stitch and reverse stocking stitch, and using small amounts of coloured wools very effectively for embroidered embellishments. The predilection for texture in classic Tyrolean knitting is apparently prompted by the desire to create a framework or space within the knitted pieces to set off to advantage the coloured motifs, which are usually embroidered and floral in style. The choice of stitches and embellishments is unlimited and offers boundless creative potential for a variety of motifs and colours. The stitches used to create the textures are usually worked in the main colour of the knitting, with different combinations and variations, which are each detailed below. Examples given are all derived from original vintage patterns for authenticity.

A rich texture of cables from the 1940s Heartfelt Waistcoat pattern originally by Bestway.

Cables

Cables are a traditional favourite of Tyrolean knitting, and are achieved by twisting and moving groups of stitches across the main fabric, worked in a different order from simple knitting. A third double-pointed needle is used to move the position and sequence of the stitches. Worked into stocking stitch knitting, classic 'rope' cables are most effectively brought out with at least one purl stitch on each side to emphasize the relief. They can also be worked in more elaborate groups of stitches as part of heavily textured knitting, adding to the visual interest, such as in the Tyrolean Needlewoman Jacket in the Pattern Collection (Chapter 4).

Cables add a very satisfying dimension to the knitting, creating effective light and shade, but can be time-consuming to produce. Before embarking on a tempting pattern with all-over cables, it is well worth knitting some trial samples to assess their difficulty, as a whole project of cables is a considerable commitment of time and effort. As a suggestion, the front pieces may be knitted first, and if the effort of cabling is too daunting, the back and sleeves can be knitted more simply in stocking stitch or other appropriate stitch without affecting the overall result. The focus of Tyrolean garments is usually the front, and the experience should be an enjoyable one. Alternative cable effects, such as those given below, can offer an easier technique which doesn't require using a third needle, but without losing the surface interest.

If the task of extensive cabling is not too daunting, this creates a highly effective texture, though an all-over cabled pattern will require significantly more yarn. Cables offer great natural elasticity to a garment and therefore a flattering fit, making them ideal for waistbands, offering a most attractive alternative to ribbing.

The Tyrolean Needlewoman design uses an intricate stitch combination of double moss stitch and cabling.

A classic cable of eight stitches is worked in the Flowers for Laura pattern, defining the space for framing embroidered panels.

A dense fabric is created in this attractive 1940s design by Teddy Wools combining all-over cables with embroidery.

Cables make a most attractive alternative to ribbing for waistband welts, as seen in the Clio's Cardigan pattern.

Classic rope cable

Classic cables are worked by slipping part of the number of stitches (usually half the number) designated for the cable onto a double-pointed cable needle and placing these either in front or behind the main work, knitting the remaining stitches first, and completed by knitting the stitches from the cable needle, and so twisting the groups of stitches around each other.

Worked on an even number of stitches. Example worked over 8 sts., repeating the cable twist every 10 rows.

1st row: K8
2nd row: P8
Rep these 2 rows once more.
5th row: Slip the first 4 sts. onto a double-pointed cable needle and place to the front of the work, then K the next 4 sts., then K the 4 sts. from the cable needle
6th row: P8
7th row: K8
Rep the last 2 rows 3 times more.
14th row: P8
15th row: As Row 5 (cable row)

Alternative instructions are given for 'mock' or 'flat' cables below, which do not require using a third needle, and create a very similar visual effect to a simple rope-style cable, but with less depth, making for a smoother fabric if this is preferred.

Note

If substituting mock cables in place of cables worked with a third double-ended needle, ensure the same number of stitches represents the cabled group being replaced – this can comprise additional purl stitches worked on either side of the mock cable to total the same number for this group of stitches.

A mock cable of six stitches can be an effective substitute for cables, worked on two rather than three needles.

Mock cable

Multiples of 7 stitches (P1, K6 for the 'cable') plus one P st. to complete. If working more than one 'cable' across a pattern, include additional purl stitches between each cable.
Over 8 rows.
If repeating across a row, work as P1, (K6 P1) and rep required number of times.

1st row: P1 K6 P1
2nd row: K1 P6 K1
3rd row: Like row 1
4th row (WS facing): K1, wool forward, slip next 3 sts. purlways, P3, wool back, pass 3 slipped sts. over the 3 purled sts., K1
5th row: P1, pick up and knit into the back of the loop before next st.; K1, knit twice into next st.; K1, pick up and knit loop before next st.; P1
This completes the pattern and resumes the original number of stitches.
6th row: Like row 2
7th row: Like row 1
8th row: Like row 2

Flat cable

The loose slipped stitch of this flat cable gives the visual effect of being a twisted cable, but without its bulk.
Multiples of 10 sts. (to include 4 purl sts. between 'cables' of 6 sts.) plus 4.
Over 10 rows.

1st row: P4, K6, P4
2nd row: K4, P6, K4
Rep these 2 rows 3 times more – 8 rows in all.
9th row: P4, slip 1, (K2tog) twice, K1, psso the last 3 sts., P4
10th row: K4 P twice into the next 3 sts., K4

Small mock cable

This is especially effective worked at the waist and sleeve cuffs instead of ribbing, and works well with finer weight yarns.
Multiples of 6 sts. (3 'cable' sts. plus 3 sts. between cables) plus 3 sts. to complete a row.
Worked over 4 rows.

1st row: P3, K3, P3
2nd row: K3, P,3 K3
3rd row: P3, wool fwd., K3, pass wool loop over the 3 knit sts., P3
4th row: Like row 2
Wider cables shaped in different ways work well with thicker yarns, such as DK or worsted, and are effective as the base for embroidery details.
Cabling is a very flexible feature and you can take the textures it creates almost anywhere across the knitting. A flowing arrangement of interlaced cables is created in Clio's Cardigan from the Pattern Collection (Chapter 4), where different-sized lozenges are worked as the background for the embroidery of stylized floral sprays.

Small mock cable worked over three stitches.

Mock cable technique

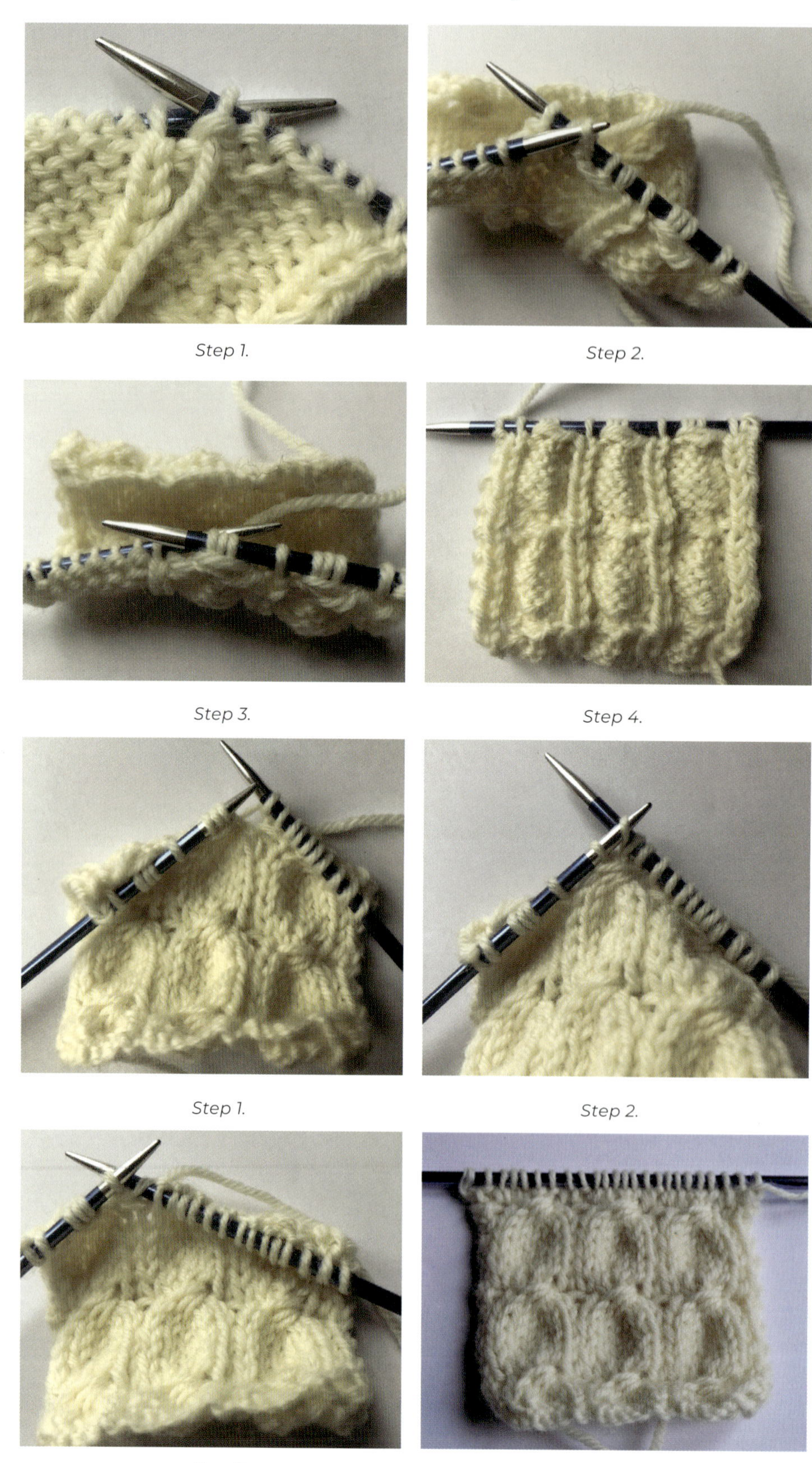

Step 1.

Step 2.

Step 3.

Step 4.

Step 1.

Step 2.

Step 3.

Step 4.

A flat cable worked over six stitches.

The 1940s Bestway booklet of Tyrolean designs features wider cables, which are then embroidered.

Flat cable technique

The first action of Row 9.

The closing of the cable in Row 9.

Bobbles

Bobbles appear on many Tyrolean-style garments, especially favoured from the 1950s and on through to today. They feature in earlier designs of the 1930s in abundance, but are less often seen in patterns of the war years and just after, as they require considerably more yarn.

Apart from being wool-guzzlers, bobbles can be very labour intensive. There are many ways to execute bobbles, with more or less complexity. As with cables, the prospect of hundreds of bobbles can be a daunting one, and it is worth trying out some of the simpler versions to substitute these where a vintage pattern demands overly complicated techniques.

Many instructions for bobbles require the work to be turned around three times for each bobble to be completed in any one row. This will greatly extend the time taken to work the pattern if the design includes many hundreds of bobbles to be worked on every piece. Some of the simpler versions of bobbles reduce the number of turns, and a selection of these is given below. It may be worth noting that the methods that do require numerous turns of the work often result in fuller and rounder bobbles, which may be a preferred result and worth the additional manoeuvres needed.

Bobble type 1

This method creates a classic bobble, standing clearly away from the main knitting and with a distinct rounded shape. It requires two turns of the work for each bobble, worked into one stitch, but is one of the more straightforward methods of working.

To make a bobble (MB):

Purl alternate rows (for wrong side of work) between each completed bobble.

Step 1: Knit into the front, back, front, back and front again of the stitch

Step 2: Turn the work and P5

Step 3: Turn the work, sl. 2, K3tog, pass 2 slipped sts. over; this completes the bobble

Step 4: Turn back to right side of work and continue with main knitting to next bobble

Bobble type 2

This method creates the bobble over three rows of the main work, with no separate turning of the work needed. The bobble is created from one stitch. It creates a distinct shape that stands clearly away from the main knitting, working more effectively with DK or thicker yarns. It is the bobble technique used for the Knitted for Best design in the Pattern Collection.

K5 in 1 = K1, P1, K1, P1, K1 all into the next stitch.

Worked over 11 sts. and 4 rows as follows:

Step 1 (in first row of main knitting): K5 in 1, K9, K5 in 1

Step 2 (in second row of main knitting): K5, P9, K5

Step 3: P5tog, K9, P5tog

Step 4: Purl

Bobble type 3

This method creates a bobble which stands away distinctly from the main knitting. It requires two turns of the work for each bobble, which is all worked into one stitch.

There are numerous ways of creating bobbles with more or less complexity. This sample illustrates one of the simpler methods.

To make a bobble (MB):

Step 1: Knit into the front of the stitch and slip the newly made stitch back onto the left-hand needle, keeping the original stitch still on the left-hand needle.

Step 2: Knit the newly made stitch and let it slip onto the right-hand needle, while still keeping the original stitch on the left-hand needle as before.

Step 3: Repeat this action until there are 6 new stitches from the original, which is still on the left-hand needle.

Step 4: Knit once again into the original stitch and let this now fall from the needle (7 sts. altogether).

Step 5: Turn the work, and taking the 7 sts. made, purl these together into one stitch.

Step 6: Turn, knit this stitch, thus completing the bobble.

To make the diamond-shaped grid of bobbles, see below.

Bobble type 1 technique

Step 1.

Step 2.

Step 3: sl. 2, K3tog.

Step 3: pass 2 slipped sts over.

Step 4.

The Knitted for Best cardigan uses a simple method of creating bobbles worked into the main rows of knitting.

Bobbles can be placed in groups to create 'frames' for embroidery, or as decorative shapes on their own.

Bobble type 2 technique

Step 1.

Step 2.

Step 3.

Step 4.

Bobble type 3 technique

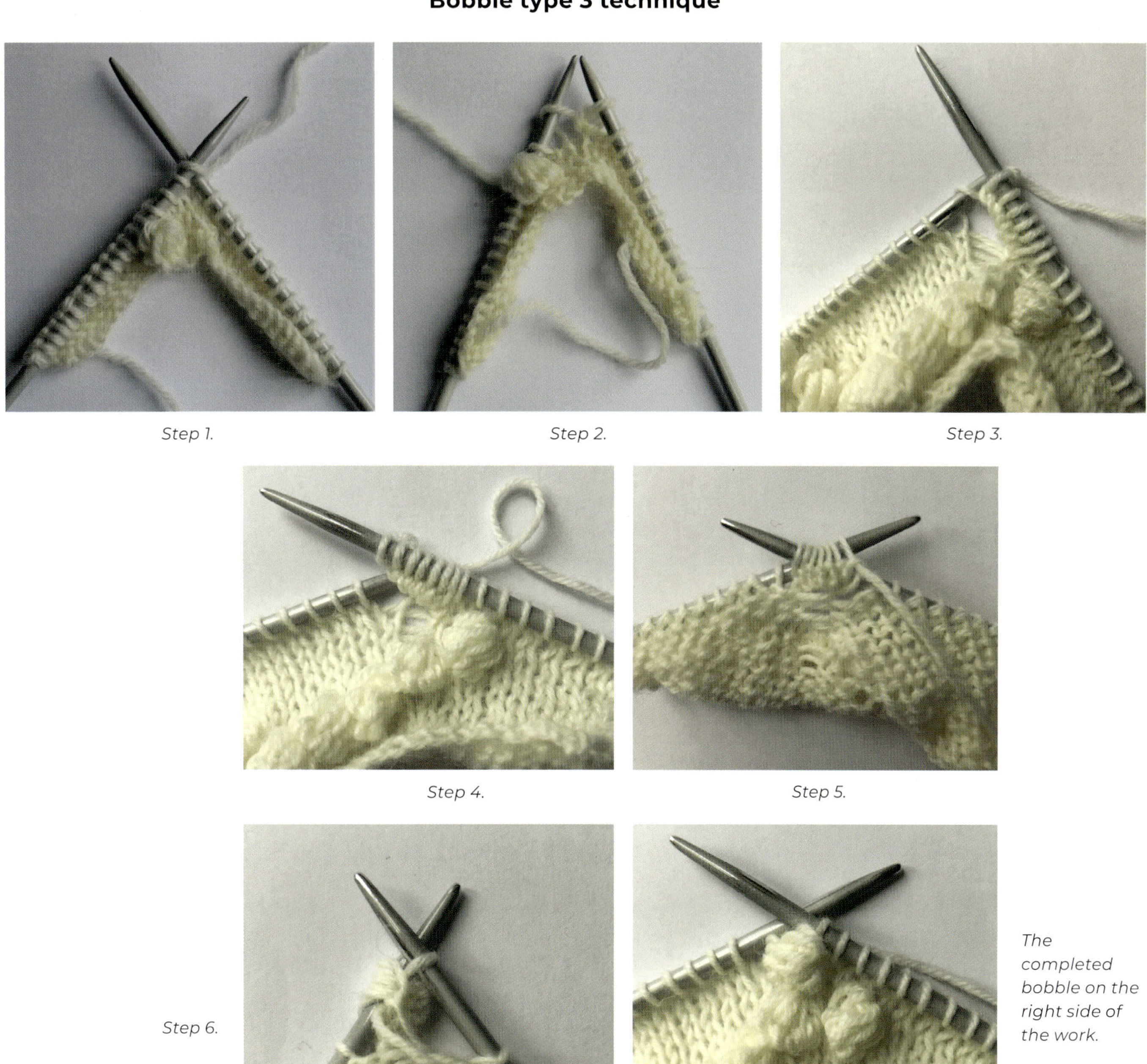

Step 1.

Step 2.

Step 3.

Step 4.

Step 5.

Step 6.

The completed bobble on the right side of the work.

Bobble grids

The sample pictured of bobbles arranged in a diamond shape is worked over 33 sts. and 18 rows, achieving 7 cm/2.75″ width x 5 cm/2″ height from outside edges of bobbles, using 4 ply and 3.75 mm/10 needles.

The shape is worked as follows (the sample was made with bobble type 3 but any of the other methods of making the bobbles can be used as they all work into one stitch):

1st row: K16, MB, K16
2nd row and every following alt row: P
3rd row: K14, MB, K3, MB, K14
5th row: K12, MB, K7, MB, K12
7th row: K10, MB, K11, MB, K10
9th row: K8, MB, K15, MB, K8
11th row: As row 7
13th row: As row 5
15th row: As row 3
17th row: As row 1

The shape can be made larger by continuing to increase the number of stitches between bobbles before starting to decrease the number of stitches, placing the bobbles so that they work back towards a point, ending in one bobble.

Stitch grids

Effective and simple 'frames' can be created by working lines of stitches which define a shape either separately or as an all-over grid across larger areas of the knitting. These can be made as simply as placing a purl stitch in a knit row at regularly spaced intervals. The size of each diamond or square can be varied according to preference, and to the space required for later embellishing.

Single stitch grid

In the sample pictured, the pattern is worked over 25 sts. (giving a diamond size of 5 cm/2″ width x 3.5 cm/1.375″ height over 15 rows, worked in 4 ply on 3.75 mm needles at a tension of 28 sts. to 10 cm/4″).

The Knitted for Best cardigan places arches of bobbles to frame simple embroidered stylized flower motifs.

1st row: K12, P1, K12
2nd row: P11, K1, P1, K1, P11
3rd row: K10, P1, K3, P1, K10
4th row: P9, K1, P5, K1, P9
5th row: K8, P1, K7, P1, K8
6th row: P7, K1, P9, K1, P7
7th row: K6, P1, K11, P1, K6
8th row: P5, K1, P13, K1, P5 (for a wider diamond continue to increase the number of centre sts. to desired width)
9th row: As row 7

The Cosy for Cold Days design from the early 1950s creates square grids of bobbles, which accentuate the shaping of the cardigan.

Working in varied stitches creates an effective texture that also offers natural spaces for embroidery, as seen in Annie's Jacket from the Pattern Collection.

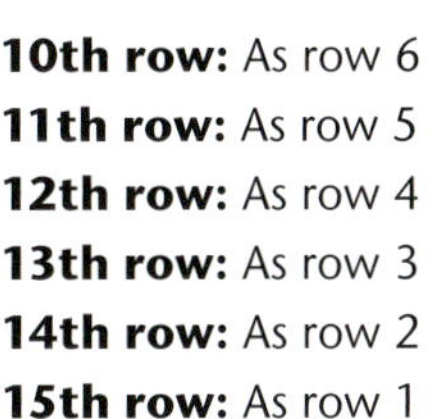

10th row: As row 6
11th row: As row 5
12th row: As row 4
13th row: As row 3
14th row: As row 2
15th row: As row 1

Triple stitch grid

The sample pictured is worked over 29 sts. to show the repeat effect (giving a diamond size of 5 cm/2" width x 3.5 cm/1.375" height worked over 14 rows in 4 ply on 3.75 mm needles at a tension of 28 sts. to 10 cm/4").

The grid effect is worked over multiples of 15 sts. and 14 rows.

1st row (WS): P1, *K3, P7, K3, P1, rep fr. *to end of row
2nd row: K2, *P3, K5, P3, K3, rep fr. *to last 2 sts., K2
3rd row: P3, *K3, P3, K3, P5, rep fr.*to last 3 sts., P3
4th row: K4, *P3, K1, P3, K7, rep fr. *to last 4 sts., K4
5th row: P5, K5, *P9, K5, rep fr. *to last 5 sts., P5
6th row: K6, P3, *K11, P3, rep fr. *to last 6 sts., K6
7th row: P5 K5 *P9 K5 rep fr. *to last 5 sts., P5
8th row: K4, *P3, K1, P3, K7, rep fr. *to last 4 sts., K4
9th row: P3, *K3, P3, K3, P5, rep fr. *to last 3 sts., P3
10th row: K2, *P3, K5, P3, K3, rep fr. *to last 2 sts., K2
11th row: P1, *K3, P7, K3, P1, rep fr.*to end
12th row: P3, *K9, P5, rep fr. *to last 3 sts., P3
13th row: K2, *P11, K3, rep fr. *to last 2 sts., K2
14th row: P3, *K9, P5, rep fr. *to last 3 sts., P3

Twist stitch grid

This grid is worked in multiples of 6 sts. (plus 2 edge stitches) over 12 rows.

In this sample, the pattern is worked over 20 sts. to show the repeat effect (three pattern repeats plus 2 edge sts.).

The twist is created with 2 stitches, picking up the second stitch on the left-hand needle and working this from in front or behind the first stitch to cross over each other.

In the Flowers for Laura design, the twist stitches are used to create larger areas for placing embroidered motifs.

Single stitch grid: working purl stitches is an easy way of creating lozenge shapes in a single stitch grid as a simple but effective texture.

Triple stitch grid: to make a more textured surface, groups of purl stitches can be worked together into a triple stitch grid.

Twist stitch grid: twisting two stitches around each other creates an extra dimension to the surface.

Row 1 (WS): P
All following odd number rows: P
2nd row: *T2F, K4, rep to last 2 sts., T2F
4th row: K1, *T2B, K2, T2F, rep fr. *to last 3 sts., T2F K1
6th row: *K2, T2B, T2F, rep fr. *to last 2 sts., K2
8th row: K3, *T2B, K4, rep fr. *to last 3 sts., K3
10th row: *K2, T2F, T2B, rep fr. *to last 2 sts., K2
12th row: K1, *T2F, K2, T2B, rep fr. *to last st., K1

This stitch can be varied by working reverse st.st in alternate diamond shapes, as with Annie's Jacket from the Pattern Collection (*see* Chapter 4).

Abbreviations

Twist 2 forward (T2F): Insert the needle into the front of the second stitch from the tip of the left needle, knit this but without letting it fall from the left needle. Then insert the right needle behind this and into the front of the first stitch still on the left needle. Knit this and let both stitches fall from the needle together.

Twist 2 back (T2B): Insert the right needle behind the first stitch and into the front of the second stitch from the tip of the left-hand needle. Knit this but without letting it fall from the left needle. Then bring the right needle to the front of the work and knit the first stitch, letting them now both fall together from the left needle.

The grid of lozenge shapes created for the Annie's Jacket design is enhanced further by varying the stitches between alternate shapes for added textural effect.

Textured Stitches

In addition to bobbles, grids and cables, surface interest can be created by alternating straightforward knit and purl stitches in sequences to make many different textured effects.

Simple but effective application of stitch textures can be seen in the garments of the Pattern Collection in this book: in the sleeves of the Warm Red Cardigan, and in the panels of the Edelweiss Jacket and Flowers for Laura, which all use a variation of double moss stitch. The Forties Favourite uses single moss stitch for the yoke and the Lilli Bolero uses very simple small garter stitch rectangles for texture.

The Edelweiss Jacket uses double moss stitch as a simple texture, contrasting with the areas of plain stocking stitch.

Moss stitch

This is worked as K1, P1, then reversed on the return row.

This stitch creates a firm fabric and is ideal for front bands, collars, or as an alternative to ribbing, as well as a neat attractive texture as part of the body.

Double moss st

This is worked as K2, P2 for 2 rows, then alternated on the following 2 rows.

Like moss stitch, this gives a firm fabric and is ideal for edgings and as part of the body.

Squares

By alternating blocks of st.st and reverse st.st, an all-over texture is achieved which can be ideal for adding embroidery.

Single moss stitch is worked to define the yoke sections of the Forties Favourite cardigan as an effective way of including texture without using extra yarn.

By reversing knit and purl sections within stocking stitch, a simple grid of squares achieves texture and spaces for embellishment.

The sleeves and edging of the Warm Red Cardigan are worked in double moss stitch.

Colourful rows of crochet stitches are used to define the neckband and edges in this design by Sirdar from the late 1940s.

Crochet

Coloured accents are created very effectively in Tyrolean garments by using crochet. The stitches used allow for colours to create vertical stripes along front borders, trimming finished edges, making looped channels for drawstrings and the cords themselves, among other features.

Almost every needleworker of the 1930s and 1940s would have had some level of skill in crochet, alongside knitting. The modern maker is generally more likely to have developed preference for one or the other, but most vintage knitting patterns call on some crochet details, especially those in the Tyrolean style. Most stitches used are straightforward as described below, but knitted alternatives are given where relevant in the patterns in this book for those who prefer to knit rather than crochet.

The designs for the Pattern Collection use nothing more complicated than a treble stitch (US dc.) and options are given for knitted substitutions where appropriate. The chart included later in the book illustrates how the various stitches are executed (*see* Appendix 1).

Creating a crochet cord for drawstrings

With double strands if using finer wool, or a single strand of DK or thicker, work a chain long enough to tie, leaving a length of around 7.5 cm/3″ at each end to use for finishing the cord.

Average length required for neckline drawstring: 90 cm/35.5″.
Average length required for waist drawstring: 122 cm/48″.

A thicker cord can be most effective, using strands of all the colours used for the embroidery, for example, worked on a larger crochet hook. Instructions for this are given with the Evergreen design in the Pattern Collection, Chapter 4.

In place of a threaded tie cord at the neck, the Forties Favourite design attaches a decorative bow made from a crochet chain of the combined colours used in the pattern.

Typical Tyrolean colours of red and green are used for the neck, waist and front edges in striking contrast to the main cream colour.

The Evergreen Jacket recreates the details of the original 1930s Tyrolean jacket with a tie cord at the waist and neck made up of strands of every colour used in the embroidered sections.

Finishing touches for drawstrings
These can be neatened and left unadorned by simply sewing in the ends left at the time of making.

If you wish to add decorative endings, thread the cord through the designated loops beforehand.

Pompoms

These can be made in one, two or multiple colours for the desired effect. They give a charming touch to the garment, though more in keeping with styles from the 1950s onwards. By far the easiest method is to use a commercially produced pompom maker, which will also have a longer life.

Tassels

These appear frequently on patterns from the 1930s in particular and are easily created in single or multiple colours.

To make tassels:
Step 1: You will need a piece of stiff card 5 cm/2″ wide for making the tassels (the short side of a plastic credit card is perfect). Using 2 strands together (the June Clyde Jacket used red and yellow together), wind firmly and evenly around the card at least 20 times. Cut a length of the double yarn about 15 cm/6″ in length and thread this under the wound yarn, tying firmly with several knots.
Step 2: Slide the wound wool off the card.
Step 3: Cut through all strands opposite where you have tied these. Use the remainder of the wool length used to tie the strands and wind around the top to form a tassel – if you do this slightly down from the top of the tied strands it creates a fuller head to the tassel. Tie the tassels securely to each of the ends of the cords. Trim the bottom edge of the tassels to neaten lengths.

Tassels are a favourite Tyrolean style embellishment for finishing tie cords, as seen in the 1936 design for June Clyde Sets a Fashion.

Pompoms can add a light-hearted touch by finishing a tie cord at the neck.

Colour Work

The coloured details in a Tyrolean design are one of its most important characteristics, along with textured stitches. To look authentically Tyrolean, a garment needs these distinctive colour accents. The look can be achieved with minimal or no texture, but not without the quintessential colour work.

The first way in which this is achieved is with coloured edgings, usually along the button bands and around the neckline, either knitted or crocheted.

The second is the characteristically coloured embroidered details, often covering the garment, typically 'framed' in

Tassels technique

Step 1.

Step 2.

The completed tassel attached to the cord ends.

textured grids or bands, at least adorning the fronts if not also along the sleeves and across the back. Most commonly the embroidery features stylized flowers, either simply stitched as 'lazy daisies' or elaborately worked in satin stitch, chain stitch or cross stitch. The types of stitches and how they are worked is explained in the 'Embroidery' section later in this chapter.

The motifs are embedded into textured stitches such as cables or grids worked into the main knitting, worked on plain

Using strong contrasting colours to work neckbands and edgings adds to the Tyrolean styling, as seen in the Edelweiss Jacket.

Crochet edgings can be simple or worked in more decorative stitches, as in the Warm Red Cardigan, which adds shell stitch edgings (instructions are given in the pattern).

The Forties Favourite works coloured floral motifs into the main knitting, which are further embellished after the work is completed.

Picot edgings add a neat decorative finish to hemmed borders, as in the original 1930s Jacket.

stocking stitch or surrounded by bobbles (please see earlier sections in this chapter for details on working with textured knitted stitches).

Colour work is usually added to the surface of the finished garment but is also found worked into the knitted stitches, then embellished after the knitting is completed with additional embroidery. This can be seen as especially effective in the Forties Favourite cardigan, where the technique is explained in the pattern.

Coloured edgings

These are mainly worked after knitting is complete, added along the front bands and across the neckline. Using crochet for this means that front bands and neck edging can be worked in one go, whereas knitting requires these to be worked separately to achieve the same vertical line effect on the bands.

Crochet buttonholes also have the advantage of achieving a neater finish than those knitted in, by the inherent nature of wool and how knitted stitches sit when cast off and cast on. It is also easier to create decorative border stitches with crochet.

Picot edging

This knitted edging creates a most effective and pretty scalloped effect, and is ideal for neat hemming. For a hem at the beginning of work (this can be worked in the main colour, as with the Evergreen Jacket in the Pattern Collection, or in a contrast colour, as in the sample pictured). Worked in stocking stitch as follows:

Using the same size needles as the main work, cast on an odd number of sts. as required and work at least 4 rows st.st, or number needed to form a suitable hem which when folded back will sit on the wrong side of the work.

Step 1 (first picot row): K1, *yo K2tog, rep fr. *to end of row
Step 2 (second picot row): Purl

The eyelets formed across the entire row are the first step in creating a picot edging.

This creates a line of eyelet holes across the row. When folded at this row, it creates a neat scalloped effect.
Step 3: Continue in st.st. for the same number of rows as worked before first picot row
Hemming can be completed at this stage as part of the work, or left until completed – as detailed below.

Hemming a picot row

A neat hem is created by folding over the picot edge at the row with eyelets.

Step 1: With right side facing, pick up and knit into each stitch of the cast-on row, together with every stitch across the last knitted row. This is best achieved by taking a spare needle and picking up each cast-on stitch so that the points of both needles are at the same end (this also allows for easier counting to ensure that every stitch has been picked up, otherwise the hem will twist slightly and not sit evenly).
Step 2: Fold at the row of eyelets and holding both needles parallel to each other, pick up one stitch from each needle and knit these together. (This is a fiddly process as the stitches on each needle tend to move across differently, but it is well worth persevering as the result is very neat.)
Alternatively, hemming can be left until work is complete and sewn down loosely to retain stretch.
If you work a picot hem along the vertical edge of knitting, casting on and hemming is the only option.

Adding a picot hem to the edge of work:
Step 1: With right side of work facing, pick up and knit enough stitches so as not to pucker the edge, but without creating a border with too many stitches as this will 'wave'. As a guide, pick up 2 of every 3 edge stitches.
Step 2: Work an odd number of rows (at least 3) for the required width of the edging, finishing so that the right side is facing for

Folding across the eyelet row creates little scallops, forming an attractive edge to a neat hem.

The neatest way to finish a picot edged hem is to work on two parallel needles to pick up stitches evenly from the cast-on edge as the next row is knitted (step 1).

Finishing a hem with a picot edge is best achieved by working from two parallel needles, picking up one stitch from the cast-on edge and knitting together with the next stitch from the main row (step 2).

the next row, which will be worked as the first picot row given above.

Work the 2 picot rows as above, then continue in st.st for the same number of rows as knitted before the first picot row plus 1 row so tha t right side is facing to cast off. Cast off loosely (this is done most easily by using a needle one size larger and working with your usual tension to cast off).

Step 3: To complete, fold over at the row with eyelets and stitch the cast-off edge to the main work on the wrong side without pulling, to retain the stretch (this is especially important at the neck edge or lower edges of bodice or sleeves).

The hem of a picot edge can be sewn down at the back of the work and as necessary when worked alongside edges, as in the Evergreen Jacket pattern.

To create a picot hem along a side edge, stitches are picked up and knitted either in the main colour or a contrast (step 1).

The eyelet row of a side edge picot hem is created to form the distinctive scalloped edge once folded and hemmed (step 2).

The Evergreen Jacket finishes every edge with a neat picot hem, all around the sleeve, body and neckband (step 3).

Integral colour work

Working with coloured wools as part of the main knitting appears less frequently in vintage Tyrolean patterns, as they tend to feature smaller areas of colour which are better rendered by working onto the knitted surface after the work is complete. Areas in blocks of colour are best worked in the intarsia method, where yarns are twisted together when there is a change of colour, worked from separate balls of wool picked up as needed. This technique requires practice as the stitches naturally tend to create uneven work by the very nature of wool.

The Forties Favourite pattern by Bestway included in the Pattern Collection (Chapter 4) has coloured motifs worked in a variation of Fair Isle technique. The pattern refers to the motifs as 'Fair Isle panels' but does not apply the usual methods of weaving or stranding the colours across an entire row.

Where small amounts of each colour are used, these are best wound onto individual wool holders to prevent tangling. As colours are changed, the wools are twisted around each other to prevent holes in the knitting.

It is helpful to anticipate where the colour will be required in the following row, by looking at the next row on the chart (or next line of the pattern if given in this way in the instructions), and 'preparing' the colour by carrying it across the next few stitches so that it is 'lined up' ready when reaching this point in the next row. This avoids having to strand the wool back and adjusting the tension accordingly to avoid puckering or holes. (For ease of working, the coloured motifs for Forties Favourite

The Forties Favourite pattern, based on Bestway pattern number 1511, is a perfect example of 1940s styling, maximizing on colour work rather than extravagant textures which would use up valuable wool in times of scarcity.

When working with many small quantities of coloured wool together, it is useful to wind these on separate spools or holders to prevent tangling.

Bestway design number 1797 named 'Tyrolean Jumper' (although a buttoned jacket) features a yoke of Fair Isle pattern in contrast colour.

Once completed, additional French knots and running stitches add embellishments to the Forties Favourite design.

have been converted to a chart in addition to the line-by-line instructions of the original pattern.)

A small number of vintage Tyrolean patterns feature colour work to be executed in Fair Isle or woven and stranded techniques of knitting with two or more colours together. The 1940s design by Bestway for a Tyrolean 'Jumper' (a buttoned cardigan) with Fair Isle yoke is an attractive example, where the flat area of colour work is set off by the deeper texture of the large bobble stitches over the rest of the cardigan.

Embroidery

Embroidered motifs add the defining touch to any Tyrolean garment, and most patterns include these details. The most elaborate ones are remarkable feats of embroidery, but the simpler stitches can be just as effective as the breathtaking mastery, and the aim is to embellish your knitted work to make it your own, adorning it with the hallmark of authentic Tyrolean style.

Annie's Jacket from the Pattern Collection features embroidery on the back and front, offset with plain stocking stitch sleeves with dramatic pleating at the shoulder.

Flowers for Laura from the Pattern Collection has embroidered flowers set into the lozenge shapes of textured stitches, edged with cables.

Floral motifs

Floral motifs are by far the favourites of all embroidery motifs in Tyrolean style. Most often these are stylized, five-petal flowers executed in simple lazy daisy stitch. They work best when fairly small, as they can look rather 'gappy' if the stitches are stretched over a larger area. They can of course be filled in with extra stitches for the larger spaces, or for a more cushioned finish.

The flowers can also resemble actual flowers more closely, and the natural choices for Tyrolean style are the native edelweiss, blue gentian and pink or red rhododendron. Whichever flowers are chosen, these are mostly executed in the pure colours in which they appear in nature, but can be varied to suit individual taste and colour preferences. Floral motifs can be executed in completely individual palettes, to suit the background colour chosen and the maker's personal choice.

These three floral motifs provide the balance of bright colours that give a Tyrolean garment much of its style. Yellow flowers, and touches of yellow at the centre of the other flowers, add a further bright note and complete the primary colour trio so favoured for Tyrolean embellishments, along with the green of the leaves and stems.

Versions of edelweiss and gentians can also look very effective when worked in crochet, especially as edelweiss has a woolly quality to its 'furry' petals, or bracts, which translates perfectly into wool. These can then be applied to knitted pieces and stitched on in lieu of embroidering, having their own stitched texture, or can be made into brooches by adding a pin at the back.

Edelweiss (Lentopodium alpinum)

These snowy white flowers work most effectively on a coloured background and are not usually featured on the classic cream background of so many Tyrolean garments as they stand out less. This endearing familiar flower can be interpreted in many ways (and even many colours), easily recognizable by the distinctive centres (capitula), which are often exaggerated in colour for both jewellery and embroidery. Simple ways of embroidering a stylized edelweiss are shown in the accompanying images.

Alpine flowers have always been popular in jewellery, especially the souvenirs of the 1940s and 1950s, a selection of which is shown here. Many of these have been the inspiration for the embroidery worked on designs from the Pattern Collection.

Vintage postcards illustrating typical Alpine flowers can give inspiration for embroidered motifs.

Lazy daisy stitch is used for many of the stylized flowers embroidered onto Tyrolean designs, such as the December 1951 pattern from Stitchcraft, *included in the Pattern Collection as the Cosy for Cold Days cardigan.*

Spring flowers from the garden can be a source of inspiration for embroidery, with their range of colours and shapes, as chosen for Annie's Jacket from the Pattern Collection.

Edelweiss flowers lend themselves to embroidery, working best on a coloured background.

An embroidered edelweiss can be made of simple long and short stitches.

Step 1: Using varied lengths of stitch with double strands of wool to set the petals.

Step 2: Filling out the flower with shorter stitches between longer petals.

Step 3: Working French knots in the centre in a contrasting colour.

Pink rhododendron

This is the mysterious little flower which so often appears in red or pink together with the more familiar edelweiss and gentian. It is the one which is most popularly stylized into a five-petal flower in lazy daisy stitch.

Embroidery stitches

The stitches which will be most useful when embroidering onto a Tyrolean garment are lazy daisy, French knot and cross stitch.

All the embroidery on the original 1930s jacket is executed in outlined chain stitch.

Lazy daisy

This can be worked with a single or double strand of yarn, to balance the thickness of the wool used for the main knitting. It can create an outline, which can then be filled in with straight stitches for a denser effect.

French knot

The French knot is an ideal stitch to highlight the centre of any flower, or clustered together to form tiny flowers on a stem, such as featured on Annie's Jacket in the Pattern Collection. They are easier to work than they might appear (*see* photos).

Cross stitch

Using cross stitch creates its own interesting texture and can be used to place coloured areas instead of intarsia work if preferred.

Other colour motifs

There are many ways to introduce colour into a Tyrolean garment which are completely in keeping with the vintage style and evoke the unmistakable identity of the style. The colour motifs applied do not necessarily have to be floral to create this look. As in some of the earliest patterns from the 1930s, the motifs can

Step 1: Work lines of chain stitch for each 'petal' of the edelweiss.

Step 2: Complete the flower with French knots at the centre.

In lazy daisy embroidery, a loop of yarn is stretched to the desired size and caught down with a stitch at the topmost part.

The 'petal' shapes created by the lazy daisy loops can be filled in with stitches for a fuller effect.

be coloured dots, as in the Needlewoman Jacket included in the Pattern Collection, or coloured stitches draw together ribbing for a smocked effect, as in the June Clyde jacket.

Running stitch

A simple line of running stitch defines separate areas. Easily executed, the stitches should maintain the natural stretch of the knitted background.

Chain stitch

As well as working well for embroidering flowers (as detailed earlier in this chapter), chain stitch is a most useful stitch as it can outline other shapes, or create defining lines between different textures, as in the Flowers for Laura cardigan (Chapter 5), worked to define the changes of stitches used between the yoke and panels, and along the edge of cabling to highlight the depth of texture.

French knots are used for the centre of stylized flowers, and also to interpret the blooms of mimosa and ceanothus on Annie's Jacket.

To make a French knot, wind the wool around the needle at least three times.

Gently pull the needle and yarn through the stitches to create a knot, guiding the yarn through to ensure this doesn't tangle, and securc on the wrong side.

The colour work on the Edeleweiss Jacket is all worked in cross stitch.

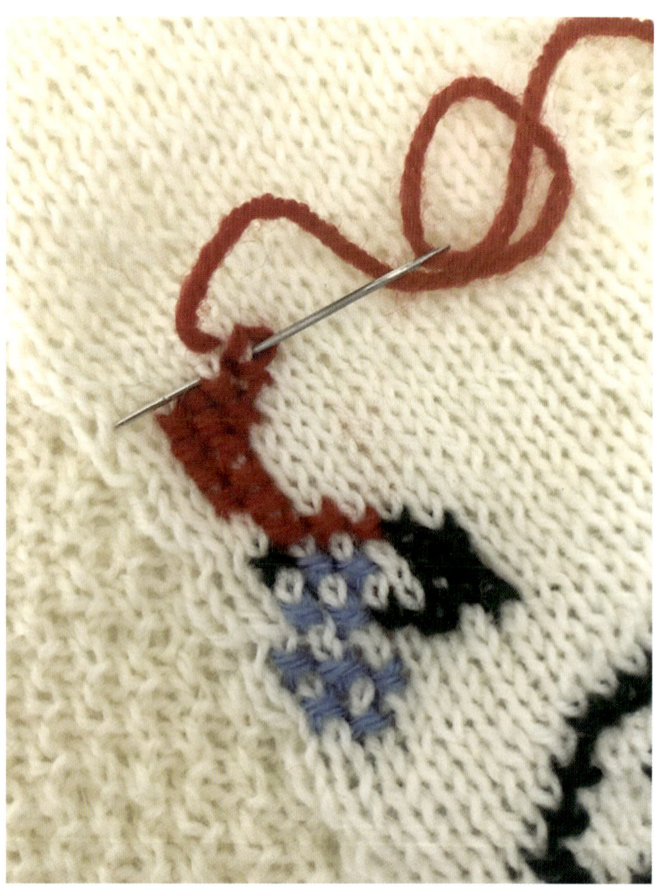

One embroidered cross of yarn covers each knitted stitch, following the chart given in the pattern for the Edelweiss Jacket.

Stylized gentian flowers are worked in lazy daisy stitch on the Flowers for Laura cardigan.

Gentians are interpreted in chain stitch on the original 1930s jacket.

Variations on the embroidered gentian flowers of the original 1930s jacket are worked in the recreated pattern of Evergreen.

The Flowers for Laura design is embroidered with little red flowers, inspired by the small red alpine rhododendron.

Beginning with a coloured ring of chain stitches makes it easier to locate the stitches for the following rows to make the edelweiss petals.

To work an edelweiss in crochet, you will need:

- Small quantities of 4 ply for each flower in cream, pale green and light brown or ochre
- A 3 mm crochet hook
- Brooch back (or safety pin)

To make the flower:

With a 3 mm crochet hook and using a light brown wool (using a contrast wool to begin sets the centre of the flower clearly and is easier to locate the stitches which follow to create the petals in cream)

Ch.3 and join the loop with a sl.st.

Ch.1 then 6 dc. into the foundation ring and close with a sl.st.

Ch.1 and cut brown wool.

Join cream and work 1st bract (petal): Sl.st. into **back** of 1st dc. then ch.6. Turn and skip 1st st. then 1 dc. in next 5 sts. Sl.st. in **back loop** of the next st. of the foundation ring.

Repeat to form another 5 petals around the ring, 6 in total (edelweiss can have up to 15 bracts).

Inner smaller bracts (petals): Ch.4, turn and skip the 1st st., then 1 dc. in next 3 sts., sl.st. into **front loop** of next st. in the foundation ring. Repeat to form another 5 smaller petals, 6 altogether.

The 'petals' naturally curl a little, and can be gently pressed, if preferred, to straighten out. (Any irregularities in the petals look all the more like the real flowers.)

For the centre florets (capitula): using light brown and light green together, ch.2, then sl.st. again in the 1st ch. *Ch.3 and sl.st. again in the 1st of these. Rep from *twice more to form 4 little bobbles in a line. Break off both wools, leaving an end to draw through, and gather the row of bobbles together and stitch this to the centre of the double rounds of petals.

A brooch pin or safety pin can be attached to the back to make a brooch.

Gentians (Gentiana) *in blue or pink*

Naturally an intense cobalt blue, or a deep pink, this bell-shaped flower adds a strong accent to any embroidered colour work.

A gentian made in its natural bright blue can make a striking embellishment to a knitted garment.

The first step of making a gentian flower is the tubular base where the petals will sit.

To work a gentian in crochet, you will need:

- small quantities of 4 ply wool in cobalt or royal blue, green and yellow
- A 3 mm crochet hook
- Brooch back (or safety pin)

To make the flower:

For the petals (corolla):

With a 3 mm crochet hook and using blue wool ch.4 and join the loop with a sl.st.

Ch.1 then work dc. into the 5 sts. of foundation ring and close with a sl.st.

Repeat the round 4 times more to form a short tube.

Work 1st outer petal: Ch.6 and turn. Skip 1st st. Sl.st. into next 2 sts. then dc. in next st., trb in net st., dc. in last st. then connect to next st. in ring with a sl.st. Repeat 4 times more (5 petals in all). Ch.1 and work 1st petal: Sl.st. into **back** of 1st dc. then ch.6. Turn and skip 1st st. then 1 dc. in next 5 sts. Sl.st. in **back loop** of the next st. of the foundation ring.

Edelweiss and gentians can be made in crochet and used as appliqués for an alternative to embroidery, or made into brooches to decorate a finished garment.

Repeat to form another 4 petals around the ring, 5 in total.

Inner smaller petals: Ch.4, turn and skip the 1st st., then 1 dc. in next 3 sts., sl. st. into **front loop** of next st. in the foundation ring. Repeat to form another 4 smaller petals, 5 altogether.

To complete: Work a French knot with yellow at the centre of the flower. Insert the flower into the green tube (calyx), leaving a little of the blue tube showing above the green, and sew this together to secure. A brooch back or safety pin can now be added along the length of the calyx.

The petals and centre of the gentian are made separately and sewn together.

The Tyrolean Needlewoman pattern from Needlework *magazine of 1937 offers an alternative to floral motifs with embroidered dots of colour, using the colours which make up the dramatically striped yoke.*

Basic running stitch creates borders for the flower motifs and accentuates the yoke line in the Forties Favourite cardigan.

In the Flowers for Laura design, contrasting lines of chain stitch are worked where textures change.

The Copley's pattern of June Clyde's jacket in the Pattern Collection of this book uses the red and yellow of the borders with simple stitches to create the smocked effect over the basic ribbing.

Running a line of chain stitches in a contrast colour against a cable gives this extra depth, as in the Flowers for Laura cardigan.

The Flowers for Laura cardigan draws inspiration from vintage designs for embellishments and embroidery.

The Hollywood Comes to Broadway waistcoat works a wide cable in thicker yarn as the base for embroidered flower motifs.

CHAPTER 4

THE PATTERN COLLECTION

This collection of Tyrolean-style patterns has been selected from the array of wonderful vintage patterns available, beginning with the 1930s when the popularity of the style first emerged and knitting patterns began to be accessible to all knitters through dedicated publications and leaflets. These are British patterns for the most part, with the inclusion of key American and Australian designs. There is of course a wealth of continental patterns, notably German, which would form a volume of their own, but the focus for this present selection is on how the Tyrolean style captured the imagination of British knitters and has continued to do so for nearly 100 years.

The fourteen designs presented in this book are selected as examples of the variety of stitchery, techniques and shaping drawn from across the three decades of the 1930s, 1940s and early 1950s. A number of these are recognizable favourites, popular as vintage knitting recreations and deserving of their place in this context, but most of those offered here have been sourced from rarer publications, or designed for this book from vintage inspiration. The patterns are exclusively adapted and simplified here for the modern knitter. The knitting skill required for each is shown by the little Tyrolean hat symbol; 1 hat = easy; 2 hats = medium; 3 hats = difficult; and 4 hats = expert. Wherever helpful, tips and suggestions are added in italics.

Of the many Tyrolean patterns available, those offered in this book have been specifically chosen as they capture the essence of each decade's distinctive styling. With their varied techniques and interpretations of what we think of as Tyrolean style, they offer something for all tastes. The patterns have also been selected across a variety of yarn weights – 3 ply, 4 ply, DK and Worsted – so that there is something to appeal to every knitter, while keeping to the types of yarns used in the original vintage patterns.

The last pattern, Flowers for Laura (featured in Chapter 5), is an original design created exclusively for this collection. It brings together the key elements of the style and invites the knitter to make their own creation completely individual, while incorporating elements that are authentically vintage, drawn from the many patterns available.

The Flowers for Laura cardigan is an exclusive pattern inspired by vintage Tyrolean style for individual creativity, given in Chapter 5.

HELTENHAM
COTSWOLD
Public
information
WHILE YOU ARE W
YOUR TRA
WHY NOT VIS
BROADWAY "GO

The Edelweiss Jacket

The Edelweiss Jacket.

The Edelweiss Jacket featured in the 1936 pattern collection 'Minerva Styles the Future'.

The theme of this collection of knitting patterns by Minerva from 1936 is gloriously Tyrolean. Two of the patterns from 'Minerva Styles the Future' were featured – probably for the first time – in an article of 19 July 1936 in *The New York Times*, 'High Style Knitting', by Virginia Pope. One of the two patterns is the Edelweiss Jacket, and the article describes the designs as follows:

> Lanz of Salburg is the author of the two sweaters shown here, or rather of their prototypes, for these were produced in this country. They are typical of the enchanting things worn in the Tyrol, with their snug collar bands and their attractive buttons. The patterns in typically gay peasant color schemes are embroidered after the knitting is complete.

The Minerva pattern does not credit Josef Lanz, a popular Austrian clothing designer from Salzburg who was shortly to emigrate to America. He founded an immensely popular brand in New York and later California, patronized by Marlene Dietrich and other glittering stars. The Edelweiss Jacket is possibly one of the first Tyrolean patterns made accessible to all knitters in America, if not further afield.

The coloured edgings are in the essential Tyrolean red and green, while the embroidery panels feature typical edelweiss flowers but unusually worked in blue, making them stand out against the cream background. Worked in cross stitch, the embroidery is executed on the plain stocking stitch panels of the front only. The recreated model has been worked following the original pattern, but the same embroidery could be effectively worked on the back and the sleeves if desired, following the same chart that is given in the adapted instructions below. The colours can also be varied, but it will work best when including the green and red used to knit the ribbing and collar (or corresponding colours if substituted).

The original pattern has a number of anomalies, so this version has been amended to navigate through these more easily.

Materials

6 (7) × 50 g balls of Cygnet Truly Wool Rich 4 Ply in Cream (1192)
1 (2) × 50 g balls Cygnet Truly Wool Rich 4 ply in Holly (402)
1 × 50 g ball of King Cole 100% Merino 4 ply in Cranberry (703)
Oddments of black, yellow and blue 4 ply wool (for embroidery)
1 pair 3 mm/11 needles
1 pair 3.25 mm/10 (3.75 mm/9) knitting needles
1 × 3 mm crochet hook
8 buttons (*9 if including an additional one at the top of the neck – though if sourcing original vintage buttons this can be an awkward number to find!*)
Piece of stiff card 5 cm/2" wide for making the tassels (*the short side of a plastic credit card is perfect*)

Measurements

To fit size 32–34" bust (34–36" given in brackets where appropriate)
Length at centre back 47 cm/18.5"
Sleeve length 46 cm/18"

Tension

28 sts. to 10 cm/4" and 8 rows to 2.5 cm/1"

Back

With 3 mm/11 needles and Green cast on 104 sts. and work ribbing (K1, P1) for 2 cm/0.75". (*Keep note of how many rows worked so this can be repeated for ribbing on fronts.*)

Change to Red and work even in ribbing for a further 2 cm/0.75".

Change to 3.25 mm/10 (3.75 mm/9) needles and Cream and work first 18 sts. in double moss st. (K1, P1 on even number of sts. for 2 rows, then P1, K1 for 2 rows), work next 19 sts in st.st, then work next 30 sts. in double moss st., work next 19 sts. in st.st and work last 18 sts in double moss st.

Continue in this manner for the entire back, working all sts. in double moss st. except the 2 bands of 19 sts. each worked in st.st. When work measures 5 cm/2" from start, inc. 1 st. each side.

Inc. 1 st. each side every inch after this for 11 more times (128 sts.), working in additional sts. in double moss st.

Work without further increases until this measures 29 cm/11.5" from the start. (*This will achieve a total length of the completed garment of 45.5 cm/17.75" measured from the drawstring to bottom edge or 49.5 cm/19.55" from topmost edge of collar. At this point you can add length as desired, and more easily than above the armhole shaping – note how many additional rows are knitted so this can be repeated for both fronts. The original pattern was to 25.5 cm/10", which results in a shorter garment.*)

Shape armhole

Cast off 7 sts. at beg. of next 2 rows.
Starting with next row (right side facing) dec. 1 st. each side every other row 9 times.
When work measures 14 cm/5.5" from start of armhole shaping, work 30 sts., and place on stitch holder (or leave on needle to work later).
Cast off next 36 sts.
Working on last 30 sts., cast off 3 sts. at inside edge every other row 3 times, then dec. 1 st. at inside edge every row 9 times.
At the same time, when work measures 18 cm/7" up from beg. of armhole shaping, cast off sts. from armhole edge every other row twice.

Pick up the 30 sts. for the other side and work in the same manner.

Right Front

With 3 mm/11 needles and Green cast on 60 sts. and work ribbing same as back, working a buttonhole when work measures 13 mm/0.5" by working 3 sts., casting off 3 sts., working across remaining sts.
Next row: Cast on 3 sts. over the cast-off sts.

Work a buttonhole in this manner every 5 cm/2" 6 more times. When work measures 2 cm/0.75" (*having worked same number of rows as back*) change to Red.

When work measures 38 mm/1.5" from start, change to 3.25 mm/10 (3.75 mm/9) needles and Cream.
Working from front edge, work 22 sts. in double moss st., work next 19 sts. in st.st, and work last 19 sts. in double moss st.

When work measures 5 cm/2" from start, inc. 1 st. at underarm side.
Inc. 1 st. at this side every 2.5 cm/1" 9 times more (70 sts.).

When work measures 29 cm/11.5" (*or desired length as for back*), cast off 7 sts. at underarm side once, then dec. 1 st. at same underarm side every row 14 times (49 sts.).

When work measures 7.5 cm/3" straight up from start of armhole shaping, cast off 15 sts. at front edge once. Dec. 1 st. at neck edge every row 17 times, then dec. 1 st. at neck edge every 4th row 5 times.

When work measures 18 cm/7" straight up from start of armhole shaping, cast off 6 sts. at armhole edge twice.

Left Front

Work to correspond to right front, omitting buttonholes.

Sleeves (Both Alike)

With 3 mm/11 needles and Green cast on 56 sts. Working in ribbing (K1, P1) for 11.5 cm/4.5" working 2.5 cm/1" in Green, 2.5 cm/1" in Red, then 6.5 cm/2.5" in Cream.

Change to 3.25 mm/10 (3.75 mm/9) needles and start working 19 sts. in double moss st., 18 sts. in st.st, and last 19 sts. in double moss st. Work the centre panel in st.st. for entire sleeve.

When work measures 12 cm/4.75" from start, inc. 1 st. each side, then inc. 1 st. each side every 2.5 cm/1" for 3 more times, then every 8 mm/0.5" 18 times (100 sts.).

When work measures 46 cm/18" from start (*or desired underarm sleeve length*), cast off 7 sts. at the beg. of each of the next 2 rows, then dec. 1 st. each side every other row 15 times, then 1 st. each side every row 15 times (26 sts.). Cast off remaining sts.

The plain stocking stitch panels may be pressed on each piece before assembly but do not press any of the ribbing or double moss stitch areas as this would flatten their texture and elasticity. Please read ball band of chosen yarn for advice before pressing. The fit of this garment means that all parts stretch comfortably to fit and do not especially need pressing.

At this stage, the embroidery details may be worked (please see below for charts and explanation) while the pieces are easily handled, or left until the fronts and back are joined at the shoulder and the collar completed. The original instructions assemble the whole garment and complete the collar before embroidering but this can make the work rather unwieldy! Also, if you choose to embroider all pieces as well as the front, it would be easier to execute before assembling.

Collar

Sew shoulder seams.

With 3 mm/11 needles and Red, pick up 192 sts. evenly around neck – 58 across top of right front, 76 across back, 58 across left front – and work in ribbing (K1, P1) for 7 mm/0.25". Then work a buttonhole as before. Work a further 2.5 cm/1". Change to Green and continue in rib (*if desired, an additional buttonhole can be worked here after 7 mm. Otherwise the drawstring cord brings the two edges together at the top of the neck*). When work measures 6.2 cm/2.5" cast off loosely in ribbing.

The collar is worked in the same essential Tyrolean colours as the welts of red and green, gathered by chain cord.

Edging

With Red and 3 mm crochet hook, work edging as follows:
*Ch.4, skip 4 sts., work 1 dc. in next st., rep fr. *up entire front edges.
With Green, work over Red in same manner, working the dc. through the ch.4 of previous row.

Cord for collar

Using 2 strands of Green together, crochet a chain around 91 cm/36″ long.
Thread this through the yoke on the line between the Green and Red at regular intervals, at ridge of every 3 ribs.

Cord for waistband

Work as for collar cord for 122 cm/48″ and thread as before.

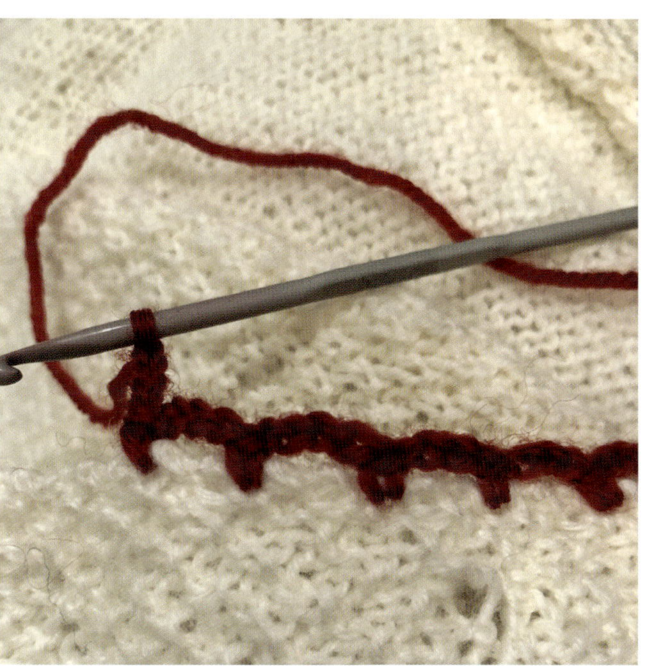

The front edges have a delicate looped chain of red and green worked in crochet.

The waist is defined by a tie cord, finished with tassels.

Make tassels × 4

(See diagrams for the June Clyde pattern below.)

Using 2 strands together of Green, wind firmly and evenly around the card 20 times. Cut a length of the double yarn about 15 cm/6" in length and thread this under the wound yarn, tying firmly with several knots. Slide the wound wool off the card and cut through all strands opposite where you have tied these. Use the remainder of the wool length used to tie the strands to wind around the top to form a tassel – if you do this slightly down from the top of the tied strands it creates a fuller head to the tassel. Tie the tassels securely to each of the 4 ends of the cords. Trim the bottom edge of the tassels to neaten lengths.

Embroidering the Panels

This is executed in cross stitch throughout, using Green, Red and adding in Black, Blue and Yellow as indicated on the chart, with each cross stitch covering one knitted stitch. (More information is given in the 'Colour Work' section in Chapter 3).

Left front

On st.st panel of left front, count up 4 rows from start of st.st after ribbing and mark with a pin.
Count in 2 sts. from right edge of st.st panel (as you are looking at it on right side of work) and mark (this will give you 1 st. clear of the embroidery on either side).

Start the embroidery on the 5th st. up and 3rd st. in from the right edge of the st.st panel using Blue.
Complete the chart and repeat the first section.

Right front

Use reversed chart and start on 5th st. up and 3rd st. in from left edge of the st.st. panel using Blue.
Complete to mirror the left front.

The two front panels of stocking stitch are the background for floral motifs worked in cross stitch.

The charts given are from the original pattern, but with reverse placings also given here for simpler working. The overlapping stitches have been included as a guide to placing.

Making Up

Sew sleeves in place.
Sew underarm and sleeve seams.
Sew on buttons to left front to correspond with buttonholes.

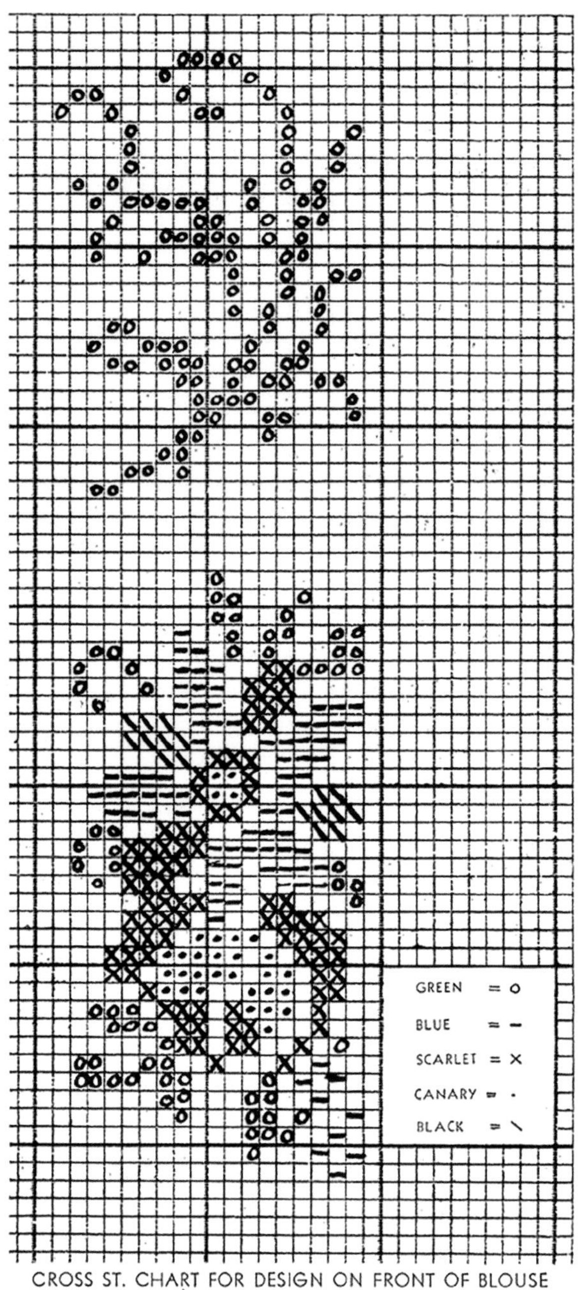

The original cross stitch chart for the left front.

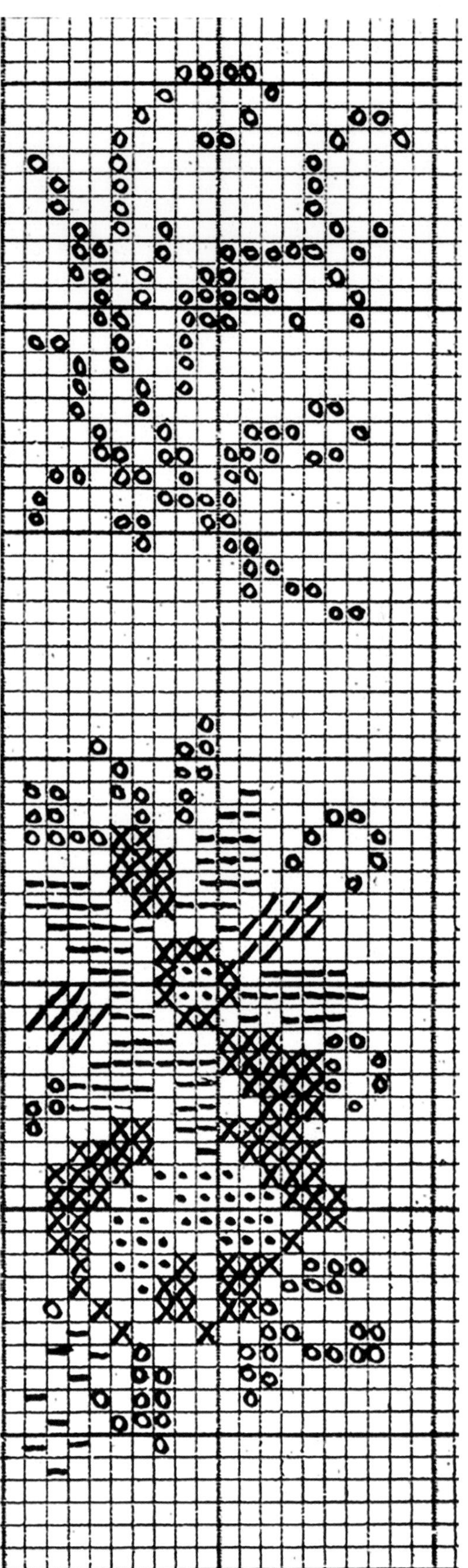

The chart for the right front, mirroring the embroidery panels.

M. H. B

June Clyde Sets a Fashion

The smocking texture was very fashionable in knitwear of the 1930s and the June Clyde Jacket has added a Tyrolean touch with contrasting coloured edgings and a tie cord.

The same smocking effect is created on the back, fronts and sleeves of the June Clyde jacket.

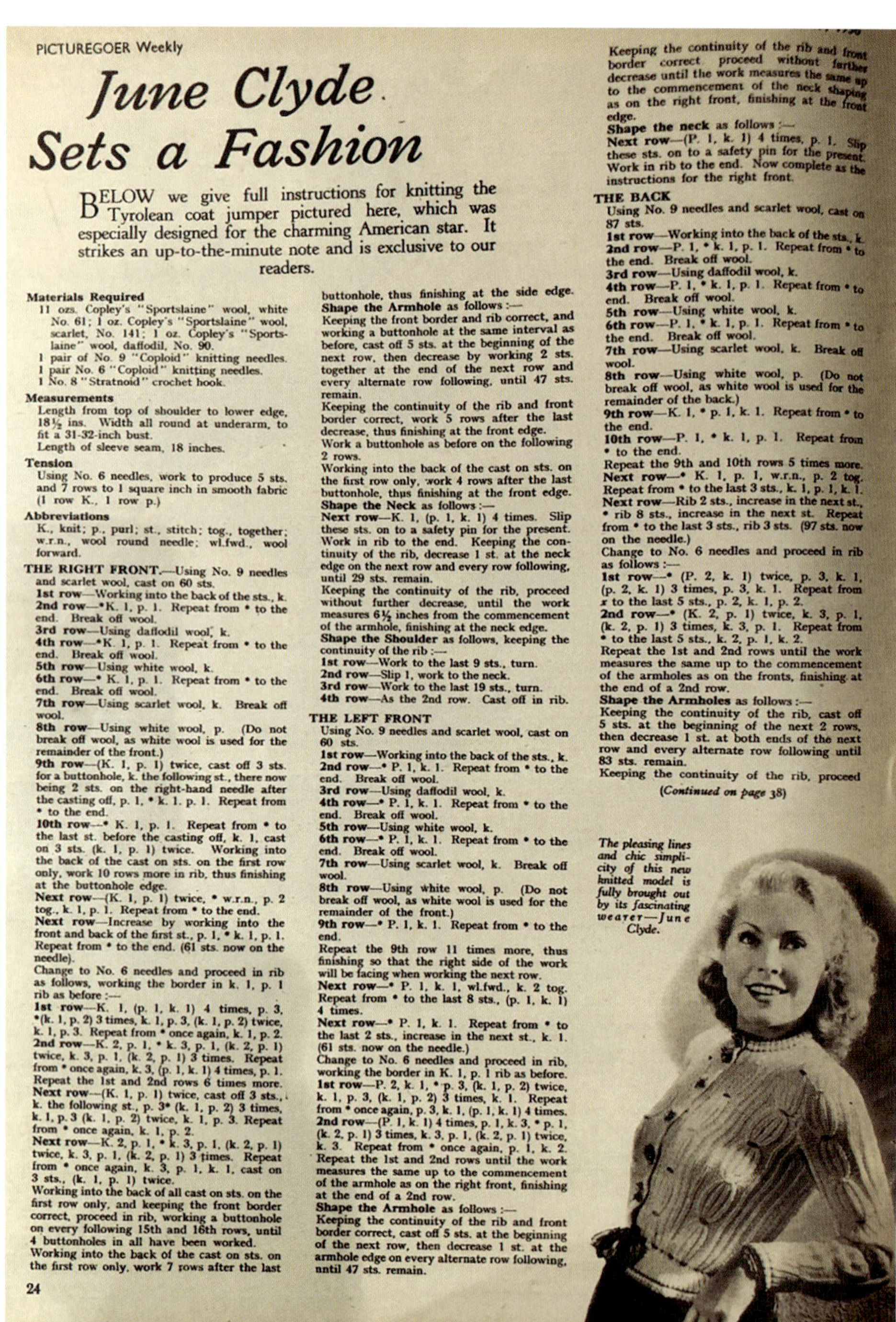

PICTUREGOER Weekly

June Clyde Sets a Fashion

BELOW we give full instructions for knitting the Tyrolean coat jumper pictured here, which was especially designed for the charming American star. It strikes an up-to-the-minute note and is exclusive to our readers.

Materials Required
11 ozs. Copley's "Sportslaine" wool, white No. 61; 1 oz. Copley's "Sportslaine" wool, scarlet, No. 141; 1 oz. Copley's "Sportslaine" wool, daffodil, No. 90.
1 pair of No. 9 "Coploid" knitting needles.
1 pair No. 6 "Coploid" knitting needles.
1 No. 8 "Stratnoid" crochet hook.

Measurements
Length from top of shoulder to lower edge, 18½ ins. Width all round at underarm, to fit a 31-32-inch bust.
Length of sleeve seam, 18 inches.

Tension
Using No. 6 needles, work to produce 5 sts. and 7 rows to 1 square inch in smooth fabric (1 row K., 1 row p.)

Abbreviations
K., knit; p., purl; st., stitch; tog., together; w.r.n., wool round needle; wl.fwd., wool forward.

THE RIGHT FRONT.—Using No. 9 needles and scarlet wool, cast on 60 sts.
1st row—Working into the back of the sts., k.
2nd row—*K. 1, p. 1. Repeat from * to the end. Break off wool.
3rd row—Using daffodil wool, k.
4th row—*K. 1, p. 1. Repeat from * to the end. Break off wool.
5th row—Using white wool, k.
6th row—* K. 1, p. 1. Repeat from * to the end. Break off wool.
7th row—Using scarlet wool, k. Break off wool.
8th row—Using white wool, p. (Do not break off wool, as white wool is used for the remainder of the front.)
9th row—(K. 1, p. 1) twice, cast off 3 sts. for a buttonhole, k. the following st., there now being 2 sts. on the right-hand needle after the casting off, p. 1, * k. 1. p. 1. Repeat from * to the end.
10th row—* K. 1, p. 1. Repeat from * to the last st. before the casting off, k. 1, cast on 3 sts. (k. 1, p. 1) twice. Working into the back of the cast on sts. on the first row only, work 10 rows more in rib, thus finishing at the buttonhole edge.
Next row—(K. 1, p. 1) twice, * w.r.n., p. 2 tog., k. 1, p. 1. Repeat from * to the end.
Next row—Increase by working into the front and back of the first st., p. 1, * k. 1, p. 1. Repeat from * to the end. (61 sts. now on the needle).
Change to No. 6 needles and proceed in rib as follows, working the border in k. 1, p. 1 rib as before :—
1st row—K. 1, (p. 1, k. 1) 4 times, p. 3, *(k. 1, p. 2) 3 times, k. 1, p. 3, (k. 1, p. 2) twice, k. 1, p. 3. Repeat from * once again, k. 1, p. 2.
2nd row—K. 2, p. 1, * k. 3, p. 1, (k. 2, p. 1) twice, k. 3, p. 1, (k. 2, p. 1) 3 times. Repeat from * once again, k. 3, (p. 1, k. 1) 4 times, p. 1.
Repeat the 1st and 2nd rows 6 times more.
Next row—(K. 1, p. 1) twice, cast off 3 sts., k. the following st., p. 3* (k. 1, p. 2) 3 times, k. 1, p. 3 (k. 1, p. 2) twice, k. 1, p. 3. Repeat from * once again, k. 1, p. 2.
Next row—K. 2, p. 1, * k. 3, p. 1, (k. 2, p. 1) twice, k. 3, p. 1, (k. 2, p. 1) 3 times. Repeat from * once again, k. 3, p. 1, k. 1, cast on 3 sts., (k. 1, p. 1) twice.
Working into the back of all cast on sts. on the first row only, and keeping the front border correct, proceed in rib, working a buttonhole on every following 15th and 16th rows, until 4 buttonholes in all have been worked.
Working into the back of the cast on sts. on the first row only, work 7 rows after the last buttonhole, thus finishing at the side edge.
Shape the Armhole as follows :—
Keeping the front border and rib correct, and working a buttonhole at the same interval as before, cast off 5 sts. at the beginning of the next row, then decrease by working 2 sts. together at the end of the next row and every alternate row following, until 47 sts. remain.
Keeping the continuity of the rib and front border correct, work 5 rows after the last decrease, thus finishing at the front edge.
Work a buttonhole as before on the following 2 rows.
Working into the back of the cast on sts. on the first row only, work 4 rows after the last buttonhole, thus finishing at the front edge.
Shape the Neck as follows :—
Next row—K. 1, (p. 1, k. 1) 4 times. Slip these sts. on to a safety pin for the present. Work in rib to the end. Keeping the continuity of the rib, decrease 1 st. at the neck edge on the next row and every row following, until 29 sts. remain.
Keeping the continuity of the rib, proceed without further decrease, until the work measures 6½ inches from the commencement of the armhole, finishing at the neck edge.
Shape the Shoulder as follows, keeping the continuity of the rib :—
1st row—Work to the last 9 sts., turn.
2nd row—Slip 1, work to the neck.
3rd row—Work to the last 19 sts., turn.
4th row—As the 2nd row. Cast off in rib.

THE LEFT FRONT
Using No. 9 needles and scarlet wool, cast on 60 sts.
1st row—Working into the back of the sts., k.
2nd row—* P. 1, k. 1. Repeat from * to the end. Break off wool.
3rd row—Using daffodil wool, k.
4th row—* P. 1, k. 1. Repeat from * to the end. Break off wool.
5th row—Using white wool, k.
6th row—* P. 1, k. 1. Repeat from * to the end. Break off wool.
7th row—Using scarlet wool, k. Break off wool.
8th row—Using white wool, p. (Do not break off wool, as white wool is used for the remainder of the front.)
9th row—* P. 1, k. 1. Repeat from * to the end.
Repeat the 9th row 11 times more, thus finishing so that the right side of the work will be facing when working the next row.
Next row—* P. 1, k. 1, wl.fwd., k. 2 tog. Repeat from * to the last 8 sts., (p. 1, k. 1) 4 times.
Next row—* P. 1, k. 1. Repeat from * to the last 2 sts., increase in the next st., k. 1. (61 sts. now on the needle.)
Change to No. 6 needles and proceed in rib, working the border in K. 1, p. 1 rib as before.
1st row—P. 2, k. 1, * p. 3, (k. 1, p. 2) twice, k. 1, p. 3, (k. 1, p. 2) 3 times, k. 1. Repeat from * once again, p. 3, k. 1, (p. 1, k. 1) 4 times.
2nd row—(P. 1, k. 1) 4 times, p. 1, k. 3, * p. 1, (k. 2, p. 1) 3 times, k. 3, p. 1, (k. 2, p. 1) twice, k. 3. Repeat from * once again, p. 1, k. 2.
Repeat the 1st and 2nd rows until the work measures the same up to the commencement of the armhole as on the right front, finishing at the end of a 2nd row.
Shape the Armhole as follows :—
Keeping the continuity of the rib and front border correct, cast off 5 sts. at the beginning of the next row, then decrease 1 st. at the armhole edge on every alternate row following, until 47 sts. remain.
Keeping the continuity of the rib and front border correct proceed without further decrease until the work measures the same up to the commencement of the neck shaping as on the right front, finishing at the front edge.
Shape the neck as follows :—
Next row—(P. 1, k. 1) 4 times, p. 1. Slip these sts. on to a safety pin for the present. Work in rib to the end. Now complete as the instructions for the right front.

THE BACK
Using No. 9 needles and scarlet wool, cast on 87 sts.
1st row—Working into the back of the sts., k.
2nd row—P. 1, * k. 1, p. 1. Repeat from * to the end. Break off wool.
3rd row—Using daffodil wool, k.
4th row—P. 1, * k. 1, p. 1. Repeat from * to end. Break off wool.
5th row—Using white wool, k.
6th row—P. 1, * k. 1, p. 1. Repeat from * to the end. Break off wool.
7th row—Using scarlet wool, k. Break off wool.
8th row—Using white wool, p. (Do not break off wool, as white wool is used for the remainder of the back.)
9th row—K. 1, * p. 1, k. 1. Repeat from * to the end.
10th row—P. 1, * k. 1, p. 1. Repeat from * to the end.
Repeat the 9th and 10th rows 5 times more.
Next row—* K. 1, p. 1, w.r.n., p. 2 tog. Repeat from * to the last 3 sts., k. 1, p. 1, k. 1.
Next row—Rib 2 sts., increase in the next st., * rib 8 sts., increase in the next st. Repeat from * to the last 3 sts., rib 3 sts. (97 sts. now on the needle.)
Change to No. 6 needles and proceed in rib as follows :—
1st row—* (P. 2, k. 1) twice, p. 3, k. 1, (p. 2, k. 1) 3 times, p. 3, k. 1. Repeat from x to the last 5 sts., p. 2, k. 1, p. 2.
2nd row—* (K. 2, p. 1) twice, k. 3, p. 1, (k. 2, p. 1) 3 times, k. 3, p. 1. Repeat from * to the last 5 sts., k. 2, p. 1, k. 2.
Repeat the 1st and 2nd rows until the work measures the same up to the commencement of the armholes as on the fronts, finishing at the end of a 2nd row.
Shape the Armholes as follows :—
Keeping the continuity of the rib, cast off 5 sts. at the beginning of the next 2 rows, then decrease 1 st. at both ends of the next row and every alternate row following until 83 sts. remain.
Keeping the continuity of the rib, proceed

(*Continued on page* 38)

The pleasing lines and chic simplicity of this new knitted model is fully brought out by its fascinating wearer—June Clyde.

24

'June Clyde Sets a Fashion' pattern from Picturegoer magazine of Saturday, 17 October 1936.

Of the leading knitting pattern designer-publishers of the day, Copley's was way ahead of its competitors in launching leaflets for Tyrolean jackets. Evidence points to them being credited with publishing the very first pattern bearing the name of Tyrolean as early as 1936, even before the first British magazines began to feature these.

Having first come across this design as Copley's leaflet[1], the hunt began to track down which issue of *Picturegoer* had featured the pattern, as mentioned on the leaflet cover. The detective work eventually revealed the exact issue, which very satisfyingly gives us a precise date for when the pattern was first launched.

Who would have thought it possible to be able to pinpoint this so precisely, but here we have the charming American actress, June Clyde, living and working in England at the time, endorsing the new Tyrolean style which she promotes as her own (and why not!). The article does not name the designer, but uses Copley's wools, and shortly afterwards the same pattern is published by them as leaflet number 637 with a delightful quote by June Clyde to strengthen its promotion. Their listings show that they also issued another Lady's Tyrolean Jacket pattern at the same time – number 636 – but unfortunately this pattern has so far proved elusive.

Picturegoer seems a most unlikely publication to feature knitting instructions and possibly the very first named Tyrolean knitted jacket pattern. This was neither a needlework nor a general lady's magazine, but a widely popular British publication of a weekly issue centred around the thriving cinema industry. With its huge following, the magazine reflected the power and reach of the cinema and its idols, which should not be even slightly underestimated at this time. This popular publication had a far-reaching influence, presenting 'behind the scenes' stories about the stars, with the ability to promote any message to their audience by association with featured celebrities. This is still a most powerful vehicle and as familiar to us today as it was then, but bear in mind that there was not the competition from wider platforms which we know today. Their message was stronger for being more focused.

The wording on the leaflet seems to indicate that *Picturegoer* had agreed some exclusivity for the launch of the pattern before Copley's released the pattern as their own. This gives some indication of the force of the market, where the magazine ensured it was first to publicize a Tyrolean pattern. The endearing editorial notes by June Clyde on the cover of the Copley's leaflet refer to the earlier *Picturegoer* article of which she was so proud, and her obvious enthusiasm for this new style.

This year's loveliest hand-knits seem to have been inspired by the Tyrol – and isn't mine the prettiest of all? Look at these cute 'buttons' which are just tufts of gay wool. And the cable effect – simply ribbing drawn together at intervals by two or three colourful stitches! I felt it would be a shame to keep such a gem all to myself so I gladly agreed to let the instructions be published. You'll find it easy and quick to make and I hope you'll love it as much as I do.

What makes it all the more intriguing is that *Picturegoer* did not feature knitted fashions on a regular basis and, with only a few of their weekly issues offering patterns for knitwear endorsed by a leading lady, we find here what is most probably the very first Tyrolean knitting pattern bearing the glorious title 'June Clyde sets a fashion!'

If it is possible to set a precise date to the first publicly available Tyrolean knitting pattern in Britain, here it is: Saturday, 17 October 1936.

With great faith that this is one of the first – if not the *very* first – published Tyrolean pattern available in Britain, it is included here in all its glory, with updated instructions and knitted up in a modern yarn that matches the original perfectly.

It is simple to knit, and the 'smocking' effect which is created after knitting was very fashionable at the time, as found in many contemporary patterns. The added embellishments of coloured edgings and tassels are unmistakably Tyrolean in style.

Thicker yarns were very popular in the 1930s as home knitting evolved, and would no doubt have continued in favour for their speed of work and extra warmth, had the war not impacted so greatly on wool supplies. The thickness of June Clyde's jacket gives this an added contemporary feel for today, and finding a compatible substitute for the yarn was straightforward with the tension recommended perfectly matching the Worsted yarn (a thickness between DK and Aran) used to re-create the original.

However, the size of the original pattern was a slim 31–32", and the worsted used achieves the same tension of 20 sts. to 10 cm/4" (when knitted on the brand's recommended 4.5 mm/7 needles). The whole piece is knitted in a rib, which is then cleverly drawn together to create a smocking effect, and this does have elasticity, but for a more forgiving size a larger needle is suggested for the main work in the instructions below.

Frivolous touches are often seen in 1930s knitting patterns, such as pompoms, bows and other decorative details, and though their practicality may not be ideal, the tufted 'buttons' of this jacket give delightful and unusual embellishments. The button bands are knitted integrally.

The unusual closure for the June Clyde jacket of coloured wool tufts.

No. **637**

Instructions for knitting June Clyde's pet woollie appeared recently in the "Picturegoer" and are reproduced in this leaflet by permission of that paper and Miss Clyde Here is what she says :

This year's loveliest hand-knits seem to have been inspired by the Tyrol— and isn't mine the prettiest of all? Look at those cute "buttons", which are just tufts of gay wool. And the cable effect—simply ribbing drawn together at intervals by two or three colourful stitches! I felt it would be a shame to keep such a gem all to myself so I gladly agreed to let the instructions be published.

You'll find it easy and quick to make and I hope you'll love it as much as I do.

June Clyde

June Clyde's TYROLEAN COAT

IN

"SPORTSLAINE" Wool

Price 3d

Leaflet No. **637**

L. COPLEY—SMITH & SONS LTD
MANCHESTER AND LONDON

The cover of Copley's pattern 637, with June Clyde's charming endorsement.

Materials

The recreated model used Sirdar's 'Country Classic' worsted (50% merino wool and 50% acrylic)
6 × 100 g balls Main colour (M) in Clotted Cream 659 (cream)
1 × 100 g ball Port 654 (red)
1 × 100 g ball Vanilla 675 (yellow)
7 × buttons if you prefer these to the tufts
1 pair 4 mm/8 needles
1 × pair 4.5 mm/7 (5 mm/6) needles
1 × 4 mm crochet hook

Measurements

The original pattern is for size 31–32", and knitted to match comes up true to this size
For a more generous fit to a size 34–36" use 5 mm/6 needles

Tension

Pattern recommends 20 sts. to 10 cm/4" and the Sirdar worsted yarn used matches this by using 4.5 mm/7 needles – but please note measurements above for a more generous fit

Right Front

Using 4 mm/8 needles and Red wool, cast on 60 sts.
1st row: Working into the back of the sts., knit
2nd row: *K1, P1, rep fr. *to the end. Break off Red wool
3rd row: Using Yellow wool, knit
4th row: *K1, P1, rep fr. *to the end. Break off Yellow wool
5th row: Using Cream wool, knit
6th row: *K1, P1, rep fr. *to the end. Break off cream wool
7th row: Using red wool, knit. Break off red wool
8th row: Using cream wool, purl. (Do not break off cream wool as this is used for the remainder of the front)
9th row: (K1, P1) twice, cast off 3 sts. for a buttonhole. K the following st., there now being 2 sts. on the right-hand needle after the casting off. P1, *K1, P1, rep fr. *to the end
10th row: *K1, P1, rep fr. *to the last st. before the casting off, K1, cast on 3 sts. (K1, P1) twice.
Working into the back of the cast-on sts. on the 1st row only, work 10 rows more in rib, thus finishing at the buttonhole edge
Next row: (K1, P1) twice, *w.r.n., P2tog, K1, P1, rep fr. *to the end
Next row: Inc. by working into the front and back of the first st., P1, *K1, P1, rep fr. *to the end (61 sts. now on needle)

Change to 4.5 mm/7 (5 mm/6) needles and proceed in rib as follows, working the border in K1, P1 rib as before:
1st row: K1, (P1, K1) 4 times, P3 *(K1, P2) 3 times, K1, P3, (K1, P2) twice, K1, P3, rep fr. *once again, K1, P2
2nd row: K2, P1, *K3, P1, (K2, P1) twice, K3, P1, (K2, P1) 3 times, rep fr. *once again, K3, (P1, K1) 4 times, P1
Rep the 1st and 2nd rows 6 times more.
Next row: (K1, P1) twice, cast off 3 sts., K the following st., P3 *(K1, P2) 3 times, K1, P3, (K1, P2) twice, K1, P3, rep fr. *once again, K1, P2
Next row: K2, P1 *K3, P1, (K2, P1) twice, K3, P1, (K2, P1) 3 times, rep fr. *once again, K3, P1, K1. Cast on 3 sts. (K1, P1) twice
Working into the back of all cast-on sts. on the 1st row only, and keeping the front border correct, proceed in rib, working a buttonhole on every following 15th and 16th rows, until 4 buttonholes in all have been worked.
Working into the back of the cast-on sts. on the 1st row only, work 7 rows after the last buttonhole, thus finishing at the side edge.

Shape armhole

Keeping the front border and rib correct, and working a buttonhole at the same interval as before, cast off 5 sts. at the beginning of the next row, then decrease by working 2 sts. together at the end of the next row and every alternate row following, until 47 sts. remain.

Keeping the continuity of the rib and front border correct, work 5 rows after the last decrease, thus finishing at the front edge.

Work a buttonhole as before on the following 2 rows.

Working into the back of the cast-on sts. on the 1st row only, work 4 rows after the last buttonhole, thus finishing at the front edge.

Shape neck

Next row: K1, (P1, K1) 4 times. Slip these sts. onto a safety pin for the present. Work in rib to the end.

Keeping the continuity of the rib, decrease 1 st. at the neck edge on the next row and every row following until 29 sts. remain.

Keeping the continuity of the rib, proceed without further decrease, until the work measures 16.5 cm/6.5″ from the commencement of the armhole, finishing at the neck edge.

Shape shoulder

Keeping the continuity of the rib:
1st row: Work to the last 9 sts., turn
2nd row: Slip 1, work to the neck
3rd row: Work to the last 19 sts., turn
4th row: As the 2nd row
Cast off in rib.

Left Front

Using 4 mm/8 needles and Red wool, cast on 60 sts.
1st row: Working into the back of the sts., knit
2nd row: *P1, K1, rep fr. *to the end. Break off wool
3rd row: Using Yellow wool, knit
4th row: *P1, K1, rep fr. *to the end. Break off wool
5th row: Using Cream wool, knit
6th row: *P1, K1, rep fr. *to the end. Break off wool
7th row: Using Red wool, knit. Break off wool
8th row: Using Cream wool, purl. (Do not break off Cream wool, as this is used for the remainder of the front)
9th row: *P1, K1, rep fr. *to the end
Rep the 9th row 11 times more, thus finishing so that the right side of the work will be facing when working the next row.
Next row: *P1, K1, wl. fwd., K2tog, rep fr. *to the last 8 sts., (P1, K1) 4 times
Next row: *P1, K1, rep fr. *to the last 2 sts., inc. in the next st., K1 (61 sts. on the needle)
Change to 4.5 mm/7 (5 mm/6) needles and proceed in rib, working the border in K1, P1 rib as before.
1st row: P2, K1, *P3, (K1, P2) twice, K1, P3, (K1, P2) 3 times, K1, rep fr. *once again, P3, K1, (P1, K1) 4 times
2nd row: (P1, K1) 4 times, P1, K3, *P1, (K2, P1) 3 times, K3, P1, (K2, P1) twice, K3, rep fr.*once again, P1, K2
Rep the 1st and 2nd rows until the work measures the same up to the commencement of the armhole as on the right front, finishing at the end of a 2nd row.

Shape armhole

Keeping the continuity of the rib and front border correct, cast off 5 sts. at the beg. of the next row, then dec. 1 st. at the armhole edge on every alternate row following until 47 sts. remain.

Keeping the continuity of the rib and front border correct, proceed without further decrease until the work measures the same up to the commencement of the neck shaping as on the right front, finishing at the front edge.

Shape neck

Next row: (P1, K1) 4 times, P1. Slip these sts. onto a safety pin for the present. Work in rib to the end.
Now complete as the instructions for the right front.

Back

Using 4 mm/8 needles and Red wool cast on 87 sts.
1st row: Working into the back of the stitches, knit
2nd row: P1, *K1, P1, rep fr. *to the end. Break off wool
3rd row: Using Yellow wool, knit
4th row: P1, *K1, P1, rnep fr. *to the end. Break off wool
5th row: Using Cream wool, knit
6th row: P1, *K1, P1, rep fr. *to the end. Break off wool
7th row: Using Red wool, knit. Break off wool
8th row: Using Cream wool, purl (do not break off cream wool as this is used for the remainder of the back)
9th row: K1, *P1, K1, rep fr. *to the end
10th row: P1, *K1, P1, rep fr. *to the end
Rep the 9th and 10th rows 5 times more.
Next row: *K1, P1, w.r.n., P2tog, rep fr. *to the last 3 sts., K1, P1, K1
Next row: Rib 2 sts., inc. in the next st., *rib 8 sts., inc. in the next st., rep fr. *to the last 3 sts., rib 3 sts. (97 sts. now on the needle)

Change to 4.5 mm/7 (5 mm/6) needles.
1st row: *(P2, K1) twice, P3, K1, (P2, K1) 3 times, P3, K1, rep fr. *to the last 5 sts., P2, K1, P2
2nd row: *(K2, P1) twice, K3, P1, (K2, P1) 3 times, P1, rep fr. *to the last 5 sts., K2, P1, K2
Rep the 1st and 2nd rows until the work measures the same up to the commencement of the armholes as on the fronts, finishing at the end of a 2nd row.

Shape armholes

Keeping the continuity of the rib, cast off 5 sts. at the beginning of the next 2 rows, then dec. 1 st. at both ends of the next row and every alternate row following until 83 sts. remain.

Keeping the continuity of the rib, proceed without further decrease until the work measures 16.5 cm/6.5″ from the commencement of the armhole, finishing so that the right side of the work will be facing when working the next row.

Shape shoulders

Keeping the continuity of the rib:
1st row: Work to the last 9 sts., turn
2nd row: Slip 1, work to the last 9 sts., turn
3rd and 4th rows: Slip 1, work to the last 19 sts., turn
5th row: Slip 1, work to the last 29 sts., turn
6th row: Slip 1, work to the last 29 sts. Break off wool
Slip all the sts. onto one needle, turn and re-joining the wool, with the right side of the work facing, cast off as follows:
Next row: Cast off 29 sts., work the following 24 sts. in rib, there now being 25 sts. on the right-hand needle, cast off the remaining 29 sts. Break off wool
Slip the remaining 25 sts. onto a stitch holder or spare needle.

Sleeves (Both Alike)

Using 4 mm/8 needles and Red wool, cast on 38 sts.
Working into the back of the sts. on the 1st row only, work rows 1–8 inclusive as worked at the commencement of the right front.

Now proceed as follows:
Using Cream wool, work 16 rows in K1, P1 rib, increasing 1 st. at the end of the last row.
Change to 4.5 mm/7 (5 mm/6) needles and using Cream wool, proceed in rib as follows:
1st row: P3, (K1, P2) 3 times, K1, P3, (K1, P2) twice K1, P3, (K1, P2) 3 times, K1, P3
2nd row: K3, (P1, K2) 3 times, P1, K3, (P1, K2) twice, P1, K3, (P1, K2) 3 times P1, K3
Rep these 2 rows twice more.
Keeping the continuity of the rib, increase at both ends of the next row and every following 6th row, until there are 65 sts. on the needle.
Keeping the continuity of the rib, proceed without further increases until the work measures 44.5 cm/17.5" (or desired length) from the commencement, finishing so that the right side of the work will be facing when working the next row.

Shape top

Keeping the continuity of the rib, cast off 5 sts. at the beginning of the next 2 rows, then decrease 1 st. at both ends of the next row and every alternate row until 43 sts. remain.

Now dec. 1 st. at both ends of every row following until 11 sts. remain. Cast off purlwise.
Work a second sleeve in the same manner.

Collar

Join the shoulders of the back and fronts together.

Slip the border sts. of the right front from the safety pin onto a 4 mm/8 needle, the point to the inside edge. Join the Cream wool and knit up 20 sts. along the side of the neck.

Slip the 25 sts. of the back onto a spare needle and then slip them onto a second spare needle, thus the point will be towards the right shoulder. P1, (K1, P1) 12 times across these sts. Knit up 20 sts. along the left side of the neck. Slip the border sts. of the left front onto a 4 mm/8 needle, the point to the inside edge, K1 (P1, K1) 4 times across these sts. (83 sts. now on the needle).

Now proceed as follows:
1st row: Using Cream wool, P1, *K1, P1, rep fr. *to the end
2nd row: K1, *P1, K1, rep fr. *to the end
3rd row: As the 1st row. Break off wool
4th row: Using Red wool, knit. Break off wool
5th row: Using Cream wool, purl
6th and 7th rows: As the 2nd and 3rd rows
8th row: Using Yellow wool, K4, cast off 3 for a buttonhole, K to the end
9th row: *P1, K1, rep fr. *to the casting off, cast on 3 sts. (K1, P1) twice. Break off wool

The collar of the June Clyde jacket is worked in the red and yellow contrasts.

10th row: Using Red wool and working into the back of the cast-on sts., knit
11th row: P1, *K1, P1, rep fr. *to the end
Using Red wool, cast off in rib.

Embroidery

Mark out each front as shown, commencing 3 cm/1.25″ from the K1, P1 ribbing at the lower edge, joining together the first group of four K1 ribs.

Leaving 5 cm/2.5″ between each 'join' continue joining each group of four K1 ribs alternately, leaving a group of three K1 ribs between each stripe of 'joins'.

Work over these 'joins' as follows:
Using Yellow wool and commencing at the 'join' nearest the lower edge, work over the four K1 ribs drawing them together with a 12 mm/0.5″ loop.
Work over the 'join' several times in the same manner and fasten off securely on the wrong side.
Using Red wool, work in the same manner over the next 'join'.
Using Yellow and Red wool alternately, work over the remaining 'joins' as before.
Embroider the back and sleeves in the same manner.

Marking out the stitches that gather together the lines of ribbing into 'smocked' details.

The width of the gathering stitches needs to be equal each time to create the regularity of the effect.

The coloured wool is passed under the knit stitches of the ribbing to create the 'smocking'.

Making Up

Pressing is not recommended as this would flatten the natural elasticity of the ribbing.
Stitch the sleeves into position.

Strands of the yellow and red contrast colours are alternated for gathering the rib lines together.

Join the side and sleeve seams.

Make the 'tufts' for fastening in the following manner:

Cut 12 strands each of Yellow and Red wool 37 mm/1.5″ in length.

Place the strands together and secure by winding Cream wool several times firmly round the middle.

Fasten off securely.

Trim the ends neatly to leave a 'tuft' 32 mm/1.25″ in length.

Make 6 more 'tufts' in the same way.

Attach the 'tufts' on to the left front to correspond with the buttonholes.

Waist tie cord

Using the crochet hook and one strand of each of the Yellow and Red wools together, work a chain 91.5 cm/36″ in length, fasten off.

Thread the cord through the holes at the waist and finish off each end by attaching a small tassel (*see* Chapter 3, 'Finishing Touches' for drawstrings).

Attach the tassels firmly and trim as needed.

Small lengths of red and yellow wool are cut equally to create tufts which will be placed instead of buttons to close the jacket.

The red and yellow contrast wools are crocheted together to make the tie cord, which is threaded through the eyelets at the waist, finished with tassels.

Annie's Jacket

The detail of Annie's Jacket.

The back and fronts of Annie's Jacket are embroidered, contrasting with the sleeves in plain stocking stitch featuring dramatic pleating at the shoulder.

Copley's were one of the first to design and publish patterns in the Tyrolean style. This is the 'Lady's Tyrolean Coat 891' from around 1936–37.

This pattern dates from the later 1930s, and as number 891 it post-dates Copley's June Clyde pattern (*see* above) by about a year or more, therefore probably dating it to around 1937–38.

The varied colour combinations suggested are a real joy to see, showing that even in the early days of the fashion there was no restriction to 'traditional' Tyrolean colourways. These more adventurous choices of colours do not seem to have been as popular, however, until at least the 1950s. Here is an opportunity to recreate a 1930s Tyrolean pattern in delightful colours, pastel or vibrant, as an alternative to the classic cream background, knowing them to be true to their time.

For this recreated model the colours chosen were as close as possible to 'Beauty Pink, edged with Mermaid'. Some of the suggested names, although so charmingly lyrical, give no clue at all as to their actual colour! So the message is to enjoy putting them together to your own individual choice.

The original pattern uses 4 ply, but this is vintage 4 ply, which is slightly thicker than our modern yarn of the same name (this is explained in detail in Chapter 2 in the section on matching vintage yarns).

The original is for a small size – to fit a 32–33" bust – knitted with a recommended tension of 30 sts. to 4 cm on 3.25 mm needles, which with the weight of yarn used would have given a dense fabric. The beautifully styled volume of the sleeves needs a similar yarn that will give a firm knitted fabric to support the shape and create the desired effect. The yarn chosen accordingly for knitting this model is a modern 4 ply which, though finer than vintage 4 ply, holds its shape while allowing for draping of the pleats at the top of the sleeves. Knitted on 3.25 mm needles it achieves a finished size which fits a 34–35" bust (tension of 28 sts. to 4 cm). For a size 36–38" bust, work with 3.75 mm needles throughout (other modern 4 ply yarns are suggested at the beginning of the pattern for a similar firm finish).

The embroidery worked on the recreated model is more elaborate than the pattern's suggested stitches, which would be simpler to work – you can of course be as simple or as complicated as you wish, and can omit embroidering the back – or the entire garment altogether – if preferred. Even if left without embroidery, the coloured edgings and textured stitch trellis give an unmistakable Tyrolean flair. The sleeves are plain stocking stitch and their statement is in the fullness and dramatically pleated tops. As these are otherwise unadorned, the back could also be knitted plain and just the fronts knitted with the grid stitch detail, if preferred, for a quicker knit.

The original pattern explains every row line by line, and has been adapted here with a few amendments, noted in the instructions where appropriate. Lengthy patterns like this one do not necessarily mean complicated instructions, and in this one they offer a fool-proof way of keeping check at every row, and become quite reassuring as each stage is clearly confirmed.

Lady's Tyrolean Coat

For warm sunny days make this model, alive with tropical flowers, on a cool white background. Otherwise pastel shades such as Beauty Pink 1085 edged with Mermaid 1017 and flowers in Stadium Blue 1081, St. Moritz 1082, Jade 32, Hunting Yellow 1037 and Purple 222. Or Iris Blue 127, edging Bloom A1065, embroidered Sunflower 160, Charleston Rose 42, New Delphinium 1041, Parrot Green 200, Symphony 1073, Bloom A1065. Or it will be just as attractive in Black 60 or Navy 85 with bright coloured flowers.

Copley's 891 suggested some delightful variations on traditional cream background colours, and Annie's Jacket followed the suggestion of 'Beauty Pink edged with Mermaid'.

Materials

10 × 50 g balls of 4 ply (M): Debbie Bliss 4 Ply Rialto 100% Merino in 'Blush' (034)

1 × 50 g ball 4 ply contrast (C): King Cole 100% Merino 4 ply in 'Ivy' (3293)

Oddments of 4 contrasting shades of 4 ply for embroidery

1 pair 3.25 mm knitting needles (3.75 mm for larger size)

1 × 3 mm crochet hook

6 × buttons (*please see note on buttonhole band shaping for amendments – as it is generally easier to source 6 vintage buttons than 7*)

Measurements

Bust 34" (36")

Length at centre back 48 cm/19"

Sleeve seam length 47 cm/18.5"

Tension

28 sts. to 10 cm/4" on 3.25 mm/10 needles

Right Front

Using main colour (M), cast on 60 sts.

Working into the back of the sts. P 1 row (*if this is not done, the work has a tendency to curl when finished as there is no edging*).

Now proceed as follows:
1st row: K1 *T2F, K6, rep fr. *to last 3 sts., T2F, K1
2nd row: K1, P to last st., K1
3rd row: K2, *T2B, K4, T2F, rep fr. *to last 2 sts., P1, K1
4th row: K1, *K2, P6, rep fr. *to last 3 sts., K3
5th row: K1, *P2, take wool to back of work, T2B, K2, T2F, rep fr. *to last 3 sts., P2, K1
6th row: K4, *P4, K4, rep fr. *to end
7th row: K1, P3, *take wool to back of work, T2B, T2F, P4, rep fr. *to last 8 sts., take wool to back of work, T2B, T2F, P3, K1
8th row: K5, *P2, K6, rep fr. *to last 7 sts., P2, K5
9th row: K1, P4, *take wool to back of work, T2B, P 6, rep fr. *to the last 7 sts., take wool to back of work, T2B, P4, K1
10th row: As 8th row
11th row: K1, P3, *take wool to back of work, T2F, T2B, P4, rep fr. *to last 8 sts., take wool to back of work, T2F, T2B, P3, K1
12th row: As 6th row
13th row: K1, P2, *take wool to back of work, T2F, K2, T2B, P2, rep fr. *to last st., K1
14th row: As 4th row
15th row: K1, P1, take wool to back of work, *T2F, K4, T2B, rep fr. *to last 2 sts., P1, K1
16th row: As 2nd row
These 16 rows complete one pattern.
Repeat rows 1–16 inclusive once again, then repeat rows 1–4 inclusive.
Begin increasing at the side edge as follows:
(*Continue to take the wool to the back of the work after each purl section and before twisting the stitches at T2F or T2B. This action will not be referred to again.*)
1st row: K1, *P2, T2B, K2, T2F, rep fr. *to last 3 sts., P1, increase by working into front and back of next st., K1
2nd row: K5, *P4, K4, rep fr. *to the end
3rd row: K1, P3, *T2B, T2F, P4, rep fr. *to last st., K1
4th row: *K6, P2, rep fr. *to last 5 sts., K5
5th row: K1, P4, *T2B, P6, rep fr. *to last 8 sts., T2B, P5, K1
6th row: As 4th row
7th row: K1, P3, *T2F, T2B, P4, rep fr. *to last st., K1
8th row: As 2nd row
9th row: K1, P2, *T2F, K2, T2B, P2, rep fr. *to last 2 sts., K2
10th row: K1, P1, *K2, P6, rep fr. *to last 3 sts., K3
11th row: K1, P1, *T2F, K4, T2B, rep fr. *to last 3 sts., T2F, K1
12th row: K1, P to last st., K1
13th row: K1, *T2F, K6, rep fr. *to last 4 sts., T2F, K2
14th row: As 12th row
15th row: K2, *T2B, K4, T2F, rep fr. *to last 3 sts., K1, inc. in next st., K1
16th row: K1, P2, *K2, P6, rep fr. *to last 3 sts., K3
17th row: K1, *P2, T2B, K2, T2F, rep fr. *to last 5 sts., P2, T2B, K1
18th row: K1, P1, K4, *P4, K4, rep fr. *to end
19th row: K1, P3, *T2B, T2F, P4, rep fr. *to last 2 sts., P1, K1
20th row: K1, *K6, P2, rep fr. *to last 5 sts., K5
21st row: K1, P4, *T2B, P6, rep fr. *to last st., K1
22nd row: As 20th row
23rd row: K1, P3, *T2F, T2B, P4, rep fr. *to last 2 sts., K2
24th row: As 18th row
25th row: K1, P2, *T2F, K2, T2B, P2, rep fr. *to last 3 sts., T2F, K1
26th row: As 16th row
27th row: K1, P1, *T2F, K4, T2B, rep fr. *to last 4 sts., T2F, K2
28th row: As 12th row
29th row: K1, *T2F, K6, rep fr. *to last 5 sts., T2F, K1, inc. in next st., K1
30th row: As 12th row
31st row: K2, *T2B, K4, T2F, rep fr. *to last 5 sts., T2B, K3
32nd row: K1, P3, *K2, P6, rep fr. *to last 3 sts., K3
33rd row: K1, *P2, T2B, K2, T2F, rep fr. *to last 6 sts., P2, T2B, K2
34th row: K1, P2, K4 *P4, K4, rep fr. *to end
35th row: K1, P3, *T2B, T2F, P4, rep fr. *to last 3 sts., T2B, K1
36th row: K1, P1, *K6, P2, rep fr. *to last 5 sts., K5
37th row: K1, P4, *T2B, P6, rep fr. *to last 2 sts., K2
38th row: As 36th row
39th row: K1, P3, *T2F, T2B, P4, rep fr. *to last 3 sts., T2F, K1
40th row: As 34th row
41st row: K1, P2, *T2F, K2, T2B, P2, rep fr. *to last 4 sts., T2F, K2
42nd row: As 32nd row
43rd row: K1, P1, *T2F, K4, T2B, rep fr. *to last 5 sts., T2F, K1, inc. in next st., K1
44th row: As 12th row
45th row: K1, *T2F, K6, rep fr. *to last 7 sts., T2F, K5
46th row: As 12th row
47th row: K2, *T2B, K4, T2F, rep fr.*to last 6 sts., T2B, K4
48th row: K1, P4, *K2, P6, rep fr. *to last 3 sts., K3
49th row: K1 *P2, T2B, K2, T2F, rep fr. *to last 7 sts., P2, T2B, K3
50th row: K1, P3, K4, *P4, K4, rep fr. *to end
51st row: K1, P3, *T2B, T2F, P4, rep fr. to last 4 sts., T2B, K2
52nd row: K1, *P2, K6, rep fr. *to last 7 sts., P2, K5
53rd row: K1, P4, *T2B, P6, rep fr. *to last 3 sts., T2B, K1
54th row: As 52nd row
55th row: K1, P3, *T2F, T2B, P4, rep fr. to last 4 sts., T2F, K2
56th row: As 50th row
57th row: K1, P2, *T2F, K2, T2B, P2, rep fr. *to last 5 sts., T2F, K1, inc. in next st., K1
58th row: K1, P5, *K2, P6, rep fr. *to last 3 sts., K3
59th row: K1, P1, *T2F, K4, T2B, rep fr. *to last 7 sts., T2F, K5
60th row: As 12th row
61st row: K1, *T2F, K6, rep fr. *to end
62nd row: As 12th row

63rd row: K2, *T2B, K4, T2F, rep fr. *to last 7 sts., T2B, K5
64th row: As 58th row
65th row: K1, *P2, T2B, K2, T2F, rep fr. *to last 8 sts., P2, T2B, K4
66th row: K1, *P4, K4, rep fr. *to end
67th row: K1, P3, *T2B, T2F, P4, rep fr. *to last 5 sts., T2B, T2F, K1
68th row: K2, *P2, K6, rep fr. to last 7 sts., P2, K5
69th row: K1, P4, *T2B, P6, rep fr. *to last 4 sts., T2B, P1, K1
70th row: As 8th row
71st row: K1, P3, *T2F, T2B, P4, rep fr. *to last 5 sts., T2F, K1, inc. in next st., K1 (66 sts. now on needle)
72nd row: K2, *P4, K4, rep fr. *to end
73rd row: K1, P2, *T2F, K2, T2B, P2, rep fr. *to last 7 sts., T2F, K2, T2B, K1
74th row: K1, *P6, K2, rep fr. *to last st., K1
75th row: K1, P1, *T2F, K4, T2B, rep fr. *to last 8 sts., T2F, K4, P1, K1
76th row: As 12th row
77th row: K1, *T2F, K6, rep fr. *to last st., K1
78th row: As 12th row
79th row: K2, *T2B, K4, T2F, rep fr. *to last 8 sts., T2B, K4, P1, K1
80th row: As 74th row
81st row: K1, *P2, T2B, K2, T2F, rep fr. *to last st., K1

Shape armhole

1st row: Cast off 13 sts., K the following 4 sts., there now being 5 sts. on the right-hand needle. *P4, K4, rep fr. *to end
2nd row: K1, P3 *T2B, T2F, P4, rep fr. *to last st., K1
3rd row: Cast off 2 sts., K following 3 sts., *P2, K6, rep fr. *to last 7 sts., P2, K5
4th row: K1, P4, *T2B, P6, rep fr. *to last 6 sts., T2B, P4
5th row: Cast off 2 sts., K following st., *P2, K6, rep fr. *to last 7 sts., P2, K5
6th row: K1, P3, *T2F, T2B, P4, rep fr. *to last 5 sts., T2F, T2B, K1
7th row: P2tog, P3, K4, *P4, K4, rep fr. *to end
8th row: K1, P2, *T2F, K2, T2B, P2, rep fr. *to last 5 sts., T2F, K1, K2tog
9th row: P2tog, P2, *K2, P6, rep fr. *to last 3 sts., K3
10th row: K1, P1, *T2F, K 4, T2B, rep fr. *to last 2 sts., T2F, K2tog
11th row: P2tog, P to last st., K1
This completes the armhole shaping (44 sts. remain).
Now rep the original 16 pattern rows twice, as worked at the commencement of the front.

Shape neck

1st row: Cast off 4 sts., K the following 4 sts., *T2F, K6, rep fr. *to last 3 sts., T2F, K1
2nd row: K1, P to end
3rd row: Cast off 3 sts., the st. on the right-hand needle counting as K1, T2F, *T2B, K4, T2F, rep fr. *to last 2 sts., P1, K1
4th row: K1, *K2, P6, rep fr. *to last 4 sts., K2, P2
5th row: Cast off 3 sts., the st. on the right-hand needle counting as P1, *T2B, K2, T2F, P2, rep fr. *to last st., K1
6th row: *K4, P4, rep fr. *to last 2 sts., K2
7th row: Cast off 2 sts., K following st., *T2F, P4, T2B, rep fr. *to last 6 sts., T2F, P3, K1
8th row: K5, *P2, K6, rep fr. *to last 3 sts., P2, K1
9th row: Cast off 2 sts., the st. on the right-hand needle counting as K1, *P6, T2B, rep fr. *to last 5 sts., P4, K1
10th row: K5, *P2, K6, rep fr. *to last st., P1
11th row: Cast off 1 st., the st. on the right-hand needle counting as K1, *P4, T2F, T2B, rep fr. *to last 4 sts., P3, K1 (29 sts. remain)
12th row: K4, P4, K4, rep fr. *to last st., K1
13th row: K2, *P2, T2F, K2, T2B, rep fr. *to last 3 sts., P2, K1
14th row: K3, *P6, K2, rep fr. *to last 2 sts., P1, K1
15th row: K1, T2B, T2F, K4, rep fr. *to last 4 sts., T2B, P1, K1
16th row: K1, P to last st., K1
17th row: K2, *T2F, K6, rep fr. *to last 3 sts., T2F, K1
18th row: As 16th row
19th row: K1, *T2F, T2B, K4, rep fr. *to last 4 sts., T2F, P1, K1
20th row: As 14th row

Shape shoulder

1st row: K2, (P2, T2B, K2, T2F) twice, P2, T2B, turn
2nd row: P1, (K4, P4) twice, K5
3rd row: K1, P4, T2B, T2F, P4, T2B, turn
4th row: P1, K6, P2, K6
5th row: K1, P5, T2B, turn
6th row: P2, K6
Cast off knitwise.

Left Front

Work this exactly as the instructions for the Right Front, up to the commencement of the side increase.
Now inc. as follows:
1st row: Inc. in 1st st., P2, *T2B, K2, T2F, P2, rep fr. *to last st., K1
2nd row: K4, *P4, K4, rep fr. *to last st., K1

3rd row: K1, *P4, T2B, T2F, rep fr. *to last 4 sts., P3, K1
4th row: K5, *P2, K6, rep fr. *to end
5th row: K1, P5, *T2B, P6, rep fr. *to last 7 sts., T2B, P4, K1
6th row: As 4th row
7th row: K1, *P4, T2F, T2B, rep fr. *to last 4 sts., P3, K1
8th row: As 2nd row
9th row: K2, *P2, T2F, K2, T2B, rep fr. *to last 3 sts., P2, K1
10th row: K3, *P6, K2, rep fr. *to last 2 sts., P1, K1
11th row: K1, *T2B, T2F, K4, rep fr. *to last 4 sts., T2B, P1, K1
12th row: K1, P to last st., K1
13th row: K2, T2F, K6, rep fr. *to last 3 sts., T2F, K1
14th row: As 12th row
15th row: Inc. in 1st st., K2, *T2B, K4, T2F, rep fr. *to last 2 sts., P1, K1
16th row: K3, *P6, K2, rep fr. *to last 3 sts., P2, K1
17th row: K1, T2F, P2, *T2B, K2, T2F, P2, rep fr. *to last st., K1
18th row: K4, *P4, K4, rep fr. *to last 2 sts., P1, K1
19th row: K1, P1, *P4, T2B, T2F, rep fr. *to last 4 sts., P3, K1
20th row: K5, *P2, K6, rep fr. *to last st., K1
21st row: K1, *P6, T2B, rep fr. *to last 5 sts., P4, K1
22nd row: As 20th row
23rd row: K2, *P4, T2F, T2B, rep fr. *to last 4 sts., P3, K1
24th row: As 18th row
25th row: K1, T2B, *P2, T2F, K2, T2B, rep fr. *to last 3 sts., P2, K1
26th row: As 16th row
27th row: K2, *T2B, T2F, K4, rep fr. *to last 4 sts., T2B, P1, K1
28th row: As 12th row
29th row: Inc. in 1st st., K2, *T2F, K6, rep fr. *to last 3 sts., T2F, K1
30th row: As 12th row
31st row: K3, *T2F, T2B, K4, rep fr. *to last 4 sts., T2F, P1, K1
32nd row: K3, *P6, K2, rep fr. *to last 4 sts., P3, K1
33rd row: K2, T2F, P2. *T2B, K2, T2F, P2, rep fr. *to last st., K1
34th row: K4, *P4, K4, rep fr. *to last 3 sts., P2, K1
35th row: K1, T2F, *P4, T2B, T2F, rep fr. *to last 4 sts., P3, K1
36th row: K5, *P2, K6, rep fr. *to last 2 sts., P1, K1
37th row: K2, *P6, T2B, rep fr. *to last 5 sts., P4, K1
38th row: As 36th row
39th row: K1, T2B, *P4, T2F, T2B, rep fr. *to last 4 sts., P3, K1
40th row: As 34th row
41st row: K2, T2B, *P2, T2F, K2, T2B, rep fr. *to last 3 sts., P2, K1
42nd row: As 32nd row
43rd row: Inc. In 1st st., K2, *T2B, T2F, K4, rep fr. *to last 4 sts., T2B, P1, K1
44th row: As 12th row
45th row: K5, *T2F, K6, rep fr. *to last 3 sts., T2F, K1
46th row: As 12th row
47th row: K4, *T2F, T2B, K4, rep fr. *to last 4 sts., T2F, P1, K1
48th row: K3, *P6, K2, rep fr. *to last 5 sts., P4, K1
49th row: K3, T2F, P2, *T2B, K2, T2F, P2, rep fr. *to last st., K1
50th row: K4, *P4, K4, rep fr. *to last 4 sts., P3, K1
51st row: K2, T2F, *P4, T2B, T2F, rep fr. *to last 4 sts., P3, K1
52nd row: K5, *P2, K6, rep fr. *to last 3 sts., P2, K1
53rd row: K1, T2B, *P6, T2B, rep fr. *to last 5 sts., P4, K1
54th row: As 52nd row
55th row: K2, T2B, *P4, T2F, T2B, rep fr. *to last 4 sts., P3, K1
56th row: As 50th row
57th row: Inc. in 1st st., K2, T2B, *P2, T2F, K2, T2B, rep fr. *to last 3 sts., P2, K1
58th row: K3, *P6, K2, rep fr. *to last 6 sts., P5, K1
59th row: K5, *T2B, T2F, K4, rep fr. *to last 4 sts., T2B, P1, K1
60th row: As 12th row
61st row: *K6, T2F, rep fr. *to last st., K1
62nd row: As 12th row
63rd row: K5, T2F, *T2B, K4, T2F, rep fr. *to last 2 sts., P1, K1
64th row: As 58th row
65th row: K4, T2F, P2, *T2B, K2, T2F, P2, rep fr. *to last st., K1
66th row: *K4, P4, rep fr. *to last st., K1
67th row: K1, T2B, T2F, *P4, T2B, T2F, rep fr. *to last 4 sts., P3, K1
68th row: K5, *P2, K6, rep fr. *to last 4 sts., P2, K2
69th row: K1, P1, *T2B, P6, rep fr. *to last 7 sts., T2B, P4, K1
70th row: As 68th row
71st row: Inc. in 1st st., T2F, T2B, *P4, T2F, T2B, rep fr. *to last 4 sts., P3, K1 (66 sts.)
72nd row: *K4, P4, rep fr. *to last 2 sts., K2
73rd row: K1, *T2F, K2, T2B, P2, rep fr. *to last st., K1
74th row: K1, *K2, P6, rep fr. *to last st., K1
75th row: K6, T2B, *T2F, K4, T2B, rep fr. *to last 2 sts., P1, K1
76th row: As 12th row
77th row: K1, *K6, T2F, rep fr. *to last st., K1
78th row: As 12th row
79th row: K6, Y2F, *T2B, K4, T2F, rep fr. *to last 2 sts., P1, K1
80th row: As 74th row

Shape armhole

1st row: Cast off 13 sts., K following st., P2, *T2B, K2, T2F, P2, rep fr. *to last st., K1
2nd row: *K4, P4, rep fr. *to last 5 sts., K5
3rd row: Cast off 2 sts., P following 2 sts., T2B, T2F, *P4, T2B, T2F, rep fr. *to last 4 sts., P3, K1
4th row: K5, P2, *K6, P2, rep fr. *to last 4 sts., K4
5th row: Cast off 2 sts., P following st., T2B, *P6, T2B, rep fr. *to last 5 sts., P4, K1
6th row: K5, P2, *K6, P2, rep fr. *to last 2 sts., K2
7th row: P2tog, K1, *T2B, P4, T2F, rep fr. *to last 6 sts., T2B, P3, K1

8th row: K4, *P4, K4, rep fr. *to last 4 sts., P2, P2tog
9th row: K2tog, T2B, P2, *T2F, K2, T2B, P2, rep fr. *to last st., K1
10th row: K3, *P6, K2, rep fr. *to last 3 sts., P1, P2tog
11th row: K2tog, P1, *T2F, K4, T2B, rep fr. *to last 2 sts., P1, K1
12th row: K1, P to last st., K1
This completes the armhole shaping (44 sts. remain).
Now repeat rows 1–16 inclusive as worked at the commencement of the right front, then repeat rows 1–15 inclusive of the same instructions, thus finishing at the front edge.

Shape neck

1st row: Cast off 4 sts., P to last st., K1
2nd row: K1, *T2F, K6, rep fr. to last 7 sts., T2F, K5
3rd row: Cast off 3 sts., P to last st., K1
4th row: K2, *T2B, K4, T2F, rep fr. *to last 3 sts., T2B, K1
5th row: Cast off 3 sts., the st. on the right-hand needle counting as K1, *P6, K2, rep fr. *to last st., K1
6th row: K1, *P2, T2B, K2, T2F, rep fr. *to last st., P1
7th row: Cast off 2 sts., P following 3 sts., K4, P4, K4, rep fr. *to end
8th row: K1, P3, *T2B, T2F, P4, rep fr. *to last 4 sts., T2B, K2
9th row: Cast off 2 sts., the st. on the right-hand needle counting as P1, *K6, P2, rep fr. *to last 5 sts., K5
10th row: K1, P4, *T2B, P6, rep fr. *to last st., P1
11th row: Cast off 1 st., K following 5 sts., P2, *K6, P2, rep fr. *to last 5 sts., K5 (29 sts.)
12th row: K1, P3, *T2F, T2B, P4, rep fr. *to last st., K1
13th row: K1, *P4, K4, rep fr. *to end
14th row: K1, *P2, T2F, K2, T2B, rep fr. *to last 4 sts., P2, K2
15th row: K1, P1, *K2, P6, rep fr. *to last 3 sts., K3
16th row: K1, P1, *T2F, K4, T2B, rep fr. *to last 3 sts., T2F, K1
17th row: K1, P to last st., K1
18th row: K1, T2F, K6, rep fr. *to last 4 sts., T2F, K2
19th row: As 17th row
20th row: K2, *T2B, K4, T2F, rep fr. *to last 3 sts., T2B, K1

Shape shoulder

1st row: K1, P1 (K2, P6) twice, K2, P2, turn
2nd row: K2, P2 (T2B, K2, T2F, P2) twice, P1, K1
3rd row: K5, P4, K4, P2, turn
4th row: K2, P4, T2B, T2F, P4, K1
5th row: K6, P2, turn
6th row: K2, P5, K1
Cast off purlwise.

Back

Using M, cast on 92 sts.
Working into the back of the sts., P one row.
Now proceed exactly as the instructions for the right front up to the commencement of the side increase, thus finishing so that the right side of work is facing when working next row.

Now inc. as follows:
1st row: Inc. in 1st st., *P2, T2B, K2, T2F, rep fr. *to last 3 sts., P1, inc. in next st., K1
2nd row: K5, *P4, K4, rep fr. *to last st., K1
3rd row: K1, P4, *T2B, T2F, P4, rep fr. *to last st., K1
4th row: K6, *P2, K6, rep fr. *to end
5th row: K1, P5 *T2B, P6, rep fr. *to last 8 sts., T2B, P5, K1
6th row: As 4th row
7th row: K1, P4, *T2F, T2B, P4, rep fr. *to last st., K1
8th row: As 2nd row
9th row: K2, *P2, T2F, K2, T2B, rep fr. *to last 4 sts., P2, K2
10th row: K1, P1, *K2, P6, rep fr. *to last 4 sts., K2, P1, K1
11th row: K1, *T2B, T2F, K4, rep fr. *to last 5 sts., T2B, T2F, K1
12th row: K1, P to last st., K1
13th row: K2, *T2F, K6, rep fr. *to last 4 sts., T2F, K2
14th row: As 12th row
15th row: Inc. in 1st st., K2, *T2B, K4, T2F, rep fr. *to last 3 sts., K1, inc. in next st., K1
16th row: K1, P2, *K2, P6, rep fr. *to last 5 sts., K2, P2, K1
17th row: K1, *T2F, P2, T2B, K2, rep fr. *to last 7 sts., T2F, P2, T2B, K1
18th row: K1, P1, *K4, P4, rep fr. *to last 6 sts., K4, P1, K1
19th row: K1, P5, T2B, *T2F, P4, T2B, rep fr. *to last 8 sts., T2F, P5, K1
20th row: K7 *P2, K6, rep fr. *to last st., K1
21st row: K1, *P6, T2B, rep fr. *to last 7 sts., P6, K1
22nd row: As 20th row
23rd row: K2, *P4, T2F, T2B, rep fr. *to last 6 sts., P4, K2
24th row: As 18th row
25th row: K1, *T2B, P2, T2F, K2, rep fr. *to last 7 sts., T2B, P2, T2F, K1
26th row: As 16th row
27th row: K2, *T2B, T2F, K4, rep fr. *to last 6 sts., T2B, T2F, K2
28th row: As 12th row
29th row: Inc. in 1st st., K2, *T2F, K6, rep fr. *to last 5 sts., T2F, K1, inc. in next st., K1
30th row: As 12th row
31st row: K3, *T2F, T2B, K4, rep fr. *to last 7 sts., T2F, T2B, K3
32nd row: K1, P3, *K2, P6, rep fr. *to last 6 sts., K2, P3, K1
33rd row: K2, *T2F, P2, T2B, K2, rep fr. *to end
34th row: K1, P2, *K4, P4, rep fr. *to last 7 sts., K4, P2, K1
35th row: K1, *T2F, P4, T2B, rep fr. *to last st., K1

36th row: K1, P1, *K6, P2, rep fr. *to last 8 sts., K6, P1, K1
37th row: K2, *P6, T2B, rep fr. *to last 8 sts., P6, K2
38th row: As 36th row
39th row: K1, *T2B, P4, T2F, rep fr. *to last st., K1
40th row: As 34th row
41st row: K2, *T2B, P2, T2F, K2, rep fr. *to end
42nd row: As 32nd row
43rd row: Inc. in 1st st., K2, *T2B, T2F, K4, rep fr. *to last 7 sts., T2B, T2F, K1, inc. in next st., K1
44th row: As 12th row
45th row: K5, *T2F, K6, rep fr. *to last 7 sts., T2F, K5
46th row: As 12th row
47th row: K4, *T2F, T2B, K4, rep fr. *to end
48th row: K1, P4, *K2, P6, rep fr. *to last 7 sts., K2, P4, K1
49th row: K3, *T2F, P2, T2B, K2, rep fr. *to last st., K1
50th row: K1, P3, *K4, P4, rep fr. *to last 8 sts., K4, P3, K1
51st row: K2, *T2F, P4, T2B, rep fr. *to last 2 sts., K2
52nd row: K1, P2, *K6, P2, rep fr. *to last st., K1
53rd row: K1, *T2B, P6, rep fr. *to last 3 sts., T2B, K1
54th row: As 52nd row
55th row: K2, *T2B, P4, T2F, rep fr. *to last 2 sts., K2
56th row: As 50th row
57th row: Inc. in 1st st., *K2, T2B, P2, T2F, rep fr. *to last 3 sts., K1, inc. in next st., K1
58th row: K1, P5, *K2, P6, rep fr. *to last 8 sts., K2, P5, K1
59th row: K1, *K 4, T2B, T2F, rep fr. *to last 5 sts., K5
60th row: As 12th row
61st row: K6, *T2F, K6, rep fr. *to end
62nd row: As 12th row
63rd row: K1, *K4, T2F, T2B, rep fr. *to last 5 sts., K5
64th row: As 58th row
65th row: K4, T2F, P2, *T2B, K2, T2F, P2, rep fr. *to last 6 sts., T2B, K4
66th row: K1, P4, *K4, P4, rep fr. *to last st., K1
67th row: K1, *T2B, T2F, P4, rep fr. *to last 5 sts., T2B, T2F, K1
68th row: K2, P2, *K6, P2, rep fr. *to last 2 sts., K2
69th row: K1, P1, *T2B, P6, rep fr. *to last 4 sts., T2B, P1, K1
70th row: As 68th row
71st row: Inc. in 1st st., *T2F, T2B, P4, rep fr. *to last 5 sts., T2F, K1, inc. in next st., K1 (104 sts.)
72nd row: K2, P4, *K 4, P4, rep fr. *to last 2 sts., K2
73rd row: K1, *T2F, K2, T2B, P2, rep fr. *to last 7 sts., T2F, K2, T2B, K1
74th row: K1, P6, *K2, P6, rep fr. *to last st., K1
75th row: K1, P1, K4, *T2B, T2F, K4, rep fr. *to last 2 sts., P1, K1
76th row: As 12th row
77th row: K1, *K6, T2F, rep fr. *to last 7 sts., K7
78th row: As 12th row
79th row: K1, P1, K4, *T2F, T2B, K4, rep fr. *to last 2 sts., P1, K1
80th row: As 74th row

Shape armholes

1st row: Cast off 5 sts., K following st., *P2, T2B, K2, T2F, rep fr. to last st., K1
2nd row: Cast off 5 sts., K following 4 sts., *P4, K4, rep fr. *to last st., K1
3rd row: P2tog, P3, *T2B, T2F, P4, rep fr. *to last st., P1
4th row: K2tog, K4, *P2, K6, rep fr. *to last 7 sts., P2, K5
5th row: P2tog, P3 *T2B, P6, rep fr. *to last 7 sts., T2B, P5
6th row: K2tog, K3, *P2, K6, rep fr. *to last 6 sts., P2, K4
This completes the armhole shaping. 90 sts. remain.

Continue as follows:
1st row: K1, P2, *T2F, T2B, P4, rep fr. *to last 7 sts., T2F, T2B, P2, K1
2nd row: K3, P4, *K 4, P4, rep fr. *to last 3 sts., K3
3rd row: K1, P1, *T2F, K2, T2B, P2, rep fr. *to last 8 sts., T2F, K2, T2B, P1, K1
4th row: K2, *P6, K2, rep fr. *to end
5th row: K1, *T2F, K4, T2B, rep fr. *to last st., K1
6th row: K1, P to last st., K1
7th row: K2, *K6, T2F, rep fr. *to last 8 sts., K8
8th row: As 6th row
9th row: K1, *T2B, K4, T2F, rep fr. *to last st., K1
10th row: As 4th row
11th row: K1, P1, *T2B, K2, T2F, P2, rep fr. *to last 8 sts., T2B, K2, T2F, P1, K1
12th row: As 2nd row
13th row: K1, P2, *T2B, T2F, P4, rep fr. *to last 7 sts., T2B, T2F, P2, K1
14th row: K4, *P2, K6, rep fr. *to last 6 sts., P2, K4
15th row: K1, P3, *T2B, P6, rep fr. *to last 6 sts., T2B, P3, K1
16th row: As 14th row
Repeat rows 1–16 inclusive twice more, then repeat rows 1–8 inclusive.

Shape shoulders

1st row: K1, T2B, K4, T2F, rep fr. *to last 9 sts., T2B, turn
2nd row: P1, *K2, P6, rep fr. *to last 10 sts., K2, P1, turn
3rd row: K1, *P2, T2B, K2, T2F, rep fr. *to last 18 sts., P2, T2B, turn
4th row: P1, *K4, P4, rep fr. *to last 19 sts., K4, P1, turn
5th row: K1, *P4, T2B, T2F, rep fr. *to last 27 sts., P4, T2B, turn
6th row: P1, *K6, P2, rep fr. *to last 28 sts., K6, P1, turn
7th row: P1, *P6, T2B, rep fr. *to last 36 sts., P7, turn
8th row: K1, *K6, P2, rep fr. *to last 36 sts., K6, P1. Break off the wool

Slip all the sts. onto one needle, turn and rejoining the wool, with the right side facing, cast off knitwise across all sts.

Sleeves (Both Alike)

With M cast on 46 sts.
Proceed in stocking st. as follows:
1st row: Working into the back of the sts., knit
2nd row: K1, P to last st., K1
3rd row: Knit
4th row: As 2nd row
Repeat 3rd and 4th rows until 5 cm/2" of st.st. have been worked, finishing at the end of P row.
Continue in st.st., inc. in first st. and last st. but one on next row and every following 8th row until there are 56 sts. on the needle.
Now inc. at both ends of every following 6th row until there are 64 sts. on the needle, then inc. at both ends of every following 4th row until there are 84 sts.
Continue increasing at both ends of every following 3rd row (so increases will be worked on a P row and K row alternately) until there are 112 sts. on the needle.
Proceed without further increases until the work measures 45 cm/17.75" from the beginning, finishing at the end of a P row.

Shape top

Continue in st.st., cast off 8 sts. at beg. of next 2 rows. Now cast off 4 sts. at beg. of next 2 rows, then cast off 3 sts. at beg of next 2 rows.
Cast off 2 sts. at beg. of the following 6 rows (70 sts. remaining).
Now decrease 1 st. at both ends of next row and every following 4th row until 50 sts. remain.
Work 3 rows after the last dec. row.
Now dec. 1 st. at beg. of following 10 rows.
Cast off 2 sts. at beg. of next 4 rows. Now cast off 3 sts. at beg. of next 2 rows, then cast off 4 sts. at beg. of following 2 rows.
Cast off remaining 18 sts.
Work another sleeve in the same manner.

Buttonhole Border

The original pattern knits the border bands in garter stitch, but this can look uneven, so the suggested stitch used in the instructions is a neat moss stitch, as used in the recreated model.

Please note the buttonhole spacings are amended to be worked every 33rd and 34th rows if 6 buttonholes rather than 7 are required.

With C wool, cast on 10 sts.
Proceed in moss st. as follows:
Working into back of sts., on first row only:
1st row: K1, P1 to end
2nd row: P1, K1 to end
Repeat these 2 rows once more, then the first row again.
Next row: K3, cast off 4 for buttonhole, K to end
Next row: K3, cast on 4, K3
Working into the back of all cast-on sts., on 1st row only, continue in moss st. as set, working a buttonhole on every following 29th and 30th rows (for 7 buttonholes) (*33rd and 34th rows for 6 buttonholes*). Continue until required number of buttonholes made.
Working into back of cast-on sts., on first row only, work 2 rows after last buttonhole.
Cast off.

Omitting the buttonholes, work another border band exactly the same length for the left front.

The pattern suggested garter stitch for the borders but single moss stitch has been used to recreate Annie's Jacket.

Making Up

Using a warm iron over damp cloth, pin out to size and press all pieces of work on the wrong side, being careful not to stretch any edges. (*Press the lower edges of the back and fronts with care but firmly until they are flat, as they will have a tendency to curl.*)

With a 3 mm crochet hook and using C, work a row of dc. along lower cast on edge of sleeves.

Complete embroidery before assembling for ease of handling.

Embroidery

Embroider the knit side of every alternate complete diamond of the front and back pieces.

The original pattern works simple stitches, using long st., short st., and lazy daisy, alternating colours as desired, using green for the stems and leaves.

The recreated model worked with a variety of flower motifs in the same stitches, including French knots, as explained in the 'Embroidery' section of Chapter 3.

Crochet edging gives a finishing touch and dash of colour to the edgings of Annie's Jacket.

The diamond lattice pattern of Annie's Jacket is ideal for embroidering, where alternate shapes of stocking stitch are embellished with floral motifs.

Join shoulders of back and fronts together.
Join side seams.
Form the pleats on each edge of one sleeve top as follows:

Step 1: With right side of work facing, mark a point 14 cm/5.5″ from the commencement of the armhole shaping.

The original pattern for Annie's Jacket suggested simple motifs for embroidery.

Pleating the sleeve top: marking the starting point (step 1).

Marking out the spacings for pleating the sleeve tops (step 2).

Pinning and tacking the sleeve top pleats (step 3).

Step 2: Mark the centre of the top cast-off edge. Form the material between these two points into 3 pleats at each side of the centre of the top of the sleeve, each lying towards the centre, the fold of the upper one being exactly to the

How the sleeve top pleats sit, seen from the top (step 3).

The sleeve top pleats tacked in place on either side of the centre point, ready for setting into the jacket (step 3).

centre of the cast-off edge. The fold of the middle one lies 2.5 cm/1″ below, and the fold of the lower one 2.5 cm/1″ below the middle one.

The set-in sleeve of Annie's Jacket with simple stocking stitch setting off its dramatic fullness, achieved by deep pleating.

Step 3: Repeat the pleating with mirrored spacings for the other half of the sleeve top. Tack the pleats into position. Complete the top pleating of the second sleeve in the same manner.

Join the sleeve seams and stitch the sleeves into position, placing the centre of the cast-off edge of the sleeve top exactly to the shoulder seam.

Stitch buttonhole band to right front edge and button band to left front so that these just overlap the edges and finish at the neck edge on each side.

Neck edging

With 3 mm crochet hook and using C, start at the extreme edge of the right front border and work a row of dc. all around the neck, finishing at the extreme edge of the left front border.

Lower edging

With 3 mm crochet hook, and using C, start at the corner of the left front border and work a row of dc. all along the lower edge to the bottom corner of the right front border. Fasten off.

Attach the buttons on the left front to correspond with the buttonholes.

Remove tacking threads from tops of sleeves.

The finished moss stitch borders and vintage buttons of Annie's Jacket. The crochet neck edging adds a defining line of the contrast colour, bringing the borders together.

The Tyrolean Needlewoman Jacket

The back of the Tyrolean Needlewoman is left unadorned and shows the textured stitches to advantage.

The Tyrolean Jumper (in fact a buttoned cardigan-jacket) from Needlewoman *magazine of February 1937, recreated as the Tyrolean Needlewoman for this Pattern Collection.*

The title of 'jumper' seemed to prevail generally for knitted garments in the 1930s and 1940s, and this jacket is one of the earliest to be featured in a needlework magazine. Based on original Tyrolean style, the caption in *Needlewoman* magazine of February 1937 proudly states:

> This is a true Tyrolean jumper knitted in the traditional stitch and having the triple coloured yoke and embroidered spots of the native product.

The original pattern is knitted with four strands of finer wool worked together, which is perfectly substituted with our modern double knitting. It has an intricate texture created by interwoven cabling and moss stitch panels, making a stretchy fabric for a good fit, but originally designed for a small size. The pattern has been adapted below to allow for a more generous fit if preferred.

As part of the Pattern Collection, and for those who prefer a bolder colour statement without the more typical floral motifs, it offers a strong colour combination at the yoke, echoed in a simpler embellishment of coloured spots. Most usefully, the pattern offers a clear chart for placement and colour sequence of the spots (reproduced below).

The original pattern endearingly refers to buttons 'the size of a shilling', and here is a contemporary shilling from 1937, measuring 23 mm.

The buttons featured are endearingly described as 'the size of a shilling' rather than being given an actual measurement. For reference, a contemporary 1937 shilling is shown here, measuring 7/8" or 23 mm (fractionally smaller than a decimal 10p piece).

Materials

In keeping with 1930s fit, and if knitted to the equivalent tension stated of 22 sts. to 4 cm, this is a close-fitting, short cardigan. If you prefer an easier fit, use needles one size up, as suggested. You can add to the length by increasing the number of rows in the ribbing, but make sure you allow for the extra spacing with the buttonholes on the right front. Alternatively, you can keep the same number of rows in the ribbing and instead add an extra complete pattern repeat to each bodice piece before the armhole shaping – this will add approximately 8 cm/3.25" to the length of the body, depending on your own tension and yarn selected.

8 × 50 g balls of DK: Cygnet 100% Superwash DK in Cream 2195
1 × 50 g ball DK in each of the following colours: Cygnet 100% Superwash Wook DK in Tartan (2150), Gold (2155), Cranberry (298), Mocha (972)
1 pair each 3.25 mm/10 (3.75 mm/9) and 4 mm/8 (4.5 mm/7)
1 × 4 mm (4.5 mm) cable needle
1 × 4 mm crochet hook
7 buttons of 23 mm diameter

Measurements

Instructions are given below to fit size 34" (36") bust
For 38–40" bust substitute a slightly thicker worsted weight and work on 4.5 or 5 mm needles/7 or 6
Finished centre back length 43 cm/17"
Sleeves 46 cm/18"

Tension

22 sts. to 4 cm with DK (or 20sts to 4 cm with Worsted)

Right Front

With Cream wool and 3.25 mm (3.75 mm) needles, cast on 54 sts. Work 2 rows in K2, P2 rib.

The stitch pattern of the Tyrolean Needlewoman is a richly textured combination of moss stitch and cabling.

3rd row: K2, cast off 4 sts., rib to end
4th row: Rib until 2 sts. remain, cast on 4 sts., rib 2
Continue in rib, making a buttonhole on every 11th and 12th rows until there are 3 in all.
Work 2 rows after the last buttonhole, inc. 1 st. at the beg. of the 2nd row (30 rows).

Change to 4 mm (4.5 mm) needles and pattern as follows:
1st row: K13, P2, K1, then (K1, P1) 3 times, K1, P2, K12, P2, K1, then (K1, P1) 3 times, K1, P2, K6
2nd row: P6, K2, P1, then (P1, K1) 3 times, P1, K2, P12, K2, P1, then (P1, K1) 3 times, P1, K2, P12, K1
Repeat these 2 rows twice more.
7th row: K1, *sl. the next 4 sts. on to the cable needle and place at the back of the work, K the next 4 sts., then K the 4 sts. from the cable needle (this will now be referred to as C4B), K4, K2, then (K1, P1) 3 times, K1, P2, rep fr. *once more, sl. the next 3 sts. onto the cable needle and place at the back of the work, K the next 3 sts., then K the 3 sts. from the cable needle (this will now be referred to as C3B)
8th row: As 2nd row
Repeat the 1st and 2nd rows twice more.

13th row: K5, *sl. the next 4 sts. on to the cable needle and place in front of the work, K the next 4 sts., then K the 4 sts. from the cable needle (this will now be referred to as C4F), P2, K1, then (K1, P1) 3 times, K1, P2
Repeat from *once more, K to end.
14th row: As 2nd row
15th row: K1, *P2, K1, then (K1, P1) 3 times, K1, P2, K12, rep fr. *once more, P2, K1,
P1, K1, P1
16th row: P1, K1, P2, *K2, P12, K2, P1, (P1, K1) 3 times, P1, rep fr. *once more, K3
17th row (buttonhole row): K1, P1, cast off 3 sts., K1, P1, K1, P1, K1, P2, K12, P2, K1, (K1, P1) 3 times, K1, P2, K12, P2, K1, P1, K1, P1
18th row: P1, K1, P2, K2, P12, K2, P1, (P1, K1) 3 times, P1, K2, P12, K2, P1, (P1, K1) twice, P1, cast on 3 sts., K2
19th row: As 15th row
20th row: As 16th row
21st row: K1, *P2, K1, (K1, P1) 3 times, K1, P2, C4B, K4, rep fr. *once more, P2, K1, P1, K1, P1
22nd row: As 16th row
Now repeat the 15th and 16th rows twice more.

27th row: K1, *P2, K1 (K1, P1) 3 times, K1, P2, K4, C4F, rep fr. *once more, P2, K1, P1, K1, P1
28th row: As 16th row
These 28 rows form one complete pattern and are repeated throughout.
Repeat the 28 rows once more, then the first 7 rows once, **but at the same time** making buttonholes on every 17th and 18th rows from the previous one until there are 6 in all. The row numbers for these fall as follows:
The 4th and 5th buttonholes will fall on rows 7/8 and 25/26 respectively of the second rep of the full pattern, **NB** the original pattern places the 6th buttonhole rows 17/18 of 3rd rep of full pattern, following armhole shaping, which doesn't look wrong, but if you wish to maintain the exact spacing place this buttonhole at row 15/16.

Shape armhole

8th row of pattern: Cast off 3 sts., patt. to end
9th row: Patt.
10th row: Cast off 2 sts., patt. to end
11th row: Patt.
12th row: Cast off 2 sts., patt. to end
13th row: Patt.
14th row: K2tog, patt. to end (47 sts.)
15th row: K1, *P2, K2, (K1, P1) 3 times, K1, P2, K12, P2, K1, (K1, P1) 3 times, K1, P2, K10
16th row: P10, K2, P1, (P1, K1) 3 times, P1, K2, P12, K2, P1, (P1, K1) 3 times, P1, K3
17th row (buttonhole row): K1, P1, cast off 3 sts., K1, P1, K1, P1, K1, P2, K12, P2, K1, (K1, P1) 3 times, K1, P2, K10
18th row: P10, K2, P1, (P1, K1) 3 times, P1, K2, P12, K2, P1, (P1, K1) 3 times, P1, cast on 3, K2

Shape yoke

19th row: Cast off 5 sts., K1, P1, K1, P1, K1, P2, K12, P2, K1, (K1, P1) 3 times, K1, P2, K10
20th row: P10, K2, P1, (P1, K1) 3 times, P1, K2, P12, K2, P1, (P1, K1) twice, K1
21st row: Cast off 4 sts., K1, P2, C4B, K4, P2, K1, (K1, P1) 3 times, K1, P2, C4B, K2
22nd row: P10, K2, P1, (P1, K1) 3 times, P1, K2, P12, K2, P1, K1
23rd row: Cast off 3 sts., K12, P2, K1, (K1, P1) 3 times, K1, P2, K10
24th row: P10, K2, P1, (P1, K1) 3 times, P1, K2, P12, K1
25th row: Cat off 3 sts., K9, P2, K1, (K1, P1) 3 times, K1, P2, K10
26th row: P10, K2, P1, (P1, K1) 3 times, P1, K2, P10
27th row: K2tog, C4F, P2, K1, (K1, P1) 3 times, K1, P2, K3, sl. the next 3 sts. onto cable needle and place in front of work, K the next 4 sts., K the 3 sts. from cable needle
28th row: P10, K2, P1, (P1, K1) 3 times, P1, K2, P7, P2tog
29th row: K2tog, P1, K1, P1, K1, P2, K12, P2, K1, (K1, P1) 3 times, K1
30th row: P1, (P1, K1) 3 times, P1, K2, P12, K2, P2, K1, P2tog
31st row: K2tog, P1, K1, P2, K12, P2, K1, (K1, P1) 3 times, K1
32nd row: P1, (P1, K1) 3 times, P1, K2, P12, K2, P1, K2tog
33rd row: K2tog, P2, K12, P2, K1 (K1, P10) 3 times, K1
34th row: P1, (P1, K1) 3 times, P1, K2, P12, K2, P1
35th row: P2tog, P1, C4B, K4, P2, K1, (K1, P1) 3 times, K1
36th row: P1, (P1, K1) 3 times, P1, K2, P12, K2
37th row: P2tog, K12, P2, K1, (K1, P1) 3 times, K1
38th row: P1, (P1, K1) 3 times, P1, K2, P12, K1
39th row: K2tog, K11, P2, K1, (K1, P1) 3 times, K1
40th row: P1, (P1, K1) 3 times, P1, K2, P12
41st row: K2tog, K2, C4F, P2, K1, (K1, P1) 3 times, K1
42nd row: P1, (P1, K1) 3 times, P1, K2, P9, P2tog
43rd row: K2tog, (P1, K1) 3 times, P2, K10
44th row: P10, K2, P1, (P1, K2) twice, K2tog
45th row: K2tog, P1, K1, P1, K1, P2, K10
46th row: P10, K2, P2, K1, P2tog.
47th row: K2tog, P1, K1, P2, K10
48th row: P10, K2, P1, K2tog
49th row: K2tog, P2, C4B, K2
50th row: P10, K1, K2tog
51st row: P2tog, K10
52nd row: P9, P2tog
53rd row: K2tog, K8
54th row: Cast off 4 sts., P2, P2tog
55th row: Cast off remaining 4 sts.

Left Front

With 3.25 mm (3.75 mm) needles and Cream, cast on 62 sts.
1st row: *K2, P2, rep fr. *until 8 sts. remain, K8
2nd row: K, rib to end
Continue in rib, keeping the 8 border sts. in garter st. until 30 rows have been worked from the beginning.
Change to 4 mm (4.5 mm) needles and patt. as follows:
K6, *P2, K1, (K1, P1) 3 times, K1, P2, K12, rep fr. *once more, K8
2nd row: K8, *P12, K2, P1, (P1, K1) 3 times, P1, K2, rep fr. *once more, P6
Continue in patt. as arranged and work exactly like the right front with all shapings at opposite edges and omitting buttonholes.

Back

With 3.25 mm (3.75 mm) needles and Cream, cast on 70 sts. and work 29 rows in K2, P2 rib.

30th row: *Rib 6 sts., P twice into the next st, rep fr. *to end (80 sts.)

Change to 4 mm (4.5 mm) needles and patt. as follows:

1st row: K10, *P2, K1, (K1, P1) 3 times, K1, P2, K12, rep fr. *finishing K10 instead of K12

2nd row: P10, *K2, P1, (P1, K1) 3 times, P1, K2, P12, rep fr. *finishing P10

Continue in patt. until 4 rows of pattern have been worked from the beginning.

Shape armhole

Cast off 2 sts. at beg. next 4 rows, then dec. 1 st. at both ends of every row until 62 sts. remain. Continue in pattern until 3 complete patterns have been worked from the beginning, then work 4 more rows in pattern.

Shape neck

1st row: Patt. 24 sts., cast off 14 sts., patt. 23 sts.

Continue on the last 24 sts., dec. 1 st. at neck edge on every row until 12 sts. remain, then dec. 1 st. at the same edge on every alternate row until 8 sts. remain, finishing at the armhole edge.

Shape shoulder

1st row: Cast off 4 sts., patt. 3 sts.

2nd row: Cast off

Join the yarn at the neck edge of the other side and work this to match the first.

Sleeves (Both Alike)

These are knitted from the top down.

With 4 mm (4.5 mm) needles and Cream, cast on 18 sts.

1st row: K12, P2, K2, P1, K1

2nd row: Cast on 2 sts., (K1, P1) 3 times, K2, P12

3rd row: Cast on 2 sts., P2, K12, P2, K1 (K1, P1) twice, K1

4th row: Cast on 2 sts., P1, (P1, K1) 3 times, P1, K2, P12, K2

5th row: Cast on 2 sts., P1, K1, P2, K12, P2, K1 (K1, P1) 3 times, K1

6th row: Cast on 2 sts., K2, P1, (P1, K1) 3 times, P1, K2, P12, K2, P2

7th row: Cast on 2 sts., (P1, K1) twice, P2, C4B, K4, P2, K1, (K1, P1) 3 times, K1, P2

8th row: Cast on 2 sts., P2, K2, P1, (P1, K1) 3 times, P1, K2, P12, K2, P2, K1, P1

9th row: Cast on 2 sts., (P1, K1) 3 times, P2, K12, P2, K1 (K1, P1) 3 times, K1, P2, K2

10th row: Cast on 2 sts., P4, K2, P1, (P1, K1) 3 times, P1, K2, P12, K2, P1, (P1, K1) twice, P1

11th row: Cast on 2 sts., K1, (K1, P1) 3 times, K1, P2, K12, P2, K1 (K1, P1) 3 times, K1, P2, K4

12th row: Cast on 2 sts., P6, K2, P1, (P1, K1) 3 times, P1, K2, P12, K2, P1, (P1, K1) 3 times, P1

13th row: Cast on 2 sts., P2, K1, (K1, P1) 3 times, K1, P2, K4, C4F, P2, K1 (K1, P1) 3 times, K1, P2, K6

14th row: Cast on 2 sts., P8, K2, P1, (P1, K1) 3 times, P1, K2, P12, K2, P1, (P1, K1) 3 times, P1, K2

15th row: Cast on 2 sts., P2, K12, P2, K1 (K1, P1) 3 times, K1, P2, K12, P2, K1 (K1, P1) twice, K1

16th row: Cast on 2 sts., *P1, (P1, K1) 3 times, P1, K2, P12, K2, rep fr. *once more

17th row: Cast on 2 sts., P1, K1, *P2, K12, P2, K1, (K1, P1) 3 times, K1, rep fr. *once more

18th row: Cast on 2 sts., K2, *P1, (P1, K1) 3 times, P1, K2, P12, K2, rep fr. *once more, P2

19th row: Cast on 2 sts., (P1, K1) twice, P2, K12, P2, K1 (K1, P1) 3 times, K1, rep fr. *once more, P2

20th row: Cast on 2 sts., K4, *P1, (P1, K1) 3 times, P1, K2, P12, K2, rep fr. *once more, P2, K1, P1

21st row: Cast on 2 sts., (P1, K1) 3 times, *P2, C4B, K4, P2, K1, (K1, P1) 3 times, K1, rep fr. *once more, P2, K2

22nd row: Cast on 2 sts., P4, K2, *P1, (P1, K1) 3 times, P1, K2, P12, K2, rep fr. *once more, P1, (P1, K1) twice, P1

23rd row: Cast on 2 sts., K1, (K1, P1) 3 times, K1, *P2, K12, P2, K1, (K1, P1) 3 times, K1, rep fr. *once more, P2, K4

24th row: Cast on 2 sts., P6, K2, *P1, (P1, K1) 3 times, P1, K2, P12, K2, rep fr. *once more, P1 (P1, K1) 3 times, P1

25th row: Cast on 2 sts., P2, K1, (K1, P1) 3 times, K1, *P, K12, P2, K1, (K1, P1) 3 times, K1, rep fr. *once more, P2, K6

26th row: Cast on 2 sts., P8, K2, *P1, (P1, K1) 3 times, P1, K2, P12, K2, rep fr. *once more, P1, (P1, K1) 3 times, P1, K2

27th row: Cast on 2 sts., K2, P2, K1 (K1, P1) 3 times, K1, *P2, K4, C4F, P2, K1, (K1, P1) 3 times, K1, rep fr. *once more, P2, K4, sl. next 2 sts. onto cable needle and place in front of work, K next 2 sts., K the 2 sts. from the cable needle

28th row: Cast on 2 sts., P10, K2, *P1, (P1, K1) 3 times, P1, K2, P12, K2, rep fr. *once more, P1, (P1, K1) 3 times, P1, K2, P2

29th row: Cast on 2 sts., P1, K1, *P2, K12, P2, K1, (K1, P1) 3 times, K1, rep fr. *twice more

30th row: Cast on 2 sts., K2, *P1, (P1, K1) 3 times, P1, K2, P12, K2, rep fr. *twice more, P2 (76 sts.)

Continue in pattern on these sts., dec. 1 st. at both ends of the 11th row, then on every 10th row following until 56 sts. remain. Continue without further dec. until 5 complete patterns have been worked from the beginning. Work 8 rows more in pattern.
Next row: K4, K2tog, *K2, k2tog, rep fr. *until 6 sts. remain, K6 (44 sts.)
Change to 3.25 mm (3.75 mm) needles and work 7.5 cm in K2, P2 rib. Cast off.

Yoke

With 4 mm (4.5 mm) needles and Brown, cast on 167 sts. Work 3 rows in moss st.
4th row: Moss st. 34 sts., K2tog, *moss st. 12 sts., K2tog, rep fr. *6 times more, moss st. 33 sts. (159 sts.). Cut Brown yarn and join on Yellow
5th row: K. Now work 3 rows moss st. Cut Yellow and join on Brown
9th row: K. Cut Brown and join on Red
10th row: P. Work 2 rows moss st.
13th row: Moss st. 33 sts., K2tog, *moss st. 11, K2tog, rep fr. *6 times more, moss st. 33 sts. (115 sts.). Cut Red yarn and join on Brown
14th row: P. Cut Brown and join on Green
15th row: K. Work 3 rows in moss st. Cut Green and join on Brown
19th row: K. Work 2 rows in moss st.
22nd row: Moss st. 33 sts., K2tog, *moss st. 10 sts., K2tog, rep fr. *6 times more, moss st. 32 sts. (143 sts.). Cut Brown and join on Yellow
23rd row: K. Work 3 rows in moss st. Cut Yellow and join on Brown
27th row: K. Cut Brown and join Red
28th row: P. Work 2 rows in moss st. Cast off. Darn in all ends.

Making Up

Press work on the wrong side with a warm iron and damp cloth (*check ball bands of yarn for special instructions*).

A row of crochet loops is worked along the top edge of the yoke as a channel for the tie cord.

The crochet row finishes the yoke edging, worked in the main cream colour.

The yoke of the Tyrolean Needlewoman jacket is finished with a looped row of crochet through which the characteristic tie cord is threaded.

The finished crochet row for the neckline of the Tyrolean Needlewoman jacket.

The crochet tie cord is drawn up at the neck to finish the Tyrolean Needlewoman jacket.

Join shoulders, sew in sleeves and press seams. Sew up side and sleeve seams and press.

With 4 mmm (4.5 mm) crochet hook and Cream, work 1 row dc. down right front.

Sew yoke round neck edge.

With crochet hook and Cream work an edge around the neck edge as follows:

1 dc. into 1st st., *6 ch., miss 5 sts., 1 dc. into next st., rep fr. *to end.

Take 4 strands of Cream, place them tog and work a chain about 91.5 cm in length. Thread it through the loops around neck.

Tie off the ends with a neat knot and darn in ends.

Sew on buttons to correspond with the buttonholes.

Using the coloured wools, embroider 2 spots on every moss st. section on the right and left fronts, (*following the chart for placement of colours*).

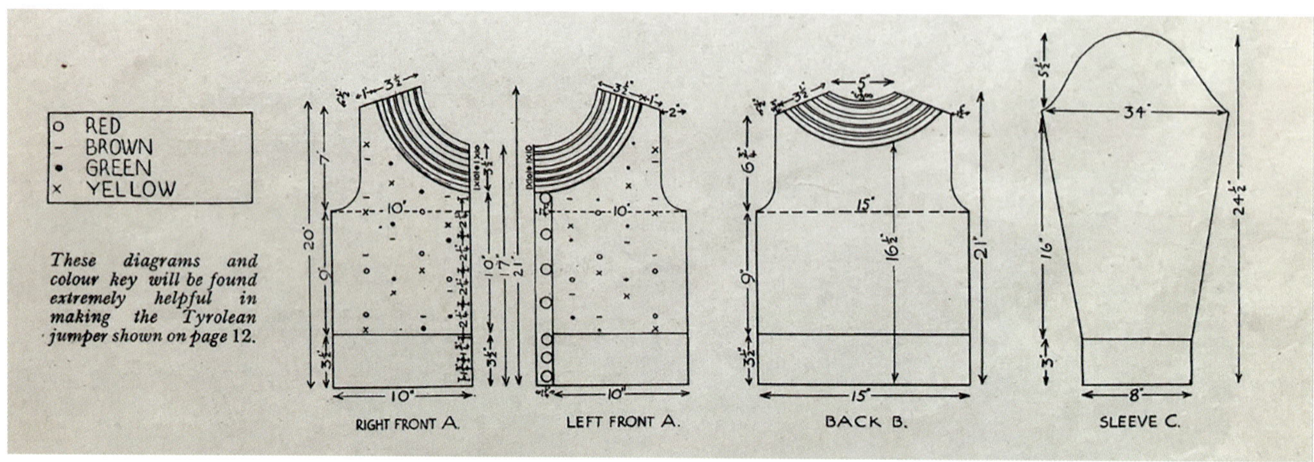

The original pattern gives a most useful chart for placing the coloured embroidered dots onto the finished jacket fronts.

Simple dots embroidered in the colours of the yoke of the Tyrolean Needlewoman jacket are an effective alternative to floral motifs.

The tie cord at the neck of the Tyrolean Needlewoman is an enduring feature of the style.

The Evergreen Jacket

This splendid original vintage jacket dates from the late 1930s, with all the hallmarks of timeless Tyrolean style in knitwear. In perfect condition for its eighty-plus years, it features cables, strong colours and embroidered flowers, with substantial draw-strings at waist and neck bringing together so many of the classic elements of the style. Exclusive to this book, the pattern is adapted directly from the original garment as faithfully as possible, interpreted in modern double knitting as the perfect match for the original yarn used.

The striking contrast of the coloured yoke against cabled bodice and sleeves would work equally well in any number of combinations, and is recreated here matching the original strong green and dark flecked charcoal of the main colour. A pure black, navy, or dark green would also work well, with the yoke in red, blue or cream, or reverse the effect with a cream main colour and vibrant red or green for the yoke.

Little decorative scallops finish the jacket edges, created by knitting a picot stitch for the hems and bands. On the original the yoke and neckband are in the same contrast green, and in the adapted design the main charcoal colour has been continued around these edges. These would also be effective worked in the same contrast colour as the yoke all around the jacket – indeed any combination would work well. (Full instructions on working the picot hems are given in the 'Coloured Edgings' section of Chapter 3.)

The Evergreen pattern is a new recreation taken from the 1930s original jacket, adapted for modern knitting.

Tie cords at the waist are a strong Tyrolean feature, and the Evergreen pattern recreates the thicker chain of colours seen in the 1930s original.

The Evergreen design recreates the textures, colours and shaping of the original 1930s Tyrolean jacket.

The embroidered flowers on the back and front yokes of the Evergreen design are an interpretation of the chain stitch embroideries of the 1930s original jacket.

The rather quirky construction of the jacket has been simplified, but the essence of the original design has been kept. Back and front lower panels are worked alike as straight pieces, with the cabling creating the natural fit to the body, enhanced by the drawstring at the waist. The completed lower panels are joined to the yoke sections, which are begun separately to create the shaping and then knitted together.

Edelweiss and gentians form the main part of the embroidered decoration on the yoke, worked in thick wool stitches and French knots for textured relief. The original flowers are all worked in edged chain stitch, but they can be worked in any preferred stitches. They have been recreated here with the original stitch for the edelweiss, but with variations on filled lazy daisy and stem stitch for the gentians and stylized flowers representing the little rhododendrons of the typical alpine trilogy.

The cables are worked as in the original, a classic rope cable of six stitches, but which could easily be replaced if preferred with the mock cable stitches suggested in Chapter 3 in the 'Stitches' section.

If you prefer to work the mock cables over 6 sts. (as given in Chapter 3) remember that these are worked over 2 rows, as opposed to the single row of a classic cable worked with a third double-pointed needle, as given in this pattern. When counting the 'twists' take the first row of the mock cable, worked on the wrong side, as the row to be counted and count the second row (which completes the mock cable) as the 4th row of the 8-row pattern given in the instructions below.

Materials

4 x 100 g balls main colour (M) Stylecraft Life DK (75% acrylic, 25% wool) in Charcoal (2323)
Or 7 x 50 g balls Cygnet Naturally Soft Superwash DK 100% wool in Black (217)
3 x 50 g balls of DK in contrast colour (C) for yoke (and edgings if preferred)
Small quantities of 4 ply wool for embroidery in cream, blue, red, light green, yellow, mustard
1 x pair 3.75 mm/9 needles
1 x pair 4 mm/8 (4.5 mm/7)
4 mm crochet hook
7.5 mm/1 x crochet hook
5 x buttons

Measurements

To fit a size 34–36" (38")
Length at centre back 48 cm/19"
Sleeve length 45.5 cm/18"

Tension

22 sts. to 10 cm/4" on 4 mm/8 needles
20 sts. to 10 cm/4" on 4.5 mm/7 needles

Lower Back Panels

Both knitted alike.
(*Using the same size needles to create the picot hem edging creates an extra 'lift' for the peplum effect. If you prefer a flatter edge, use needles one size smaller for the hem edging only.*)

With main yarn (M) and 4 mm/8 (4.5 mm/7) needles cast on 56 sts.
Stocking stitch (1 row knit, 1 row purl) for 6 rows.
Next row (picot row): K1, (yo, K2tog) rep to last st., K1
Beginning with a purl row, st.st. a further 5 rows.

Now create the picot hem:
With right side of work facing, and folding the work along the picot row, pick up and knit the next row and the cast-on stitches together, working one stitch from each set of stitches together (explained in the 'Stitches' section of Chapter 3 for picot edging).

Change to 4 mm/8 (4.mm/7) needles.
Next row (wrong side facing): K3, (P6, K5) 4 times, K6, P3
This sets the pattern; continue as follows:
1st row: P3, (K6, P5) 4 times, K6, P3
2nd row: K3 (P6, K5) 4 times, P6, K3
3rd row: P3 (C6B, P5) 4 times, C6B, P3
4th row: As row 2
5th row: As row 1
Rep the last 2 rows once more then 2nd row.
These 8 rows form the pattern.**
Repeat the 8 pattern rows 6 times more, until the 7th cable twist has been completed (counting the first twist made at row 3 as the first), ending with row 4 of the pattern.
Leave all the stitches on a spare needle or stitch holder.
Make another panel piece in the same way.

When both panel pieces have been worked, with right sides facing:
Next row (5th row of pattern): pattern across 56 sts. of first side panel.
Cast on 10 sts., then pattern across second side panel (122 sts.).

Continue on these stitches, working the cast-on stitches at the centre into the pattern as set, but without cabling them:
Next row: (6th row of pattern) K3, (P6, K5) 10 times, P6, K3
There are now 11 groups of stitches set for cables, but only continue to cable the first 4 and last 4 sets for one further cable twist, leaving the middle 3 sets without working the cabling twist.

Continue across all stitches and complete the 8th cable twist across the first and last 4 cables only.
End with row 4 of the pattern.

The lower panels of the back are worked separately and worked together to form a single row before adding the contrast yoke.

Now work 6 rows of stocking stitch across all stitches and leave on a spare needle.

Back Yoke

With C and 4 mm/8 (4.5 mm/7) needles, cast on 2 sts. and K2. Work in st.st., increasing one st. each side of every row (by working twice into first and last st.) until there are 14 sts.
Now inc. each end of every alternate row (i.e. on every K row) until there are 22 sts.
Working into the back of the new stitches at the start of each row to form a firm neat edge, continue as follows:
Cast on 20 sts. at beginning of next 4 rows. Cast on 10 sts. at beginning of next 2 rows (122 sts.).
Beginning with a purl row, work 2 rows st.st across all sts., completing the point shaping of the back yoke.

Now join the yoke to the lower panels:
Place the 122 sts. of the joined lower back sections behind the contrast colour yoke point, with the right sides of both pieces facing you.
Knit across the row in C, picking up 1 st. from the front needle (yoke) and 1 st. from the back needle (lower panels) and knitting these together all along the rows of the parallel needles.

The contrast yoke of Evergreen is begun separately then added to the lower panels by working both sections together in one row, as in the original 1930s jacket.

Now continue with C only in st.st, and starting with a purl row work 3 further rows.

Begin armhole shaping

Cast off 6 sts. at the beginning of the next 2 rows.
Dec. 1 st. at each end of the following 9 rows by K2tog (92 sts.).
Continue straight on these sts. without further shaping until back measures 45.5 cm/18".

Shape shoulders

With right side facing:
Cast off 11 sts. at the beginning of the next 2 rows.
Cast off 14 sts. at beg. of following 2 rows.
Leave the remaining 42 sts. on a spare needle.

Lower Front Panels

Both panels worked alike.
With M and 4 mm/8 needles, work as for lower back panels to**.
Repeat the 8 pattern rows until 6th cable twist has been worked (counting the first twist made at row 3 as number 1) and complete the 8th row of this pattern.
Work first 2 rows of next pattern repeat.
Next row (3rd row of pattern and 7th cable twist): P3, C6B, P5, C6B, P5, K6, P5, C6B, P5, C6B, P3
Complete the 8th row of the pattern as now set, without cabling the central 6 sts.
Work first 2 rows of next pattern.
Next row (3rd row of pattern): P3, C6B, P5, K6, P5, K6, P5, K6, P5, C6B, P3 (this completes the 8th cable twist)
Work 6 rows st.st across all sts. and leave these on a spare needle.

Make the second lower front panel in the same way.

Left Front Yoke

With C and 4 mm/8 (4.5 mm/7) needles cast on 2 sts. and K2.
Work in st.st., increasing 1 st. at each end of next K row and every following row until there are 14 sts.
Work 1 row purl.
Now inc. at each end of next K row and every alternate row until there are 18 sts.

Working into the back of the new cast-on sts., continue as follows:
With right side facing, cast on 2 sts at beg. of next row.
Next row: Purl
Next row: Cast on 2 sts.
Cast on 4 sts. at beg. of next 2 rows (30 sts.).
Next row: Cast on 6 sts. at beg.
Next row: Cast on 4 sts. (40 sts.)
Rep the last 2 rows once more.
Next row: Cast on 6 sts. at beg. of row (56 sts.)
Next row: Purl

Using C, join the yoke point to one of the lower front panels as before, with both pieces right side facing and the yoke point in front of the cabled panel, working across both sets of stitches together.
Continue in C, and starting with a purl row, st.st. 3 rows straight.

Shape armhole

Cast off 6 sts. at beg. of next row.
Dec. 1 st. at armhole edge on next 6 rows (44 sts.).
Now work 34 rows straight in st.st. ending with wrong side facing for next row.

Shape neck

Cast off 6 sts. at beg. of next row (neck edge).
Dec. 1 st. at neck edge on next 11 rows (27 sts.).
Work 8 rows straight st.st.

Shape shoulder

Cast off 12 sts. at beg. of next row.
Next row: Purl
Cast off remaining sts.

Right Front Yoke

With C and 4 mm/8 (4.5 mm/7) needles cast on 2 sts. and K2.
Work 1 row purl.
Work in st.st., increasing 1 st. at each end of next and every following row until there are 14 sts.
Work 1 row purl.
Now inc. at each end of next K row and every alternate row until there are 18 sts.
Working into the back of the new cast on sts., continue as follows:
Cast on 2 sts at beg. of next 2 rows.
Cast on 4 sts. at beg. of next 3 rows (34 sts.).
Next row (purl): Cast on 6 sts. (40 sts.)
Next row: Cast on 4 sts.
Cast on 6 sts at beg. of next 2 rows (56 sts.).
Next row: Purl

Using C, join the yoke point to the remaining lower front panel as before, with both pieces right side facing and the yoke point in front of the cabled panel, working across both sets of stitches together.
Continue in C, and work 4 rows straight st.st.

Shape armhole

Cast off 6 sts. at beg. of next row (purl row).
Dec. 1 st. at armhole edge on next 6 rows (44 sts.).
Now work 34 rows straight in st.st. with right side facing for next row.

Shape neck

Cast off 6 sts. at beg. of next row (neck edge).
Dec. 1 st. at neck edge on next 11 rows (27 sts.).
Work 7 rows straight st.st.

Shape shoulder

Cast off 12 sts. at beg. of next row (purl row).
Next row: K
Cast off remaining sts.

Sleeves (Both Alike)

With M and 3.75 mm/9 needles cast on 65 sts.
Stocking stitch 6 rows.
Work picot row: K1, (yo, K2tog) to last st.
Stocking stitch another 5 rows.
Work the hem row as before, catching the sts. from the next working row to the cast-on sts.
Change to 4 mm/8 (4.5 mm/7) needles.
Next row (wrong side facing): K3, (P5, K6) 5 times, P5, K3
Pattern first 6 rows of 8 row pattern as for back.
Row 7: working in pattern as set, inc. 1 st. each end of row

Increase in this way on every following 6th row until there are 101 sts. on the needle, working the additional edge stitches in st.st without cabling until 3rd cable twist is reached, then cable the additional edge sts. in pattern as set.
Continue in pattern until 13th cable twist is complete.
Continue straight on these sts. without further shaping until the 17th cable twist is complete (or until work measures 44.cm/17.5" from beginning), then **start armhole shaping** as follows:
Cast off 7 sts. at beginning of next 2 rows.
Dec. 1 st. at each end of every following alt. row until 53 sts. remain.
Work 1 row.
Cast of 2 sts. at beg. of next 4 rows.
Cast off 1 st. at beg. of next 2 rows (43 sts.).
Cast off remaining sts.

Finishing Yoke Points

Back yoke point

With right side of work facing (the work will be upside down) and C, using 4 mm crochet hook, work 44 dc. along the edge to the beginning of the point, 14 dc. along the edge of the point to the tip, 2 dc. over the tip of the point, then 14 dc. along the second edge of the point, and 44 dc. to finish.

Left front yoke point

With right side facing and C, using 4 mm crochet hook, work an even row of dc. all along the yoke edge, picking up 27 dc. to the point, 2 dc. over the point and 36 dc. to the edge.

Right front yoke point

With right side facing (work is upside down) and C, work as for left front yoke point but working 36 dc. to the point, 2 dc. across point and 27 dc. to edge.

Embroider Back and Front Yoke Sections

The original embroidery does not place the floral motifs symmetrically, and the recreated version has followed this.

The points of the yoke on the back and fronts are finished with a neat row of crochet.

Any placement can be made as preferred, and the choice of flowers, colours and stitches can be entirely individual. Details for embroidering the chain stitch edelweiss and lazy daisy stitch gentians and stylized flowers are given in the 'Embroidery' section of Chapter 3.

Picot Edging of Lower Back Panels

Both sides worked in the same way.
With 3.75 mm/9 needles and right side facing, using M (or C if preferred) pick up and knit 50 sts. along inner central edge of one lower back panel below cast-on sts. where the two panels join together (*using the smaller needle size ensures the edgings lie flat*).
Starting with a purl row, st.st. 5 rows.
Work picot row.
St.st 5 rows and cast off.

The original 1930s jacket has embroidered stylized flowers of edelweiss, gentian and rhododendrons executed in chain stitch.

The Evergreen pattern has adapted the embroidered flowers to work the edelweiss in chain stitch, as the original 1930s jacket, and used lazy daisy stitch and stem stitch for the gentians and rhododendrons.

The separate lower back panels of Evergreen are finished with a picot edged hem, as in the 1930s original jacket.

Work other side in the same way.
Neatly sew the cast-off edges on the wrong side, using the ridge from where the first row was picked up as a guide.

Front Edging Bands

Both sides worked alike.
These can be worked in the main colour, as the original, or in the contrast colour of the yoke, or in both colours to match each section as in the original garment.
This is the number of sts. to pick up for each section:
With 3.75 mm/9 needles and right side facing, pick up and knit 50 sts. along front edge of lower cabled panel, then 32 sts. along the edge of the yoke (82 sts. in all).
Starting with a purl row, work 5 rows st.st.
Work picot row: K1, (yo, K2tog) to last st., K1
Starting with a purl row, work a further 5 rows st.st and cast off.
On each side, fold over at the picot row to create scallops and sew to inside along the line of the picked-up stitches.

Finish the yoke point trimming as follows:
Using double strands of C and a 4 mm crochet hook, make a chain long enough to fit unstretched along each of the front

The front opening sides are finished with a picot hemmed edge, worked in the main colour in Evergreen, where the original 1930s jacket uses the same colour as each section, changing from the main colour to the contrast at the yoke.

The pointed yoke of Evergreen is trimmed with a separately made crochet chain of the same colour, stitched along the lower shaped edge, as in the original 1930s jacket.

yoke sections, following the shaped point to start from where the front band edge was picked up and along to the side seam (this needs to fit unstretched above the dc. edge or it will pucker the lower yoke point).

Make a similar chain to fit along the back yoke point.

Stitch the chains invisibly (and without pulling) to each yoke section along the lower edge, just above the dc. edging row. For a more textured ridge, stitch these so that the flatter chain side sits against the yoke, as in the original garment. The recreated version has the chain side uppermost for a smoother line.

Picot Neck Band

Join shoulder seams.

With right side of work facing and starting at right front neck edge, using 3.75 mm/9 needles and M (or C) pick up and K 28 sts. along right front neck to shoulder seam, then pick up the 42 sts. from the spare needle across the back neck, and 28 sts. along left front neck (98 sts.).

1st row (wrong side facing): K (this creates a neat ridge on the right side)

Then, starting with a K row (right side facing) work 4 rows st.st.

Picot row: K2, (yo, K2tog) to last 2 sts., K2

Beginning with a P row, work 5 rows st.st.

Cast off.

Make the neck cord before stitching down the neckband.

Neck tie cord

Take 6 strands of the coloured 4 ply wools used for the embroidery, and including contrast C, leave a length 7.5 cm/3" for the tie end. With the 7.5 mm/1 crochet hook, make a chain 86.5 cm/34" long, knotting both ends and trimming.

Place the neck cord under the neckband picot edge and fold this over, stitching down loosely in place along the joining stitches but without catching the cord so it can slide freely through.

Waist tie cord

Make another cord in the same way as the neck tie cord to fit around the waist, around 137 cm/54" in length or to desired length.

Making Up

Sew in sleeves.

Join side and sleeve seams.

The neckline is finished with a tie cord, which is placed under the picot hem before sewing it in place.

Thread waist tie cord behind every cable (there is a natural gap in the stitches where the cables twist) at the second twist or at the desired height. Knot and trim the ends.

Join side and sleeve seams and set in sleeves.
Sew on buttons along left front picot band, placing one where the yoke joins the lower panels.

To finish right front edge button loops:
Mark the number of required button loops evenly along the right front of the picot edging to correspond with the buttons. Using a 4 mm crochet hook, work into one tip of a scallop and make a chain (around 6 dc.), skipping one scallop and picking up the next with a slip st. and fastening off.
Make buttonholes in this way across the right front edge, and sew in loose ends.

Crochet chain loops are placed along the front openings to correspond with the buttons, using the tips of the picot edge to start and finish each loop.

The crochet tie cord at the waist is threaded under each of the cables of the lower panels all around.

The completed crochet chain loops on the right front edge create closures for the buttons.

The Evergreen design recreates the original 1930s jacket in structure, colours and details, worked for modern knitting.

The Hollywood Comes to Broadway Waistcoat

The cabled bands of the Hollywood waistcoat offer a perfect background for embroidering flower motifs.

Coupons, rationing, make do and mend. The war years meant all of this to knitters but glamour was never out of reach! Hollywood was the pinnacle of glamour and everyone wanted to look like their favourite movie stars – who themselves were avid knitters and often seen backstage with their own busy knitting needles.

The Hollywood Knitting Book is a wonderful Australian publication by The New Idea, dating from after 1941, when coupons and rationing had begun impacting clothes and wool supplies. It has all of the hearty 'make do and mend' spirit in its motivational editorial messages:

> Straight from Hollywood, fashion centre of the world just now, come the smartest, prettiest collection of hand-knitteds we've seen for many a day. All the clever girls in the film colony knit their own these days – in between turning out socks and sweaters for their men-folk in the services – just as you and I. Here, in this book, you'll find a selection of the favorite Hollywood styles. We hope you'll like them. We know you're going to find the directions simple and sweet to follow. You know, of course, how economical it is to knit your own.... And, if you want to show how really ingenious you can be, why not unravel one of your older jumpers? Wind the yarn around a saucepan of steaming water, then knit it up again in one of these refreshing new styles![1]

There are other Tyrolean-style cardigan patterns in this lovely collection but this trim waistcoat modelled by Evelyn Keyes is

The original pattern is from the 'Fireside Fashions' feature in the 1940s Australian publication, modelled by Hollywood actress Evelyn Keyes.

an ideal way to make up a simple, striking garment – and very economical to make! (And you won't even need the saucepan.)

The waistcoat is characteristically short, in keeping with mid-1940s style, perfect for the look with blouse and trousers (you can even make the charming pompom slippers in the original pattern, to complete the cosiness of the outfit). There are simple cables on the front and back, with just the front ones embroidered in the pattern, though the back could also be embroidered if desired. In the recreated model, the embroidered flowers were inspired by the pink and blue gentians of the vintage Austrian buttons, carved from horn. These stand out against a dark navy blue as the main colour, knitted here in an economical wool mix or a 100% wool if preferred.

This is not a complicated pattern but does require much counting of rows to place cables, buttonholes and increases. Keeping careful note of the row count as the work progresses is highly recommended in order to keep track.

Original vintage buttons from Austria, made from carved antler and hand painted with blue and pink gentians.

Materials

2 × 100 g balls of Stylecraft Life DK (25% wool, 75% nylon) in Navy
(or 4 × 50 g balls DK Cygnet Superwash 100% wool in Navy [2153])
1 pair 4 mm/8 needles
1 × 4 mm cable needle
5 × buttons
Small quantity of embroidery wools (pink, blue, yellow and green were used here but any variety of colours for the flowers can be used)
Row counter recommended

Measurements

34–36"
Length 18" – if you would like a longer garment, add to the moss stitch border at the start

Tension

22 sts. to 10 cm/4"
10 rows to 2.5 cm/1"

The original vintage buttons from Austria inspired the embroidered flowers on the Hollywood Waistcoat, placing alternate colours to tie the pink and blue together in the design.

Back

With 4 mm/8 needles cast on 92 sts. and work 8 rows in moss st.
9th row (right side): K18, P2, K8, P2, K32, P2, K8, P2, K18
10th row: P18, K2, P8, K2, P32, K2, P8, K2, P18
Rep the last 2 rows 3 times more.

The larger cables worked into the Hollywood waistcoat are left unadorned in the original.

17th row: K18, slip next 3 sts. on to cable needle, leave at front of work, knit next 5 sts. on left needle, then 3 sts. from cable needle (these 8 sts. will be referred to in rest of pattern as 'Cable'), P2, K32, P2, cable, P2, K18
18th Row: As 10th row
Rep 9th and 10th rows 8 times more, then rep 17th row. Continue in this way, working a cable row every 18th row.
At the same time, inc. 1 st. at each end of 41st, 51st, 61st, and 71st rows, until 5 cables have been worked (finishing at 89th row with 100 sts.).
90th row: P22, K2, P8, K2, P32, K2, P8, K2, P22
Continue in pattern, working cables every 18th row.

Shape armholes

Cast off 8 sts. at beg. of next 2 rows.
Cast off 2 sts. at beg. of foll. 2 rows.
Then work 2 sts. tog at beg. of next 4 rows (76 sts.).
Cont. in pattern with 10 sts. in st.st at each end of row until 7 cables have been worked from the beginning.
Work 11 more rows in pattern.

Shape shoulders

Cast off 10 sts. at beg. of next 2 rows.
Cast off 13 sts. at beg. of foll. 2 rows.
Cast off remaining 30 sts. for back of neck.

Right Front

Cast on 54 sts. and work 4 rows in moss st. (the first 8 sts. will form the buttonhole band).
5th row: Moss 3, cast off 2 (or 3 for larger buttons), work in moss st. to end
6th row: Moss st. to last 3 sts., cast on 2 (3), moss 3
Work 2 rows in moss st.
9th row: Moss 8, K16, P2, K8, P2, K18
10th row: P18, K2, P8, K2, P16, moss 8
Rep last 2 rows 3 times more.
17th row: Moss, K16, P2, Cable, P2, K18
18th row: As 10th row
Rep 9th and 10th rows 3 times more.
25th row: Moss 3, cast off 2 (3), moss 3 (2), K16, P2, K8, P2, K18
26th row: P18, K2, P8, K2, P16, moss 3 (2), cast on 2 (3), moss 3
Rep 9th and 10th rows 4 times more.
35th row: As 17th row
36th row: As 10th row
Rep 9th and 10th rows twice, then 9th row once more.
42nd row: Inc. in 1st st., P17, K2, P8, K2, P16, moss 8

Keeping a 'running score' of rows and where to place each of the following makes this much easier as you go.
Continue in this way, keeping 8 border sts. in moss st. and making 3 more buttonholes every 20th row as previously.
At the same time, inc. 1 st. at beg. of every 10th row 3 times more (4 increases altogether).
Work until 5 cables have been worked from the beginning.
Finish on 89th row (which is a cable row) with 58 sts.
90th row: P22, K2, P8, K2, P16, moss 8

Now start shaping for neckline, keeping 8 moss sts. at the border:
91st row: Moss 8, K2tog, K14, P2, K8, P2, K22

Shape armhole

92nd row: Cast off 8 sts., P14, K2, P8, K2, P15, moss 8
93rd row: Moss 8, K15, P2, K8, P2, K14
94th row: Cast of 2 sts., P12, K2, P8, K2, P13, P2tog, moss 8
95th row: Moss 8, K14, P2, K8, P2, K12
96th row: P2tog, P10, K2, P8, K2, P14, moss 8
97th row: Moss 8, K2tog, K12, P2, K8, P2, K11
98th row: P2tog, P9, K2, P8, K2, P13, moss 8
99th row: Moss 8, K13, P2, K8, P2, K10
100th row: P10, K2, P8, K2, P11, P2tog, moss 8
Cont. in pattern, working 2 tog inside border of 8 moss sts. every 3rd row, keeping armhole edge straight, until 7 cables have been worked since the beginning.
Cont. in pattern until there are 31 sts. on the needle.
Work 4 rows even in pattern.

Shape shoulder

With wrong side facing, cast off 23 sts. for the shoulder.

Continue on the 8 border sts. in moss st. for 15 rows (these form the back of the neckband).

Keep these 8 on a safety pin (this is so that both sides can be cast off together in one go for a neater finish – if you prefer to sew the ends together then cast the 8 sts. off here).

Left Front

Cast on 54 sts. and work 8 rows in moss st.
9th row: K18, P2, K8, P2, K16, moss 8
10th row: Moss 8, P16, K2, P8, K2, P18
Rep last 2 rows 3 times more.
17th row: K18, P2, cable, P2, K16, moss 8
18th row: As 10th row
Cont. in this way, working left front to correspond with right front but omitting buttonholes in the border.
Increases and decreases are worked at opposite ends of the work.

Making Up

The embroidery can be finished before assembling for easier handling of the pieces. The flowers are embroidered into the cables. (The original pattern does not give any guidance on how these look, other than the photograph. The flowers embroidered in the recreated model here were inspired by the buttons.)

Join moss st. borders at back of neck by transferring the 8 sts. of each side from the safety pins onto two knitting needles, ensuring the points of each needle face the top edge of the borders (away from the bodice). Place both sets of stitches parallel to each other, with right sides together, and cast off together, taking one stitch from each needle as you cast off. This gives a much neater finish at the back neck.

If you cast off the borders when finishing each front piece, join these together.

Join shoulder seams and join on the border to the back neck.

Finish armhole edges

With right side of work facing, pick up and knit 101 sts. right along armholes.
Work 5 rows in moss st.
Cast off.
Join side seams.
Sew on buttons.

A Warm Red Cardigan

The original pattern for this simple but striking cardigan appeared in one of the ever popular Odhams Press publications written by Margaret Murray and Jane Koster. The pattern here is adapted from the 1946 publication *Practical Family Knitting*,

A Warm Red Cardigan is a simpler design which could be embroidered if desired, or left as a strong colour statement as in the recreated original.

The original pattern from the later 1940s features a strong shoulder line, typical of the fashion of the time.

which features other Tyrolean-inspired garments for mothers and daughters.

With no intricate textured stitch patterns, this is simple to knit, and modern double knitting yarn is a perfect match for the original. The body is knitted all in one piece to the yoke, and the strong shoulder line creates a 1940s silhouette, which can be enhanced further with shoulder pads. The construction of the yoke gives a Tyrolean touch of textured interest, echoing the moss stitch of the sleeves and highlighted by the cream contrast. The striking block of colour is softened by a pretty crocheted shell stitch edging, and works as successfully in reverse, as red on a white background.

The recreated model has been left unadorned as in the original, and was chosen in order to offer a simpler pattern than some of the more complicated projects. The plain stocking stitch bodice is ideal for creative embellishing, if desired, and the clever increases for the back shaping provide a perfect 'frame' for embroidery.

This pattern would lend itself to any colour combination, and even the introduction of other colours for the crochet trimmed edgings, and still be in keeping with a traditional Tyrolean look – for example, black as the main colour with green yoke and red trim. There is a wealth of choice of colours in modern DK and so many excellent synthetic/wool mixes, which allow this to be a very economical project. Two modern yarn options are given for an economical or a more luxurious version.

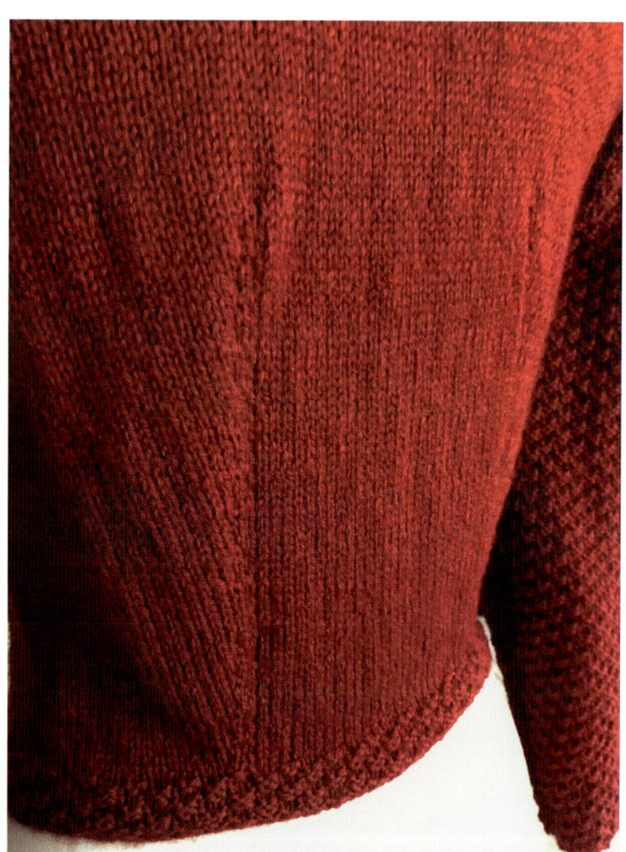

The back of the Warm Red Cardigan has a simple but clever shaping.

The original pattern for the Warm Red Cardigan is illustrated with a charmingly drawn vignette.

Materials

6 (7) × 50 g balls Cygnet 100% Superwash Wool DK in Cranberry (298)
or 3 × 100 g balls Stylecraft 'Life' DK with 25% wool in Cardinal (2306)
2 × 50 g balls contrast Cygnet 100% Superwash Wool DK in Cream (2195)
1 pair 4 mm/8 (4.50 mm/7) needles
1 × 4 mm crochet hook
1 × 3.5 mm crochet hook
9 buttons, 15 mm wide
Optional shoulder pads for accentuating

Measurements

For size 34–36" bust
Length at centre back 42 cm/16.5"
Length of sleeves 46 cm/18"

Tension

22 sts. to 10 cm/4" on 4 mm/8 needles

Body

Knitted all in one piece.

With 4 mm (4.5 mm) needles and Main colour, cast on 160 sts.

Continue in check pattern as follows:

1st row: K2, *P2, K2, rep fr. *to end

2nd row: P2, *K2, P2, rep fr. *to end

3rd row: As 2nd row

4th row: As 1st row

Rep 1st and 2nd rows once.

7th row: P2, cast off 2, patt. as 2nd row

8th row: K2, P2, rep fr. *to last 4 sts., K2, cast on 2, K2

9th row: K2, P2, K2, K57, K twice in next st., P1, K30, P1, K twice in next st., K57, K2, P2, K2

10th row: Check patt. 6 sts., P to rib st., K1, P30, K1, P to last 6 sts., check patt. 6

11th row: Check patt. 6, K to rib st., P1, K30, P1, K to last 66 sts., check patt. 66

12th row: As 10th row

13th row: Check patt. 6, K to 1 before rib st., K twice in next st., P1, K30, P1, K twice in next st., K to last 6 sts., check patt. 6

Rep last 4 rows until there are 190 sts.

At the same time, make buttonholes, as in 7th and 8th rows, in 21st and 22nd rows, and every following 14th row.

Continue in st.st. with sts. both ends in check patt., **omitting rib sts., but still making buttonholes**, until work measures 27 cm/10.5" (*this creates a short finished cardigan that will sit on the waist with a finished length of 42 cm/16.5" – work can be lengthened here if desired, in multiples of 14 rows to allow for additional buttonholes*).

Divide for fronts and back

Next row: Check patt. 6, K40, cast off 6 sts., K86, including st. already on right-hand needle, cast off 6 sts., K40, check patt. 6

Work on left front as follows:

Keeping 6 sts. at front edge in check patt., working rest of row in st.st., dec. 1 st. at armhole edge every row until 40 sts. remain.

Continue on these sts. until work measures 33 cm/13" (*adding any extra length if previously lengthened before dividing work*) ending at front edge.

Next row: Check patt. 6 and leave these 6 sts. on a safety pin.

Cast off 16 sts., work to end.

Continue in st.st, dec. 1 st. at neck edge every K row until only 1 st. remains.

Fasten off.

Back and Fronts

Dec. 1 st. both ends of every row until 74 sts. remain.

Continue without shaping until work measures 33 cm (adding in any previously worked length), ending with a row on wrong side.

Next row: K19, cast off 36 sts., K19

Work on last set of sts., dec. 1 st. at inner edge every row until only 1 st. remains. Fasten off.

Work on other set of sts. to correspond.

Work right front as left front, but continuing to make buttonholes.

Back Yoke

With right side of work facing, using main colour, pick up and K 35 sts. down side of back, 36 sts. that were cast off, and 35 sts. up to other shoulder.

Work 6 rows in check patt., dec. 1 st. both ends of alternate rows (100 sts.).

Change to contrasting yarn and P 1 row.

2nd row: *P2, K1, P2, rep fr. *to end

3rd row: *K2, P1, K2, rep fr. *to end, rep last 2 rows once more

6th row: P2, K1, *P1, P2tog, P1, K1, rep fr. *to last 2 sts., P2

7th row: K2, *P1, K3, rep fr. *to last 3 sts., P1, K2

8th row: P2, *K1, P3, rep fr. *to last 3 sts., K1, P2

Rep last 2 rows once more, then 7th row again.

12th row: P2tog, *K1, P2tog, P1, rep fr. *to last 3 sts., K1, P2tog

13th row: *K1, P1, K1, rep fr. *to end

14th row: *P1, K1, P1, rep fr. *to end

Rep last 2 rows once more, then 13th row again.

Change to main shade and K 1 row.

19th row: Purl

20th row: K2tog, K6, K2tog, K7, K2tog, K7, K2tog, K4, K2tog, K7, K2tog, K7, K2tog, K6, K2tog

21st row: Purl

22nd row: K2tog, K to last 2 sts., K2tog

Rep last 2 rows once more, then 21st row again.

Cast off.

Right Front Yoke

With right side of work facing, using main colour, pick up and K 51 sts., leaving 6 border sts. on safety pin.

The finished yoke uses stitch decreases with a ridged effect, accentuating the shaping at the neck.

Work 6 rows in K2, P2 check patt., dec. 1 st. at shoulder edge alternate rows (48 sts.). Change to contrasting wool and P 1 row.
2nd row: *K1, P4, rep fr. *to last 3 sts., K1, P2
3rd row: K2, *P1, K4, rep fr. *to last st., P1
Rep last 2 rows once more.
6th row: *K1, P1, P2tog, P1, rep fr. *to last 3 sts., K1, P2
7th row: K2, *P1, K3, rep fr. *to last 3 sts., K1, P2
Rep last 2 rows once more, then 7th row again.
12th row: *K1, P2tog, P1, rep fr. *to last 3 sts., K1, P2tog
13th row: K1, *P1, K2, rep fr. *to last st., P1
14th row: *K1, P2, rep fr. *to last 2 sts., K1, P1
Rep last 2 rows once more, the 13th row again.
Change to main colour and K 1 row.
19th row: Purl
20th row: K7, K2tog, K7, K2tog, K7, K2tog, K2
21st row: Purl
22nd row: Cast off 7 sts., K to last 2 sts., K2tog
23rd row: Purl
Rep last 2 rows once more.
Cast off remaining sts.

Left Front Yoke

With right side of work facing, using main colour, pick up and K 51 sts.
Work 6 rows in K2, P2 check patt., dec. 1 st. at shoulder edge alternate rows (48 sts.).
Change to contrasting yarn, and P 1 row.
2nd row: P2, K1, *P4, K1, rep fr. *to end
3rd row: *P1, K4, rep fr. *to last 3 sts., P1, K2
Rep last 2 rows once more.
6th row: P2, K1 *P1, P2tog, P1, K1, rep fr. *to end
7th row: *P1, K3, rep fr. *to last 3 sts., P1, K2
8th row: P2, K1 *P3, K1, rep fr. *to end
Rep last 2 rows once more, then 7th row again.
12th row: P2tog, K1 *P2tog, P1, K1, rep fr. *to end
13th row: *P1, K2, rep fr. *to last 2 sts., P1, K1
14th row: P1, K1, *P2, K1, rep fr. *to end
Rep last 2 rows once more, then 13th row again.
Change to main colour and K 1 row.
19th row: Purl
20th row: K2, K2tog, K7, K2tog, K7, K2tog, K7
21st row: Cast off 7 sts., P to last 2 sts., P2tog
22nd row: Knit
Rep last 2 rows once more.
Cast off remaining sts.

Front Bands

Sl. the 6 sts. left on safety pin to 4 mm needles and continue in K2, P2, check patt., using main colour (and continuing to make buttonholes in right side) until same length as front yoke.
Cast off.

Sleeves (Both Alike)

With main colour cast on 42 sts.
Work 6 rows of check patt.
Change to contrasting colour and P 1 row.
Next row: P1, *K1, P2, rep fr. *to last 3 sts., K1, P1
Next row: K1, *P1, K2, rep fr. *to last 2 sts., P1, K1
Rep last 2 rows 7 times more.
Change to main colour and K 1 row.
Work in check patt., inc. 1 st. both ends of 3rd and every 4th row until there are 72 sts.
Continue without further shaping until work measures 45.5 cm/18″ from the start.

The front band is worked in the same double moss stitch as the sleeves, tying the patterns together.

Shape top of sleeve

Dec. 1 st. both ends of alternate rows until there are 60 sts.
Continue without further shaping for 7.5 cm/3".
Cast off 3 sts. at beg. of next 8 rows.
Cast off remaining sts.

Making up

Join shoulder seams.
Join sleeve seams.
Sew in sleeves, marking centre point underarm and centre top of sleeve, matching seams and gathering tops of sleeves where 8 × 3 sts. were cast off, on either side of final cast-off, to fit armhole.

Sew front bands to yoke.

With 3.5 mm crochet hook and main colour, work round neck as follows:
3 ch., 1 tr., *1 ch., miss 1 st., 2 tr. Into next 2 sts., rep fr. *.

With main colour, and 4 mm crochet hook, work a neat line along right front edge. To avoid the line 'waving', work 1 dc. into every other stitch – if this tightens the edge too much you may need to work a few more stitches – the check pattern means this edge will be irregular and the line of crochet will give a better foundation for the crochet trimmed edge as follows:

With contrasting colour, join yarn to lower edge of **right front**. *Miss 1 st. of previous dc. row, then 1 tr.,1 ch., 1 tr., 1 ch., 1 tr. into the same dc. from previous row, miss 1 dc., 1 sc., rep fr. *up

The crochet border at the neck is worked in two stages of the main colour and contrast where the tie cord can be threaded.

The shell stitch edging is worked into a foundation row of double crochet for ease of counting stitches.

front and round neck, working the groups of trs. into the 1 ch. holes formed by previous row.
Work a row of dc. down left front to make a firm edge (either main colour or Cream if preferred).
Sew on buttons to match buttonholes.

For the neck tie

With 4 mm crochet hook and double strands of Cream, leave a length of around 5 cm/2″, then work chain 91 cm/36″ in length. Leave a further 5 cm/2″ and cut both strands, knotting both ends securely. Create two small tassels in Cream (*see* 'Finishing Touches for Drawstrings' section in Chapter 2) and attach with the lengths of yarn left at each end. (*The cord can be left plain, or pompoms or other trimmings attached as desired.*)

The contrast shell stitch edging of the right front border is worked at intervals of treble crochet stitch.

The right front border has added crochet detailing of a pretty shell stitch edging using the contrast colour.

The simple tassels are worked to recreate the original design, but can be replaced with decorative pompoms or tassels in two colours, as seen in the June Clyde jacket.

The shaping of the back creates a well-fitted cardigan that sits at the waist.

The Lilli Bolero

The original 1940s bolero did not add the fastenings suggested in the pattern, and is drawn in at the waist here with a Tyrolean style braid belt to complete the look.

The original 1940s pattern by Bestway for a Tyrolean Jumper (in fact a bolero), number 1640.

The discovery of a true original vintage knitted piece can only be surpassed by acquiring one made from a pattern which is already owned. To see someone's choice back in time of colours, and their skills so beautifully applied for the realization of a familiar pattern, is time-travelling joy for all enthusiasts of vintage knitting. This original piece was lovingly made at least seventy years ago, and it has survived those years to reveal jewel-like colours, true to the pattern, as a perfect lesson in knitting and embroidery as it was then.

This lovely puff-sleeved jumper was originally knitted in white, with green edges. The sprays of flowers are embroidered in bright colours in simple stitches. The front fastening is invisible.

Here is an example of the 'white' background, which in our vocabulary is 'natural' or even 'cream', together with the tantalizing choice of that special vintage green which totally eludes us in our modern yarns, at least in the finer weights. That particular green, sometimes defined as 'deco green', is a core colour in the 1930s and 1940s knitting palette, but along with other shades of green so popular at that time, it does not appear in any selection of 4 ply readily available to the modern knitter, much to our regret.

Although called a 'jumper', the pattern suggests an invisible fastening along the front edges with concealed hooks and eyes. The original garment is without a fastening, as an edge-to-edge jacket or bolero. It has currently been left as found, but it is tempting to find some appropriate fastenings, such as dirndl hooks, to finish the look.

This original vintage bolero from the 1940s used the colours suggested in the pattern.

Materials

Modern yarns to replace the original 3 ply recommended in the pattern:
6 × 50 g balls main colour (M) Cygnet Truly Wool Rich 4 ply in Cream (2614)
1 × 50 g ball contrast for edgings (C) *(suggested yarns: Cascade Heritage in Christmas Green, (5656) for a deeper green, or Debbie Bliss Rialto 4 ply Jade (50) for a softer green)*
Small amounts of wool for embroidery in lavender, red, yellow and green
1 × pair 2.75 mm/12 needles
1 × pair 3.25 mm/10 needles (or 3 mm/11 for smaller size)

Measurements

When worked to the original pattern this achieves a 35–36" bust
For a size 34" use smaller needles as above
For a size 36–38" bust use 3.75 mm/9 needles
Length at centre back 44.5 cm/17.5"
Sleeve length 11.5 cm/4.5"

Tension

28 sts. to 10 cm/4" on 3.25 mm/10 needles

The basic knitting of this cardigan is very straightforward, with no complicated textures or shaping, and the main work is in the embroidery. The maker has used the colours specified in the pattern for the embroidery, which can be taken as a model for embellishing this or other designs from the Pattern Collection, in the knowledge of this being absolutely authentic in every way. It has been given its name here in honour of the popular Bing Crosby recording of Lilli Bolero in 1948.

Back

Using C and 2.75 mm/12 needles cast on 120 sts. and work 5 rows in K1, P1 ribbing. Break off C and join in M. Now change to 3.2 mm/10 needles and work in pattern as follows:

1st row (wrong side facing): Purl
2nd and every alternate row: Knit
3rd row: P8, *K8, P16, rep fr. *to end, finish last rep with P8
5th row: P10, *K4, P20, rep fr. *to end, but finish last rep with P10

7th row: P9, *K6, P18, rep fr. *to end but finish last rep with P9
9th row: P8, *K2, P4, K2, P16, rep fr. *to end, but finish last rep with P8
11th row: As 9th row
13th row: As 7th
15th row: As 5th
16th row: Knit

These 16 rows comprise one pattern. Repeat the first 3 of these 16 rows, then, keeping continuity of the pattern, inc. 1 st. at both ends of next row and every following 8th row of work, until there are 138 sts., working the extra sts. each end of row in stocking stitch: that is, K on right side rows and P on wrong side rows. Work 12 rows straight after the last inc. row, thus completing 6th pattern from start.

Still keeping continuity of pattern, now **shape armholes** thus: Cast off 6 sts. at start of next 2 rows, and 4 sts. at start of the following 2 rows, after which dec. 1 st. at both ends of next row and every alternate row after, until 106 sts. remain.
Now work without further dec. until 9th row of 10th pattern has been finished.
Next row: K38, turn. Leaving remaining sts. on a spare needle, continue only on first 38 sts. thus:
dec. 1 st. at neck (inner) edge on every row until 32 sts. remain, then work 1 row straight, to bring you to armhole edge.

Shape shoulder

Cast off 8 sts. at start of next row and the following 2 alternate rows, then work 1 row, after which cast off remaining 8 sts.
Return to sts. on spare needle and, with right side facing you, join wool to inner end of sts. and cast off 30 sts. Then work to armhole edge.
Now dec. 1 st. at neck edge on every row until 32 sts. remain. Then shape shoulder as 1st side.

Left Front

Using C wool and 2.75 mm/12 needles, cast on 56 sts. and work in rib as back waist, working 5 rows in C and 12 rows in M. Change to 3.25 mm/10 needles
1st pattern row (wrong side): Purl
2nd and every alternate row: Knit
3rd row: *P16, K8, rep fr. *once, P8
5th row: P18, K4, P20, K4, P10
7th row: P17, K6, P18, K6, P9
9th row: *P16, K2, P4, K2, rep fr *once, P8
11th row: As 9th row
13th row: As 7th row
15th row: As 5th row
16th row: Knit
These 16 rows comprise 1 pattern. Work first 3 rows of next pattern, then inc. 1 st. at start of next row, and every following 8th row of work until there are 65 sts. Work 13 rows straight.

***__To shape the armhole__, cast off 6 sts. at start of next row, and cast off 4 sts. at start of following alternate row, after which dec. 1 st. at armhole edge on next row and every following alternate row until 49 sts. remain.
Work straight until 4th row of 10th pattern has been finished (or 3rd row of 10th pattern when working right front).

To shape the neck, cast off 9 sts. at start of next row, the dec. 1 st. at neck edge of every row until 32 sts. remain.
Work 4 rows straight.

To shape the shoulder, cast off 8 sts. at start of next 3 rows that begin from armhole end, after which work 1 row, then cast off remainder***.

Right Front

Work as left front from **to **. Then continue thus:

1st pattern row: Purl
2nd and every alternate row: Knit
3rd row: P8 *K8, P16, rep fr. *once
5th row: P10, K4, P20, K4, P18
7th row: P9, K6, P18, K6, P17
9th row: P8, *K2, P4, K2, P16, rep fr. *once
11th row: As 9th row
13th row: As 7th row
15th row: As 5th row
16th row: Knit
These 16 rows comprise 1 pattern. Work 3 rows of next pattern, then inc. 1 st. at end of next row and every following 8th row of work until there are 65 sts. Work 12 rows straight, then work as left front from ***to ***.

Sleeves (Both Alike)

With 2.75 mm/12 needles and C wool cast on 80 sts. and work in rib, working 5 rows C and 12 rows M as back waist. Change to 3.25 mm/10 needles.

Next row: *P1, P twice in next st., rep fr. *to end
Now rep 2nd to 16th rows of back, then rep 1st to 16th rows.

To shape top, cast off 6 sts. at start of next 2 rows, then dec. 1 st. at start of every row until 44 sts. remain. Cast off.

To Complete

The original pattern completes the garment before embroidering. The separate pieces can be embroidered before assembling for easier handling, if preferred. Please see the last section for making up instructions.

Right front border

With right side of work facing you, and using a 2.75 mm/12 needle and C, start at lower edge and pick up and K 6 sts. along front edge from C border, drop C, join M and pick up and K 150 sts. along remainder of front up to neck edge. Now work as follows, noting that when changing over from one colour to the other you must twist the wools over each other on wrong side, to avoid leaving a hole.

The edgings of the original 1940s bolero are worked by picking up stitches after the main work is complete, allowing for a contrast edge to be worked all around.

1st rib row: With M, *K1, P1, rep fr. *74 times, drop M, take up C, then K1, P1, alternately to end
2nd rib row: With C, *K1, P1, rep fr. *twice, drop C, take up M, then K1, P1 alternately to end
Rep these 2 rows twice more, then rep the 1st rib row again. Break off M and rib 5 rows with C.
Cast off ribwise.

Left front border

With right side of work facing you and using a 2.75 mm/12 needle and M wool, pick up and K 150 sts. along front edge, from neck to top of C border at waist, drop M, join on C, and with C pick up and K 6 sts. along edge of C border.
1st row: With C, *P1, K1, rep fr. *twice, drop C, take up M and P1, K1 alternately to end
2nd row: With M, *P1, K1, rep fr. *74 times, drop M, take up C and P1, K1 alternately to end, rep these 2 rows twice, then rep 1st row again. Break off M and C then, joining on C again, work another 5 rows rib with C. Cast off.

Neckband

Join shoulder seams. With right side of work facing and using a 2.75 mm/12 needle and C, pick up sts. round neck thus:

Pick up and K 6 sts. along neck edge across C front border, then drop C and with M pick up and K 8 sts. from M rib front border, then pick up and K 36 sts. along remainder of right front neck up to shoulder. Then pick up 80 sts. across back neck, and 36 sts. along neck of left front and 8 sts. along its M rib border, drop M, join a small ball of C and pick up and K 6 sts. along C border.

Now work 9 rows in K1, P1 ribbing, C over C and M over M. Then break off M and one ball of C and with other ball of C rib another 5 rows all across. Cast off ribwise.

Here, the original pattern works an underwrap, or facing piece, to attach to the left front border ribbing to sit under the right front for the fastening press-studs and hooks and eyes to be sewn. The finished vintage garment omitted this and was left as an edge-to-edge bolero jacket.

Underwrap

With M and 3.25 mm/10 needles cast on 18 sts.
1st row: Knit
2nd row: Purl
Rep these 2 rows until you have worked 162 rows. Cast off.

join side and sleeve seams. Sew underwrap beneath left front edge, where sts. were picked up for border; fasten right front down on to wrap with press-studs. Fasten fronts at extreme top and bottom edges with a hook and eye.

THE EMBROIDERY

Begin this as follows: In centre of each pattern block, work a cross-stitch in green wool and between the strokes of the cross work a few French knots in mauve wool. Now embroider the stocking-stitch bands with sprays of flowers, placing them in alternate positions, as photograph shows. Each flower spray is worked thus: With running stitches mark out three curving lines on garment, to represent 3 stems, the length shown in Diagram I. Work these in stem-stitch with green wool. (Diagram 2). Just below top end of each stem work a flower in lazy-daisy stitch with French knots for centre. (Diagrams 3 and 4). Each spray has two flowers in red and one in yellow, or vice versa. Each side of stem top work French knots in mauve wool, then complete lower part of each stem with short sprigs of stem-st. in green wool. Vary alternate sprays by curving the stems in reverse direction. If wished, you can trace off the whole design in Diagram I onto tissue paper, tack this to garment and work over it, then tear paper away. Turn the tissue over to other side for reversed stems.

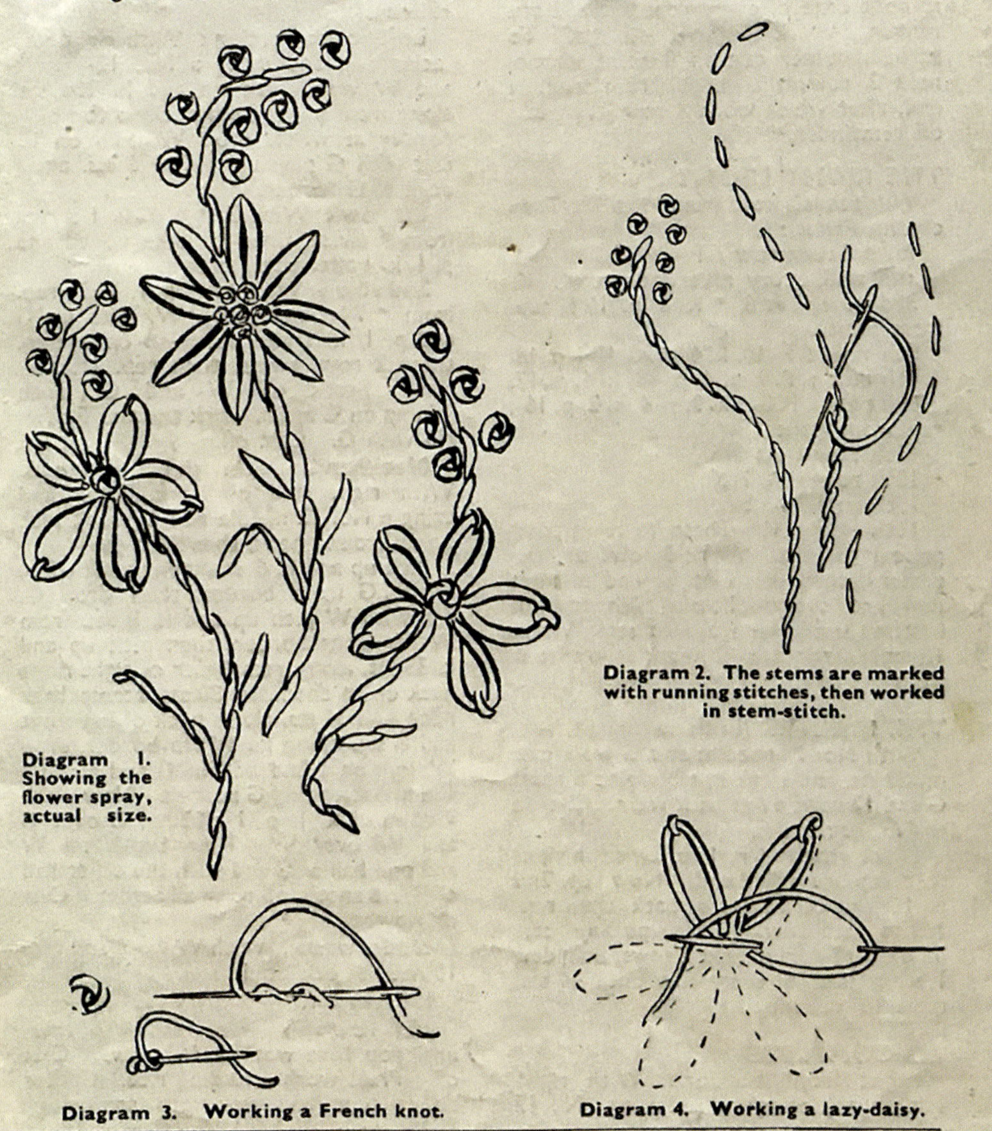

The original pattern includes a clear chart as a guide for working and placing the embroidered flowers.

Making Up

Press work, avoiding ribs.
Gather sleeve tops and sew into armholes.
Join side and sleeve seams.
Sew underwrap beneath left front edge, where sts. were picked up for border. Fasten right front down to wrap with press-studs. Fasten fronts at extreme top and bottom edge with a hook and eye.

Embroidery

Begin this as follows:
In centre of each pattern block, work a cross stitch in green wool *and between the strokes of the cross work a few French knots in lavender wool – please note this was not completed by the original maker.* Now embroider the stocking stitch bands with sprays of flowers, placing them in alternate positions as shown in the photographs.

Each flower spray is worked thus (*the diagram number references in these instructions are those in the original pattern guide, as illustrated*):

The total length of the flower sprays shown in the original pattern diagram is 9.5 cm/3.75" (Diagram 1).

With running stitches worked in green wool, mark out three curving lines on the garment, to represent 3 stems (Diagram 2).

The original 1940s knitted bolero has worked the crosses embroidered in wool as in the pattern, but has omitted the additional French knot details suggested.

Just below the top end of each stem work a flower in lazy daisy stitch with French knots for the centre (Diagrams 3 and 4).

Each spray has two flowers in red and one in yellow, or vice versa. Each side of stem top work French knots in lavender wool, then complete lower part of each stem with short sprigs of stem stitch in green wool. Vary alternate sprays by curving the stems in reverse direction.

The flower sprays embroidered on the original 1940s bolero have survived intact, giving an authentic model to follow.

The chart for embroidering the floral sprays is printed in the original pattern to actual size, which measures at 9.5 cm/3.75".

The embroidered floral sprays on the original 1940s bolero were skilfully executed exactly to the pattern.

The application involved in embroidering is well worth the time to recreate the delightful example of this original 1940s bolero.

Forties Favourite Cardigan

The Forties Favourite cardigan.

Bestway's enduringly popular pattern 1511 for a Tyrolean Jumper (as cardigans were most often named at the time) from around 1945–46.

This striking 1940s pattern is by far the single most popularly recreated of all the Tyrolean designs of that era. Social media reveals that it is knitted many times over in a multitude of colours, a testament to its longevity as a favourite. It could not be missed out of this collection, as it holds a very significant place in the enduring passion for vintage Tyrolean style.

The fashion for exaggerated shoulders reached a peak in 1945–46 (think of Joan Crawford's legendary *Mildred Pierce*) and the model's styling also strongly suggests that this pattern is probably from the immediate post-war period. The pleated fashioning of the sleeve tops is also the same as that featured in an equally popular Fair Isle top (coincidentally modelled by the same lady) in an issue of *Woman's Weekly* magazine of 1946, helping the dating to within one or two years.

The significance of the date is that this was the height of wool shortages in Britain. With some food rationing continuing on until 1954, rationing for clothing and materials was still firmly in place for many more years until 1949, and wool in ever-short supply. Though this Bestway pattern fuels the fire of fascination for Tyrolean-style knitwear, there are no wool-gobbling textures of bobbles or cables, just a simple stocking stitch body with moss stitch panel at the yoke, adorned with stylized flower motifs and touches of coloured embroidery worked from small amounts of wool – ideal for using up left-over yarn, and not in the least extravagant. The shaping of the sleeves makes the statement of fashionable 1940s style, and the last little touch of a tied cord added to the front neck gives it the hallmark of being 'Tyrolean'.

The coloured motifs are worked in a variation of Fair Isle technique, where small quantities of colour are knitted in separate blocks with the main colour stranded behind. The alternative would be to use intarsia technique, though neither of these is an especially easy technique, in that it is difficult for even experienced knitters to control the gapping that naturally occurs as colours are joined together. It is well worth practising the technique before embarking on a lovingly worked project like this cardigan.

If you prefer, you can knit the entire garment in plain stocking stitch and embroider the motifs on after knitting, where a cross stitch will be very effective, as for the Edeleweiss Jacket. Alternatively Swiss darning can be worked, which uses chain stitches placed over each original knitted stitch to look as if they have been knitted.

The original pattern does not provide a chart for the motifs, but line-by-line instructions. A coloured chart is included with the instructions as a guide for those who prefer to follow a chart, and as a template if you prefer to embroider the motifs after the knitting is completed.

The Forties Favourite cardigan knitted in one of the many alternative colourways, which work equally effectively for this striking design.

The colour work in the Forties Favourite is executed in a variation of Fair Isle technique, which strands or weaves the colours at the back of the work for each block of colour. The ends are darned in when the work is completed.

A note on the pattern's original shaping

Knitted to the recommended tension and as given in the instructions, the shoulder width is very generous, and with the accentuated sleeve tops this can result in the finished garment being very wide at the shoulders (over 2.5 cm/1" wider than average on either side). Using the smaller needles to complete the moss stitch portion of the yoke helps to redress this, and notes are given in the pattern for reducing the width of the yoke by also reducing the number of stitches. This also helps the sleeves to sit better and have the full effect of the strong shaping rather than 'drooping' off the natural shoulder line.

Materials

The original pattern suggests white as the main colour, but this would have been what we call an off-white or cream (closer to what we would call 'natural'), rather than our modern concept of pure white. The background works equally well in a light beige mix, which in vintage colours was referred to as natural, or fawn.
Short sleeves 6 × 50 g balls Cygnet Wool Rich 4 ply in Oatmeal (2046) or Cream (1992)
Long sleeves 7 × 50 g balls
1 × 50 g ball Green (G) and small amounts of Red (R), Yellow (Y) and Blue (B) for colour work (you will not use a whole ball of either of these when used for knitting, and the pattern specifies the following lengths for economy):
18 yards (16.5 m) Yellow, 24 yards (23 m) Red, 9 yards (8.5 m) Blue
12 buttons (*as this is a difficult number to source in vintage buttons, you can re-align the spacing of buttonholes worked to suit the number of buttons found, as explained in the notes with the instructions. You need around 9 to ensure a neat closing of the fronts*)

Measurements

To fit a size 34–35" bust (36–38" given in brackets)
A version for size 38–40" of this pattern is given in *Knitting Fashions of the 1940s* by Jane Waller[2]
Length 47 cm/18.5"
Short sleeves 11.5 cm/4.5"
Long sleeves 45.5 cm/18"

Tension

28 sts. to 10 cm/4" measured over stocking st. on 3.25 mm needles

Back

With 2.75 mm (3 mm) needles and M (or C if chosen) cast on 115 sts.
Work an even number of rows of K1, P1 rib for 9.5 cm/3.75".
Change to 3.25 mm (3.75 mm).
Work in st.st for 4 rows.
Row 5: Inc. at each end of K row
Continue in st.st increasing at each end of every following 6th row until there are 135 sts.
Work 15 rows straight after last inc. row.

Shape armhole

Cast off 10 sts. (8 sts.) at beg. of each of the next 2 rows.
Cast off 1 st. at beginning of next 12 rows until 103 sts. (107 sts.) remain.
Work 14 rows straight then change to 2.75 mm/12 needles and start moss st. (*using the smaller needles maintains a narrower finished shape for the yoke*).
1st row: P1, (K1, P1) to end, rep this row 51 times more (*NB original pattern states 41 times more but this makes the neck opening tight. The extra rows here allow for a more comfortable neckline*).

Shape shoulders

Cast off 8 sts. at beg. of next 8 rows.
Keep remaining 39 sts. (43 sts.) on a spare needle. (*The original pattern casts off here, but keeping them on hold to pick up for the neckband also maintains more elasticity.*)

Right Front

This can be knitted plain to the yoke and embroidered afterwards, or the motifs can be knitted in, following either the line-by-line instructions or from the chart included below. If working the motifs into the knitting, use small balls of wool held at the back of the work to pick up as the colour is needed and keep these on small holders or spools to avoid tangling. Twist the wools around each other when changing colours to avoid holes in the work. There are useful additional notes on achieving the best results in the 'Integral Colour Work' section in Chapter 3.

The motifs are reversed on each front to be symmetrical, which is explained in the instructions if knitted, but ***remember to reverse these if embroidering onto the finished knitting after this is completed***.

**With main colour M and 2.75 mm (3 mm) needles, cast on 59 sts. and work in K1, P1 rib for 9.5 cm/3.75".
Change to 3.25 mm (3.75 mm) and continue thus:
1st row: Knit
2nd row: Purl
Rep these 2 rows once more.
5th row: Knit to last st., knit twice in last st.
6th row: Purl
7th row: Knit
8th row: P33 in M, join in G, 1 G, drop G, P with M to end
9th row: K25 in M, 3 G, drop G, K with M to end
10th row: P31 M, 5 G, break off G, P with M to end
11th row: K with M to last st., K twice in last st.
12th row: P30 M, join G, 3 G, 3 M, 3 G, drop G, P with M to end

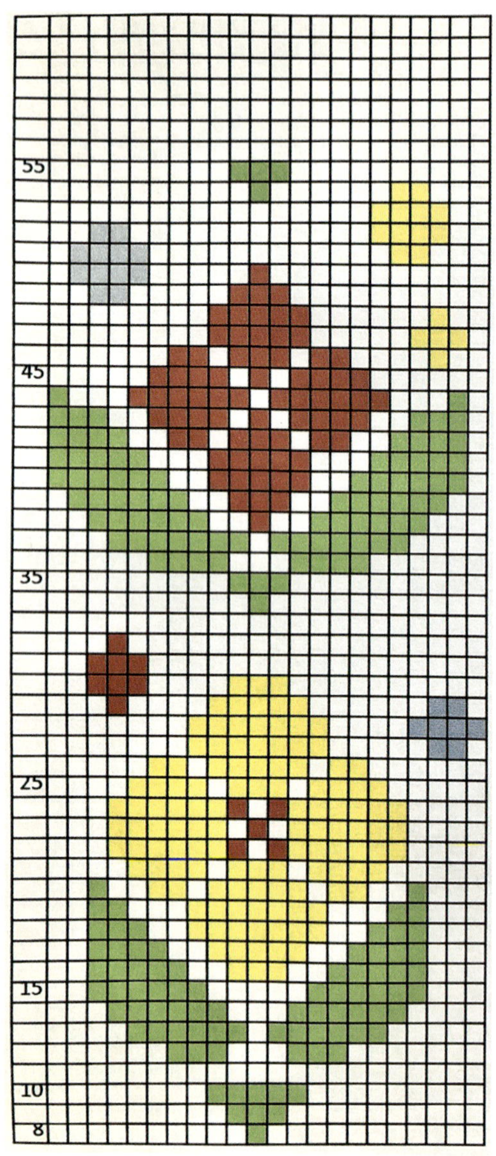

Colour stitch chart for the right front, taken from the line-by-line instructions of the original pattern.

13th row: K20 M, 6 G, 1 M, 6 G, drop G, K with M to end
14th row: P27 M, 6 G, 3 M, 6 G, drop G, P with M to end
15th row: K18 M, 6 G, 5 M, 6 G, drop G, K with M to end
16th row: P26 M, 5 G, 2 M, join in Y, 3 Y, drop Y, 2 M, 5 G, drop G, P with M to end
17th row: K18 M, 4 G, 2 M, 5 Y, drop Y, 2 M, 4 G, drop G, K with M to last st., K twice in last st.
18th row: P27 M, 3 G, 2 M, 7 Y, drop Y, 2 M, 3 G, drop G, P with M to end
19th row: K18 M, 2 G, 3 M, 7 Y, drop Y, 3 M, 2 G, drop G, K with M to end
20th row: P27 M, 1 G, 2 M, 2 Y, 1 M, 5 Y, 1 M, 2 Y, drop Y, 2 M, 1 G, break off G, P with M to end
21st row: K20 M, 4 Y, 1 M, 3 Y, 1 M, 4 Y, drop Y, K with M to end
22nd row: P28 M, 6 Y, join on R, 1 R, 1 M, 1 R, drop R, 6 Y, drop Y, P with M to end
23rd row: K19 M, 6 Y, 1 M, 1 R, drop R, 1 M, 6 Y, drop Y, K with M to last st., K twice in last st.
24th row: P29 M, 6 Y, 1 R, 1 M, 1 R, break off R, 6 Y, drop Y, P with M to end
25th row: K20 M, 4 Y, 1 M, 3 Y, 1 M, 4 Y, drop Y, K with M to end
26th row: P31 M, 2, 1 M, 5 Y, 1 M, 2 Y, drop Y, P with M to end
27th row: K16 M, join on B, 2 B, drop B, 5 M, 7 Y, drop Y, K with M to end
28th row: P33 M, 7 Y, drop Y, 4 M, 4 B, drop B, P with M to end
29th row: K16 M, 2 B, break off B, 6 M, 5 Y, drop Y, 4 M, join on R, 1 R, drop R, K with M to last st., K twice in last st.
30th row: P29 M, 3 R, drop R, 4 M, 3 Y, break off Y, P with M to end
31st row: K32 M, 3 R, drop R, K with M to end
32nd row: P30 M, 1 R, break off R, P with M to end
33rd row: K with M
34th row: P37 M, join on G, 1 G, drop G, P with M to end
35th row: K25 M, 3 G, drop G, K with M to last st., K twice in last st.
36th row: P33 M, 4 G, 3 M, 4 G, drop G, P with M to end
37th row: K19 M, 7 G, 1 M, 7 G, drop G, P with M to end
38th row: P30 in M, 6 G, 2 M, join on R, 1 R, drop R, 2 M, 6 G, drop G, P with M to end
39th row: K17 M, 6 G, 2 M, 3 R, drop R, 2 M, 6 G, drop G, K with M to end
40th row: P28 M, 6 G, 2 M, 5 R, drop R, 2 M, 6 G, drop G, P with M to end
41st row: K16 M, 5 G, 3 M, 5 R, drop R, 3 M, 5 G, drop G, K with M to last st., K twice in last st.
42nd row: P29 M, 4 G, 2 M, 2 R, 1 M, 3 R, 1 M, 2 R, drop R, 2 M, 4 G, drop G, P with M to end
43rd row: K16 M, 3 G, 2 M, 4 R, 1 M, 1 R, 1 M, 4 R, drop R, 2 M, 3 G, drop G, K with M to end
44th row: P29 M, 1 G, 3 M, 6 R, 1 M, 6 R, drop R, 3 M, 1 G, break off G, P with M to end
45th row: K21 M, 4 R, 1 M, 1 R, 1 M, 4 R, drop R, K with M to end

46th row: P35 M, 2 R, 1 M, 3 R, 1 M, 2 R, drop R, 4 M, join on Y, 1 Y, drop Y, P with M to end
47th row: K16 M, 3 Y, drop Y, 5 M, 5 R, drop R, K with M to last st., K twice in last st.
48th row: P38 M, 5 R, drop R, 6 M, 1 Y, break off Y, P with M to end
49th row: K25 M, 3 R, drop R, 5 M, join on B, 2 B, drop B, K with M to end
50th row: P31 M, 4 B, drop B, 5 M, 1 R, break off R, P with M to end
51st row: K18 M, join on Y, 2 Y, drop Y, 12 M, 4 B, drop B, K with M to end
52nd row: P32 M, 2 B, break off B, 12 M, 4 Y, drop Y, P with M to end
53rd row: K17 M, 4 Y, K with M to last st., K twice in last st.
54th row: P41 M, join on G, 1 G, drop G, 6 M, 2 Y, break off Y, P with M to end
55th row: K25 M, 3 G, drop G, K with M to end
56th row: P39 M, 5 G, drop G, P with M to end
57th row: K with M
58th row: P37 M, 3 G, 3 M,3 G, drop G, P with M to end
59th row: K20 M, 6 G, 1 M, 6 G, drop G, K with M to last st., K twice in last st. (69 sts.)
60th row: P35 M, 6 G, 3 M,6 G, drop G, P with M to end
61st row: K18 M, 6 G, 5 M, 6 G, drop G, K with M to end
62nd row: P34 M, 5 G, 2 M, join on Y, 3 Y, drop Y, 2 M, 5 G, drop G, P with M to end
63rd row: K18 M, 4 G, 2 M, 5 Y, drop Y, 2 M, 4 G, drop G, K with M to end
64th row: P34 M, 3 G, 2 M, 7 Y, drop Y, 2 M, 3 G, drop G, P with M to end
65th row: K18 M, 2 G, 3 M, 7 Y, drop Y, 3 M, 2 G, drop G, K with M to end
66th row: P34 M, 1 G, 2 M, 2 Y, 1 M, 5 Y, 1 M, 2 Y, drop Y, 2 M, 1 G, break off G, P with M to end
67th row: K20 M, 4 Y, 1 M, 3 Y, 1 M, 4 Y, drop Y, K with M to end
68th row: P35 M, 6 Y, join on R, 1 R, 1 M, 1 R, drop R, 6 Y, drop Y, P with M to end
69th row: K19 M, 6 Y, 1 M, 1 R, drop R, 1 M, 6 Y, drop Y, K with M to end
70th row: P35 M, 6 Y, 1 R, 1 M, 1 R, break off R, 6 Y, drop Y, P with M to end
71st row: As Row 67
72nd row: P37 M, 2 Y, 1 M, 5 Y, 1 M, 2 Y, drop Y, P with M to end
73rd row: K16 M, join on B, 2 B, drop B, 5 M, 7 Y, drop Y, K with M to end
74th row: P39 M, 7 Y, drop Y, 4 M, 4 B, drop B, P with M to end
75th row: K16 M, 2 B, break off B, 6 M, 5 Y, drop Y, 4 M, join on R, 1 R, drop R, K with M to end

Shape armhole

76th row: Cast off 8 sts. with M, after which you will have 1 st. on right-hand needle. P next 25 with M, 3 R, drop R, 4 M, 3 Y, break off Y, P with M to end
77th row: K32 M, 3 R, drop R, K with M to end
78th row: P2tog, P25 M, 1 R, break off R, P with M to end
79th row: K with M
80th row: P2tog, P31 M, join on G, 1 G, drop G, P with M to end
81st row: K25 M, 3 G, drop G, K with M to end
82nd row: P2tog, P25 M, 4 G, 3 M, 4 G, drop G, P with M to end
83rd row: K19 M, 7 G, 1 M, 7 G, drop G, K with M to end
84th row: P2tog, P21 M, 6 G, 2 M, join on R, 1 R, drop R, 2 M, 6 G, drop G, P with M to end
85th row: K17 with M, 6 G, 2 M, 3 R, drop R, 2 M, 6 G, K with M to end
86th row: P2tog, P18 M, 6 G, 2 M, 5 R, drop R, 2 M, 6 G, drop G, P with M to end
87th row: K16 M, 5 G, 3 M, 5 R, drop R, 3 M, 5 G, K with M to end
88th row: P2tog, P17 M, 4 G, 2 M, 2 R, 1 M, 3 R, 1 M, 2 R, drop R, 2 M, 4 G, P with M to end
89th row: K16 M, 3 G, 2 M, 4 R, 1 M, 1 R, 1 M, 4 R, drop R, 2 M, 3 G, drop G, K with M to end
90th row: P18 M, 1 G, 3 M, 6 R, 1 M, 6 R, drop R, 3 M, 1 G, break off G, P with M to end
91st row: K21 M, 4 R, 1 M, 1 R, 1 M, 4 R, drop R, K with M to end
92nd row: P24 M, 2 R, 1 M, 3 R, 1 M, 2 R, drop R, 4 M, join on Y, 1 Y, drop Y, P with M to end
93rd row: K16 M, 3 Y, drop Y, 5 M, 5 R, drop R, K with M to end
94th row: P26 M, 5 R, 6 M, 1 Y, break off Y, P with M to end
95th row: K25 M, 3 R, 6 M, join on B, 1 B, drop B, K with M to end
96th row: P19 M, 3 B, drop B, 6 M, 1 R, break off R, P with M to end
97th row: K18 M, join on Y, 2 Y, drop Y, 13 M, 3 B, drop B, K with M to end
98th row: P20 M, 1 B, break off B, 13 M, 4 Y, drop Y, P with M to end
99th row: K17 M, 4 Y, drop Y, K with M to end
100th row: P35 M, 2 Y, break off Y, P with M to end
Next row: Knit
Next row: Purl

Now continue in moss st. as follows (to keep the yoke from being too wide, change down to smaller needles):
Next row: P1, (K1, P1) to end
Rep this row 19 times more.

Shape neck

Still working in moss st., cast off 6 sts. at start of next row, then dec. 1 st. at neck edge in every row until 36 sts. remain. Work 19 rows straight after last dec. row.

Shape shoulder

Cast off 8 sts. at beg. of next 3 rows that begin from armhole edge.
Work 1 row straight.
Cast off **.

Left Front

Work as right front from **to **but read K for P and vice versa.

Sleeves (Both Alike)

Short sleeves

With 2.75 mm (3 mm) needles and M cast on 81 sts.
Work K1, P1 rib for 2.5 cm/1″.
Change to 3.25 mm (3.75 mm) and work in st.st, increasing at each end of 3rd and every following 4th row, until there are 97 sts.
Work 5 more rows straight (this gives a length of 11.5 cm/ 4.5″; add extra rows here for a longer sleeve seam as required).

Shape top
Cast off 5 sts. at beg. of next 2 rows.
Dec. 1 st. at beg. of every row until 45 sts. remain.
Cast off 15 sts. at beg. of next 2 rows then work 18 rows straight on remaining 15 sts.
Cast off.

Long sleeves

With 2.75 mm (3 mm) needles and M (or C if preferred) cast on 57 sts.
Work in K1 P1 rib for 29 rows.
30th row: Rib 7 (inc. 1 in next st., rib 5) rep to last 9 sts., inc. in next st., rib 8 (65 sts.)
Change to 3.25 mm (3.75 mm) needles and cont. in st.st., increasing at each end of 5th and every following 4th row until there are 97 sts.
Cont. straight without further shaping until work measures 45.5 cm/18″ or desired length.
Shape top as for short sleeves.

Button Bands

Left front band

Make this one first so that you can work out the spacing for the buttons.

Using 2.75 mm (3 mm) needles and M, cast on 11 sts. and work in K1, P1 rib so that this fits along the inner edge of the left front, slightly stretched (*if you knit exactly the same length this has a tendency to ripple*).

Keeping a note of the number of rows worked is helpful to replicate for the right front buttonhole band.

Sew the button band to the left front, leaving the safety pin at the neck edge, and mark out the spacings for the buttons/buttonholes, as follows:

Place the buttons along the completed button band of the left front, keeping one back for the neckband.

Place the first 1 cm/0.5″ from the bottom edge and top button at 1 cm/0.5″ from top edge of rib band.

For additional button in the neckband, equal spacing is not essential to be visually balanced.

Space the buttons equally along the left front button band and mark each with a pin. Measure and adjust spacings to correct. If you can count the number of rows between markings, note this and use to guide the intervals for the buttonholes to be worked on the right front band.

(If you have kept a note of the total number of rib rows worked for the left front band, you can calculate the spacings exactly, allowing 2 rows for each buttonhole.)

Right front buttonhole band

Using 2.75 mm (3 mm) needles and M, cast on 11 sts. and work in K1, P1 rib. Work 8 rows in rib to first buttonhole.
Make buttonholes at the regular marked/counted intervals as follows:
First buttonhole row: Rib 4, cast off 3 (or enough sts. to slide over buttons without over stretching), Rib to end.
Second buttonhole row: Rib to last 4 sts., cast on 3 sts. over cast off sts. on previous row, Rib 4.
Repeat these 2 buttonhole rows for the number of buttons (but leaving the extra button for the neckband for now), keeping the same number of rows between each. Leave the sts. on a safety pin as with left front band to pick up later for the neckband.
Stitch the buttonhole band to the right front edge, leaving the safety pin at the neck edge.

For alternative methods of creating the button bands, please see separate instructions.

Neckband

Join the shoulder seams.
With right side of work facing, using 2.75 mm (3 mm) needles and M pick up and work the 11 rib sts. left on the safety pin. then pick up and K 42 sts. along right side of neck edge up to shoulder seam. Then pick up and K 39 sts. (43 sts.) from spare needle for back neck edge, then pick up and K 39 sts. (43 sts.) along the left neck edge and finish with the 11 sts. from the safety pin at the top of the left button band. Now work 5 rows in K1, P1 rib.
Make buttonhole as before in 6th and 7th rows at right front edge. Continue in rib for another 5 rows (12 in all).
Cast off in rib.

Making Up

Complete embroidery work on front panels before sewing all pieces together.

Complete all motifs from the colour chart and/or added details to finish the small flowers. For these, add a centre dot stitch, such as a French knot, for definition. Use Yellow for each Blue and Red flower, and Green for the Yellow flowers.

Join sides of central extension at sleeve top to the 15 st. cast-off edges to form darts. Set in sleeves, then sew up side and sleeve seams.

The finished darts at the tops of the sleeves, creating the sharp distinctive look of 1940s styling.

With two strands of Red together, outline the colour work panel of each front with a running stitch on the 12th st. from front edge band, and on 41st st., working along the base of the yoke to match. A running stitch works well here, making sure to keep the stretch of the knitting and spacing the stitches equally.

Sew on all buttons.

With Red, Blue, Green and Yellow wools together (as single strands), crochet a length of chain 68.5 cm/27" long. Knot both ends and sew in loose ends. Tie the chain in a neat bow and stitch this to the neck between the top 2 buttons.

Lines of running stitch in a contrast colour are worked along the yoke edge where the stitch textures change, and to frame the colour motifs.

A bow made from a chain of the colours used in the embroidery is added as a decorative touch in Tyrolean style, in the place of a typical neck tie-cord.

A Heartfelt Waistcoat

The decorated yoke is carried across the back of the waistcoat for a colourful added effect.

The Bestway original pattern 1421 refers to this as a 'Peasant Waistcoat' on the cover, but as a 'Tyrolean Waistcoat' inside.

During the 1940s, Bestway and their contemporaries Weldons produced some of the most beautiful patterns in the Tyrolean style. Always with buttoned fronts, they designed cardigans, jackets and waistcoats that combined varied techniques for stitches and embellishments. The charming application of felt motifs to this waistcoat is just one of many options to decorate and enjoy knitted garments, making the most of small quantities of wool and other materials at a time when such resources were scarce and precious.

The pattern describes this delightful waistcoat beautifully:

This youthful and attractive design looks charming over a blouse and is fascinating to make. The main part is in cable-stitch, with a deep, ribbed welt. The yoke is stocking stitch, and afterwards trimmed with a line of chain-stitch and flowers and hearts cut from felt. The buttons are covered with crochet.

The yoke is embellished with charming felt hearts and flowers, and, in addition to the pattern, the recreated model has added slightly larger felt hearts to finish the cord that gathers the neckline.

Alternative colours and shapes would work equally well on the contrast yoke, such as these felt edelweiss and red hearts, arranged in a suggested sequence to illustrate the possibilities.

The front cover refers to this as a 'Peasant Waistcoat' but inside the pattern it is called a 'Tyrolean Waistcoat in Cable-stitch'. Many vintage patterns use Peasant and Tyrolean as interchangeable descriptions of the style. This denotes similar decorative features associated with both styles from the 1930s to the 1950s.

The original pattern uses a 3 ply and is well suited to a modern 4 ply, as the original pattern instructions were for a small size (31″ stretching to 34″), even though knitted on 4 mm needles which are larger than usual for working in fine 3 ply. The stretchiness of the stitch combination used and slightly thicker weight of modern 4 ply makes this a very comfortable fit.

The recreated model used modern 4 ply on 3.75 mm needles to make an easy-fitting size 34″ garment, which easily stretches to a 36″ bust. Using 4 mm needles as the vintage pattern suggests would easily allow for a size 38–40″. For a smaller size (32–34″), use one of the finer modern 4 ply yarns as suggested here, and 3.25 mm needles.

The appliqués to the yoke leave room for great creativity and though the hearts and flowers of the original are delightful, any combination of motifs and colours would work equally well. The cord which ties through the yoke neckline is finished with neat knots in the original pattern, but for extra detail little felt hearts were attached, inspired by one of the Tyrolean patterns in the Bestway booklet *Tyrolean Design*.

Waistcoats became increasingly popular during this decade – generally with either a yoke or V neck, as with the Hollywood Comes to Broadway design – always a popular feature of Tyrolean-style knitwear and often decorated with light-hearted motifs, such as the Tyrolean waistcoat by Weldons.

Crochet-covered buttons are a very useful solution for matching buttons to a garment, and re-using old buttons. Button moulds were easily obtainable at the time for this reason, but are more difficult to source today. The metal moulds most readily found today tend to be for covering with fabric rather than knitted pieces, which are too thick for this and tricky to locate into the mould. The best substitute is to use flat, round buttons with a shank, so that once covered they can easily be secured to the garment.

The pattern suggests 'white' wool; this would have been an off-white, closer to our idea of cream, and not a pure bleached white with which we would be familiar today.

This is a charming pattern, and could easily be adapted to a long- or short-sleeved cardigan, adding sleeves from the universal pattern given in Chapter 5 with the Flowers for Laura instructions, noting that to be in keeping with a true 1940s silhouette these should have exaggerated sleeve heads – either pleated or gathered.

Materials

4 (5) (5) × 50 g balls Cygnet Wool Rich 4 Ply Cream (1192) (King Cole Merino Blend 100% Merino in colour 'Aran' is slightly thicker for larger sizes)
1 × 100 g ball Cascade Heritage (75% Merino 25% Nylon) in Christmas Green (5656)
3.66 m/4yd Black 4 ply yarn
Small pieces of felt (pattern recommends the colour Rose)
1 pair each 2.75 mm (3 mm) (3 mm) needles (for ribbing)
1 pair 3.25 mm/10 (3.75 mm/9) (4 mm/8) needles (for main work)
1 × cable needle of the same size as the needles used for the main work
1 × 3.75 mm crochet hook (for all sizes)
3 buttons/button moulds

Measurements

To fit size 32–34" (34–36") (38–40") bust (all sizes worked to the same number of stitches but on different sized needles)
Length: original pattern 43 cm/17" – recreated model worked to 45.5 cm/18". The finished length can be adjusted by adding pattern repeats *before the armhole shaping*, as with the re-created version which added one full pattern repeat

Tension

28 sts. to 10 cm/4" knitted on 3.25 mm/10 needles

Waistcoats were a fashionable favourite during the 1940s, such as this Weldons Tyrolean waistcoat pattern 592, embellished with knitted and crocheted appliqués and an unusual lace-up front reminiscent of traditional Tyrolean bodices.

Back

With 2.75 mm (3 mm) (3 mm) needles and Cream, cast on 111 sts.
1st single rib row (right side): P1, *K1, P1, rep from *to end
2nd row: K1, *P1, K1, rep from *to end
Rep these 2 rows for 82 mm/3.25", ending with a wrong side row.

Change to 3.25 mm/10 (3.75 mm/9) (4 mm/8) needles and pattern as follows:
1st patt. row (right side): K1, *P1, K8, P1, K1 rep from *to end
2nd patt. row: K1, *P1, K1, P6, K1, P1, K1, rep from *to end
Rep 1st and 2nd rows twice more.
7th patt. row: K1, P1, K1, C6B (which is: cable 6 by slipping the next 3 sts. on to cable needle and placing behind the work, K the following 3 sts., then K 3 sts. from cable needle) K1, P1, K1, rep from *to end
8th patt. row: As 2nd row
These 8 rows comprise one pattern, rep them, and keeping the continuity of the pattern, inc. 1 st. each end of next 5th row and every following 4th row, until there are 133 sts.
Note that you should work the first 2 sts. added each end in moss st., the next 6 sts. added at each end in st.st (only cabling them when there are 6 additional stitches in st.st), and the final 3 increased sts. added each end should be in moss st.
When there are 133 sts., work straight, until you have completed 10th pattern from the start.
(Please note: the original works 8 full patterns, but you can add multiples of the pattern repeats to achieve the desired length before

Crochet coverings for buttons are an excellent solution to matching colours perfectly.

the armhole shaping, which in this case was an additional 2 repeats to achieve the extra 2.5 cm/1″ length.)

Shape armholes

Cast off 7 sts. at beg. of next 2 rows, then dec. 1 st. each end of next row and every following row until 91 sts. remain.

Then dec. 1 st. at both ends of every alternate row until 85 sts. remain.

Then work straight until 2nd row of 14th pattern has been completed.

Now shape for yoke line.

Next row: Patt. 34 sts., cast off next 17 sts., then patt. to end.

Now work on the second set of 34 sts. only as follows:

Work 1 row. **Cast off 6 sts. at beg. of next 2 rows that start from neck edge, then cast off 4 sts. at start of next 2 rows that begin from neck edge, and cast of 3 sts. at start of following row that

The combination of cables alternated with moss stitch create a soft, warm and elastic texture for this waistcoat.

begins at neck edge. After this, dec. 1 st. at neck edge on every row until 2 sts. are left. Take 2 tog and fasten off **

Now return to sts. for other side.

With wrong side facing, join yarn to inner end and work as first side from **to **.

Left Front

With 2.75 mm (3 mm) (3 mm) needles and Cream, cast on 55 sts. and work in single rib as given for back waist for 82 mm, ending with a wrong side row, and inc. 1 st. at end of this last rib row.

Now change to 3.25 mm/10 (3.75 mm/9) (4 mm/8) needles and work in pattern as given for back, but to shape side edge, inc. 1 st. at beg. of 5th row of 2nd pattern and inc. 1 st. at start of every following 4th row of knitting until there are 67 sts. Continue without further increasings until 10th pattern (or number of repeats for desired length) has been completed.

Now shape the armhole and at the same time form yoke line as follows:

****1st armhole row:** Cast off 7 sts., patt. to end

2nd row: Cast off 9 sts., patt. to end

3rd row: Take 2 tog., then patt. to end

4th row: Cast off 4 sts., patt. to 2 sts. from the end, take 2 tog

Rep 3rd and 4th rows twice more. Then rep 3rd row once again. Then dec. 1 st. at both ends of the next 6 rows.
16th row: Take 2 tog, patt. to end
17th row: Take 2 tog, patt. to 2 sts. from the end, take 2 tog
Rep 16th and 17th rows 3 times more.
Now keep armhole edge straight, but take 2 sts. tog at neck edge on next 5 alternate rows.
Work 3 rows straight.
Take 2 sts. tog at neck edge of next row.
Work another 3 rows straight.
Take 2 sts. tog and fasten off. **

Right Front

Work as for left front until waist ribbing is finished, but inc. the 1 st. at start of last rib row instead of at the end. Now change to 3.25 mm/10 (3.75 mm/9) (4 mm/8) needles and work in patt., but inc. 1 st. at end of 5th row of 2nd pattern, and inc. 1 st. at end of very following 4th row of knitting until there are 67 sts.

Continue without further increasings until 1st row of 11th pattern has been completed.

Now work as from **to **of left front.

Yoke

This is knitted separately and starts at the outer edge.
With 2.75 mm (3 mm) (3 mm) needles and Cream, cast on 185 sts. and work in rib as for back waist for 10 rows, but inc. 1 st. in centre of last rib row by knitting twice into 93rd st. Change to 3.25 mm/10 (3.75 mm/9) (4 mm/8) needles, then break off Cream and join on Green yarn, and work as follows:
1st row: Knit
2nd row: Knit
3rd row: Knit
4th row: Purl
5th row: K1, *sl. 1, K1, psso (inc. 1 in next st.) 4 times, K2tog, rep fr. *to last st., K1
There are now 232 sts.
6th row: Purl
7th row: Knit
8th row: Purl
9th row: K1, *sl.1, K1, psso, K2, (inc. 1 in next st.) twice, K2, K2tog, rep fr. *to last st., K1
There are still 232 sts.
10th row: Purl
11th row: Knit
12th row: Purl
13th row: K1, *sl.1, K1, psso, K1 (inc 1 in nxt st.) 4 times, K1, K2tog, rep fr. *to last st., K1
There are now 278 sts.
14th row: Purl
15th row: Knit
16th row: Purl
17th row: K1, *sl.1, K1, psso, K3, (inc. 1 in next st.) twice, K3, K2tog, rep fr. *to last st., K1
There are still 278 sts.
18th row: Knit. Break off Green. Join on Cream and cast off

Mark off 60 sts. at each end of yoke for fronts. Then count 28 sts. following each set and mark them to go over shoulders, the remaining (102 sts.) being for the back.
With Cream yarn sew top of fronts to position marked on yoke ends. Sew top of back to centre of yoke, leaving the sides of yoke open to form the top part of the armholes.

Armhole Bands (Both Alike)

With 2.75 mm/12 (3 mm/11) (3 mm/11) needles and Cream, pick up and K 145 sts. along armhole edge. Work in rib as given for back waist for 8 rows. Cast off.

The yoke is knitted separately and the armhole edgings are marked out, picked up and knitted in rib to complete.

Left Front Border

With 2.75 mm/12 (3 mm/11) (3 mm/11) needles and Cream, cast on 13 sts.
1st row (right side): K2, P1, *K1, P1, rep fr. *to last 2 sts., K2
2nd row: K1, *P1, K1, rep fr. *to end
Rep these 2 rows until border measures the same as left front edge, very slightly stretched (*if it is measured unstretched it may 'wave'*), keeping a note of the number of rows knitted. Cast off.

Guidance on spacing for the buttons and buttonholes is given in Chapter 5 with the Flowers for Laura pattern.

Right Front Border

Work as for left front border to position (or counted number of rows) of first pin.
1st buttonhole row: Rib 3 sts., cast off 4 sts., rib to end.
2nd buttonhole row: Work as 1st rib row, but cast on 4 sts. over those cast off in previous row.
Work in rib for required number of rows, ***, rep from ***to ***twice more. Cast off.

The Crochet Button Covers (3 Alike)

With 3.75 mm crochet hook make 3 ch., slip st. to 1st ch. to form a ring.
Next round: work 2 dc. into each ch.
Next round: work 2 dc. in each dc. of previous round.
Next round: *1 dc. in each of next 3 dc., 2 dc. in next, rep fr. *all round.
Now work 3 or 4 rounds of 1 dc. in each dc., depending on button to be covered. Fasten off. Run a length of yarn through last round, place button inside. Draw up and sew firmly.

Making Up

Lay work flat, wrong side up, with damp cloth laid over it, and pass the warm iron over work without actually pressing, and avoiding all ribbings.

Sew the front borders to the front edges, leaving a 7 mm/0.25" space open at 7 mm/0.25" below neck edge, to form slots through which to thread the cord. Sew up side seams. Stitch on the buttons.

With crochet hook and using double strands of Green, chain a cord 35.5 cm/14" long. Before finishing the ends thread this through the slots at the neck to tie together.

Trimming

With black yarn embroider a wavy line of chain st. all along the yoke, as pictured, forming one curve in each of the 23 sections of the yoke.

The felt appliqués

Using the diagrams illustrated as guides, cut small and large hearts and flowers from the felt.

You can trace these as guides but check the size for each of the pieces needed:

The size of each of the smaller hearts and flowers is 2 cm square.

The larger hearts are 2.5 cm square.

Cut the smaller heart pattern 11 times in felt and the flower pattern 12 times.

Cut the larger heart pattern 4 times (for the neck cord tie ends).

Sew the hearts onto the yoke above the stitched chain as pictured, catching them by the edges with a matching thread,

The yoke is embellished with a curving line of black against the contrast colour, working as a guide for placing the felt appliqués.

Smaller heart shape Flower shape. Larger heart shape

and sew the flowers below the chain, catching each one around the edges and through the centre with a stitch or French knot (*a contrasting thread works well for this, such as a yellow*).

Cut 4 hearts from the larger template for the ends of the cord, if desired. Position 2 of these over each of the cord ends and stitch around the edges to join together and secure to the cord.

The felt shapes are sewn on with matching coloured thread and finished with a French knot centre for the flowers.

Knitted for Best Jacket

The Knitted for Best cardigan has texture and colour interest all around each part.

The Knitted for Best cardigan.

Clothes rationing and coupons in Britain finally ended in March of 1949, nearly four long years after the end of the war, with wool supplies in those last years becoming even more scarce. By the end of 1949, and the publication of this December issue of *Stitchcraft* magazine, it really would have felt like Christmas had finally arrived for knitters!

The front cover of Stitchcraft *magazine of December 1949 featuring the pattern adapted for Knitted for Best.*

If you are lucky enough to go winter-sporting, here is the very jumper for you. Thick, white wool, gaily decorated with scattered embroidery, it is just the thing to wear ski-ing or skating. For the less fortunate, you will have a really attractive knitted for best – specially when it's cold, and you want to look smart and be warm!

Although the pattern doesn't mention Tyrolean in the description, this cardigan (called a jumper at the time) has all the hallmarks of the style: the cream wool background, the bobble 'grid' with coloured embroidered flowers are all there, and in addition there is beautifully shaped high ribbing and an attractive ruffle-effect collar. This is a truly Tyrolean cardigan by any other name.

With a softer shoulder line, longer length and defined waistline, the styling seems much more in tune with the 1950s and the fashions to come, turning away from the 1940s as that decade came to a close. The distinctive high, graduated ribbing gives a soft corset effect, reminiscent of the dirndl bodices, and heralds this style of high ribbing which became so popular in the Tyrolean knitwear of the 1970s and early 1980s, and is still favoured today as a key feature of the style.

The recommended yarn in the pattern is Patons Moorland Knitting, which was slightly thicker than our modern double knitting, though knitted on 4 mm/8 needles to give a tension of 20 sts. to 10 cm/4". When knitted with modern DK on 4 mm needles, as for the recreated model, the size achieved is a close fitting 34". (Sizing and adjustments are given in the instructions below.)

This pattern is enjoyable to knit, growing quickly and easily with the bobbles being easy to create. For authenticity, the recreated model has kept to the original placements of the embroidered flower details. These are not complicated, and are relatively bold, and could be added to more of the grid spaces in the finished cardigan, if desired.

Materials

10 (11) x 50 g balls Cygnet Naturally Soft Superwash 100% Wool DK in Cream (2195)

Small quantities of coloured wool for embroidery in Red, Blue, Pink, Yellow and Green (or any colours preferred). This works better if a finer wool is used than DK, such as a 4 ply

1 x pair 3.75 mm/9 needles

1 x pair 4 mm/8 needles (4.5 mm/7)

9 x buttons (as this is a fitted design which relies on the stretch of the deep ribbing at the waist, 9 is the minimum number of buttons needed to give effective closing without any gaping)

Measurements

34" (36")

A larger sizing will also be achieved by using a Worsted weight wool (such as the Sirdar Country Classic used in the June Clyde Jacket pattern with appropriate needles for the wool weight as indicated on the yarn ball band)

Instructions to fit size 38" for this pattern are given as the 'Tyrolean Winter Sports Cardigan' in *Knitting Fashions of the 1940s* by Jane Waller[1]

Length at centre back 52 cm/20.5"

Length of sleeves 46 cm/18"

Tension

22 sts. to 10 cm/4" on 4 mm/8 needles over stocking stitch (using modern DK as given)

20 sts. to 10 cm/4" on 4.5 mm/7 needles over stocking stitch (as original pattern)

Pattern for the Bobble Grid

Knitted over 11 sts. and 16 rows.
To make bobble: (K1, P1, K1, P1, K1) all into next st., referred throughout as K5 in 1.

1st row (wrong side facing): K5 in 1, K9, K5 in 1
2nd row: K5, P9, K5 (this is the right side of work)
3rd row: P5tog, K9, P5tog
4th row: Purl across all stitches
5th row: K1, K5 in 1, K7, K5 in 1, K1
6th row: P1, K5, P7, K5, P1
7th row: K1, P5tog, K7, P5tog, K1
8th row: Purl
9th row: K2, K5 in 1, K5, K5 in 1, K2
10th row: P2, K5, P5, K5, P2
11th row: K2, P5tog, K5, P5tog, K2
12th row: Purl
13th row: K4, K5 in 1, K1, K5 in 1, K4
14th row: P4, K5, P1, K5, P4
15th row: K4, P5tog, K1, P5tog, K4
16th row: Purl

The bobbles are placed in an arch shape accentuated by the simple coloured embroidery of stylized flowers.

Back

With 3.75 mm/9 needles, cast on 68 sts.
1st row (right side of work facing): *K3, P2, rep fr. *to last 3sts., K3
2nd row: *P3, K2, rep fr. *to last 3 sts., P3
Rep these 2 rows 18 times more.
Change to 4 mm/8 (4.5 mm/7) needles and start shaping ribbed point by gradually taking side stitches into reversed stocking stitch.
1st row (right side of work facing): P6, rib 56 thus – K2, (P2, K3) 10 times, P2, K2, P6
2nd row: K6, rib 56, K6
3rd row: P8, rib 52 thus – (P2, K3) 10 times, P2, P8
4th row: K8, rib 52, K8
5th row: Inc. in 1st stitch, P9, rib 48 thus – (K3, P2) 9 times, K3, P9, inc. in last st.
6th row: K11, rib 48, K11
7th row: P13, rib 44 thus – K1, (P2, K3) 8 times, P2, K1, P13
8th row: K13, rib 44, K13
9th row: Inc. in 1st st., P14, rib 40 thus – P1, (K3, P2) 7 times, K3, P1; P14, inc. in last st.
10th row: K16, rib 40, K16
11th row: P18, rib 36 thus – K2 (P2, K3) 6 times, P2, K2, P18
12th row: K18, rib 36, K18
13th row: Inc. in 1st st., P19, rib 32 thus – (P2, K3) 6 times, P2, P19, inc. in last st. (74 sts.)
Continue thus, working 4 sts. less in rib on alternate rows and keeping continuity of rib, and at the same time, introducing bobble pattern thus:
14th row: K2, K5 in 1, K9, K5 in 1, K8, rib 32, K8, K5 in 1, K9, K5 in 1, K2
15th row: P2, K5, P9, K5, P10, rib 28, P10, K5, P9, K5, P2
16th row: K2, P5tog, K9, P5tog, K10, rib 28, K10, P5tog, K9, P5tog, K2
17th row: Inc. in 1st st., P1, P11, P12, rib 24, P12, P11, P1, inc. in last st. (76 sts.)
18th row: K3, K1, K5 in 1, K7, K5 in 1, K1, K12, rib 24, K12, K1, K5 in 1, K7, K5 in 1, K1, K3
19th row: P3, P1, K5, P7, K5, P1, P14, rib 20, P14, P1, K5, P7, K5, P1, P3
20th row: K3, K1, P5tog, K7, P5tog, K1, K14, rib 20, K14, K1, P5tog, K7, P5tog, K1, K3
21st row: Inc. in 1st st., P2, P11, P16, rib 16, P16, P11, P2, inc. in last st. (78 sts.)
22nd row: K4, K2, K5 in 1, K5, K5 in 1, K2, K16, rib 16, K16, K2, K5 in 1, K5, K5 in 1, K2, K4
23rd row: P4, P2, K5, P5, P5, P2, P18, rib 12, P18, P2, K5, P5, K5, P2, P4
24th row: K4, K2, P5tog, K5, P5tog, K2, K18, rib 12, K18, K2, P5tog, K5, P5tog, K2, K4
25th row: Inc. in 1st st., P3, P11, P20, rib 8, P20, P11, P3, inc. in last st. (80 sts.)

26th row: K5, K4, K5 in 1, K1, K5 in 1, K4, K20, rib 8, K20, K4, K5 in 1, K1, K5 in 1, K4, K5
27th row: P5, P4, K5, P1, K5, P4, P22, rib 4 thus – K1, P2, K1, P22, P4, K5, P1, K5, P4, P5
28th row: K5, K4, P5tog, K1, P5tog, K4, K22, rib 2, pick up and knit loop, rib 2, K22, K4, P5tog, K1, P5tog, K4, K5
29th row: Inc. in 1st st., purl to last st, inc. in last st. (83 sts.)
This completes the first set of bobble patterns and ribbed point.
Next 4 rows: st.st., starting with a knit row, increasing 1 st. at each end of 4th row (85 sts.)
Next row (wrong side facing): Introduce second set of bobble patterns thus – K17, pattern 11, (K9, pattern 11) twice, K17
Continue thus until the 16 pattern rows are done, still increasing 1 stitch each end of 4th rows, twice more (89 sts.), then keep side edges straight.
Work 4 rows stocking stitch, starting with a knit row.

Shape armholes

Now introduce 3rd set of bobble patterns and shape armholes thus:
1st row: *K9, pattern 11, rep fr. *3 times more, K9
2nd row: *P9, K5, P9, K5, rep fr. *3 times more, P9
3rd row: *K9, P5tog, K9, P5tog, rep fr. *3 times more, K9
4th row: Cast off 4, purl to end
5th row: Cast off 4, K5, *K1, K5 in 1, K7, K5 in 1, K1, K9, rep fr. *twice more, pattern 11, K5
Continue in pattern, knitting 2 together at each end of every row until 73 sts. remain (leaving you with 1 instead of 9 sts. at each end of the needle before first and after last 11 pattern sts.).
Finish this 3rd line of bobble patterns, work the 4 rows stocking stitch, then another line of bobbles thus:
K11*pattern 11, K9, rep fr. *twice more, K2
Finish this pattern, work 4 rows stocking stitch, then 5th line of bobbles thus:
K1 *pattern 11, K9, rep fr. *twice more, pattern 11, K1
Work to end of 15th row.

Shape shoulders

Shape shoulders in reverse stocking stitch by casting off 7 sts. at beginning of next 6 rows. Cast off.

Left Front

With 3.75 mm/9 needles, cast on 33 sts. and work 38 rows K3, P2 rib as for back.

Change to 4 mm/8 (4.5 mm/7) needles, shape ribbed point:
1st row: P6, rib to end
2nd row: Rib to last 6 sts., K6
3rd row: P8, rib to end
4th row: Rib to last 8 sts., K8
5th row: Inc. in 1st st., P9, rib to end
6th row: Rib to last 11 sts., K11
7th row: P13, rib 21
8th row: Rib 21, K13
9th row: Inc. in 1st st., P14, rib 19
10th row: Rib 19, K16
11th row: P18, rib 17
12th row: Rib 17, K18
13th row: Inc. in 1st st., P19, rib 15

Continue thus, taking 2 sts. into reverse stocking stitch on alternate rows, and introducing bobble pattern thus:
14th row: Rib 15, K8, pattern 11, K2
15th row: P2, pattern 11, P10, rib 13
16th row: Rib 13, P1, pattern 11, P12, rib 11
17th row: Inc. in 1st st., P1, pattern 11, P12, rib 11
18th row: Rib 11, K12, pattern 11, K3
19th row: P3, pattern 11, P14, rib 9
20th row: Rib 9, K14, pattern 11, K3
21st row: Inc. in 1st st., P2, pattern 11, P16, rib 7
22nd row: Rib 7, K16, pattern 11, K4
23rd row: P4, pattern 11, P18, rib 5
24th row: Rib 5, K18, pattern 11, K4
25th row: Inc. in 1st st., P3, pattern 11, P20, rib 3
26th row: Rib 3, K20, pattern 11, K5
27th row: P5, pattern 11, P22, K1
28th row: K23, pattern 11, K5
29th row: Inc. in 1st st., purl to end
Next 4 rows: Stocking stitch, starting with a knit row and increasing at beginning of 4th row (41 sts.)

2nd bobble pattern

Next row: K13, pattern 11, K17
Complete the 16 pattern rows, inc. at beginning 4th rows twice more (43 sts.), then keep side edge straight.
Work 4 rows stocking stitch, starting with a knit row.

3rd bobble pattern

Next row: K3, pattern 11, K9, pattern 11, K9
Complete the 16 pattern rows, **shaping armhole** by casting off 4 sts. at beginning of 4th pattern row, then K2tog at this edge 4 times (35 sts.).
Work 4 rows stocking stitch, starting with a knit row.

4th bobble pattern
As for 2nd pattern but with 11 sts. at armhole edge instead of 17. Complete the 16 pattern rows, then the 4 rows stocking stitch as before.

Shape neck

Next row (wrong side facing): cast off 6, K17, pattern 11 for 5th bobble pattern, K1
Work to end of 15th pattern row, keeping stitches either side in reverse stocking stitch, and K2tog at neck edge on every row, 8 times (21 sts.); afterwards keep neck edge straight.

Shape shoulders

Shape shoulders in reverse stocking stitch by casting off 7 sts. at beginning of purl rows, 3 times.

Right Front

Work to correspond with left front, reversing pattern and shapings by reading rows backwards. Start armhole with wrong side facing and neck shaping with right side facing.

Sleeves

With 3.75 mm/9 needles, cast on 31 sts. and knit 5 rows (garter st.).
Change to 4 mm/8 (4.5 mm/7) needles and pattern.
1st row (wrong side facing): K10, pattern 11, K10
Work the 16 pattern rows thus over centre 11 sts. keeping stitches either side in reverse stocking stitch, and increasing at each end of 7th and every following 6th row (37 sts.). Work 4 rows stocking stitch.
2nd pattern: K3, pattern 11, K9, pattern 11, K3. Continue thus working the 16 pattern rows, followed by 4 rows stocking stitch and increasing each end of every 6th row as before (43 sts.).
3rd pattern: K16, pattern 11, K16. Work the 16 pattern rows, followed by 4 rows of stocking stitch, still increasing at each end of 6th pattern rows (49 sts.).
4th pattern: K9, pattern 11, K9, pattern 11, K9. Finish this pattern and the 4 rows stocking stitch, still increasing side edges (57 sts.).
5th pattern: K3, pattern 11, K9, pattern 11, K9, pattern 11, K3. Finish this pattern and the 4 rows stocking stitch, still increasing side edges (63 sts.).
6th pattern: K16, pattern 11, K9, pattern 11, K16. On the 15th row of this pattern you will be working your last pair of increasings (69 sts.).
Next row: Knit
Next row: Purl

Shape top

Next row: Cast off 4, knit to end
Next row: Cast off 4, purl to end
This completes the 4 stocking stitch rows. Now introduce the 7th line of bobbles, alternating the patterns over previous ones as before, and continue top shaping by K2tog at beginning of every row until 23 sts. remain (after 7th pattern, work the 4 stocking stitch rows, followed by 8th pattern and 2 rows stocking stitch).
Next row: K2tog, right across to last stitch, k1. Cast off.

Making Up

Embroider the pieces before assembling as this makes them easier to handle.
The original pattern embroiders daisies and leaves in the centre of the bobble patterns, arranging 4 on each front, 4 down the centre top of each sleeve and 6 across the back, as in the photographs. This creates an effective accent, but more of the bobble shapes can be embroidered if desired.

Join shoulder seams.

Neck band

Make a garter stitch band to go around the neck. (*The original pattern does not explain how to make this, and it is best worked as follows:*

With right side facing and 3.75 mm/9 needles, pick up and knit 23 sts. along right front neck, 31 sts. across the back neck and 23 sts. along the left front neck – 77 sts. Work 7 rows in garter stitch then cast off.)

Front bands

With 3.75 mm/9 needles, cast on 7 sts. and work garter stitch until band fits up left front (including neck band), when slightly stretched. Make a similar strip for right front with 9 buttonholes (or required number, measured out as explained in Chapter 5 of the Flowers for Laura pattern).

The pattern does not give details on how to interpret the flowers, but refers to the photographs for colours and stitches. The recreated model endeavours to capture the original as authentically as possible.

The added detail of a knitted frill to the collar gives a charming finish to the neckline.

To make a buttonhole:
K2, cast off 3, K2, turn, K2, cast on 3, K2
Make first buttonhole 6 mm/0.25″ up from lower edge.
Last buttonhole 6 mm/0.25″ down from top edge, and remaining buttonholes at regular intervals.

Neck trimming

With 3.75 mm/9 needles, cast on 4 sts. and work 91 cm/36″ straight in stocking stitch. Cast off. Gather the strip by running a thread at regular intervals through the middle of the strip (for the zig-zag effect in the original image) or *irregularly* to create more of a 'frill', as in the recreated model. Pull up the thread to ruche together and pin this around the neckband, easing the gathers to fit evenly around the collar. Sew the band to the collar.

Pressing is not recommended, as this will flatten out the texture, and ribbing should *never* be pressed as it will lose its elasticity.

To Complete

Join side and sleeve seams and insert the sleeves.
Sew on buttons.

Novelty buttons always add a light-hearted touch to vintage knitwear and little red Tyrolean hats are the perfect match for Knitted for Best.

Buttons matching one of the colours used to embroider the flowers create an effective combination.

RML 2

Clio's Cardigan

Combining textured stitches and familiar embroidered floral details, this 1950s cardigan design takes Tyrolean style into the new post-war decade. The softer shoulders, longer line and slim fit give a very different silhouette from the square shoulder line and shorter garments of the previous years. From the 1930s onwards, Copley's published many of the most attractive Tyrolean patterns available, always capturing the essence of the style, beautifully adapted to the fashion of the day.

Clio's Cardigan.

Clio's Cardigan goes to town on the big red bus.

Copley's original pattern number 1928 for a Lady's Tyrolean Jumper Coat.

This cabled Tyrolean cardigan dates from around 1952 and has incorporated some clever placing of fine cables to create the spaces for embroidered flowers. The delicate powder blue used for the main colour is a subtle alternative to the traditional cream background, and has been matched as closely as possible in the recreated version for this collection. The original pattern embroidered across both sets of the smaller panels, repeating the same floral motif all around.

The pattern uses very fine wool and is quite a marathon of cabling, with many twists and turns creating the texture. It is one of the more challenging patterns in the collection, but very satisfying to complete. Knitted throughout on fine 3 mm/11 needles, the work does not grow particularly quickly, but will reward the knitter for their efforts. The cabled edges offer a pretty variation from classic ribbing and the embroidery is not difficult, but the motifs are repeated many times, the challenge being to maintain regularity of the repeated motifs. Each line of the pattern is given separately, which gives reassuring step-by-step guidance and clear instructions. Setting up the stitches is the hardest part, and once established, the sequences become more intuitive.

If you are looking for a project that will require dedicated application, this will be a most satisfying accomplishment. For a simpler project, you may wish to start with the fronts (as given in these instructions) to gauge the work involved before committing to cabling the entire cardigan. However, the cabled welts should ideally be worked as in the pattern to retain the distinctive style of this model. It would also work well with the back and sleeves above the welt knitted in the same reverse stocking stitch, but omitting the cables. With embroidery on the fronts only, this would still be in keeping with the Tyrolean-style decorative focus on the front of the garment. Just as a note, if the embroidery is omitted completely, this would still be a pretty cardigan, but would lose its Tyrolean touch. Even without embroidered details, if the neck and front bands were worked in a contrast colour this would bring it closer to the style. As these are worked in crochet in the original, they lend themselves to the striped effect seen in so many Tyrolean patterns.

Note: The pattern states that the first row after casting on for each piece should be worked into the back of the stitches. This would usually create an edge which is rather tight but in the case of the all-over cables in this pattern it is highly recommended, as it prevents the edge from curling back on itself.

The cabled welt of Clio's Cardigan is a pretty alternative to ribbing and in keeping with the fine cabling of the entire design.

Materials

The recreated model was knitted using Susan Crawford Fenella 100% wool in pale blue colour 'Porcelana', as close to the original as possible. Labelled as a 2 ply yarn, it is very close in weight to vintage 3 ply (which is recommended in the original pattern) to result in a 34" size. Please see under 'Measurements' for suggested alternatives and for a larger size.

11 x 25 g skeins of Susan Crawford Fenella 100% wool (colour 'Porcelana')
Small quantities of wool for embroidering in Pink, Maroon, Yellow and Green
1 x pair 3 mm/11 needles
1 x 3 mm double-pointed cable needle
1 x 3 mm crochet hook
9 x 13 mm buttons

Measurements

To fit bust 34"
For a size 36" use a fine 4 ply and work on 3.25 mm/10 needles (please note these are not noted in the instructions as the only change is in the needle size used): Cygnet Truly Wool Rich 4 ply or Cascade 220 Fingering
Length at centre back 51 cm/20"
Sleeve length 46 cm/18"

Tension

30 sts. to 10 cm/4" on 3 mm/11 needles

Right Front

Cast on 65 sts.

1st row: Working into back of the sts., *P2, K6, rep fr. *to last st., P1 (*working into back of the sts. on the first row creates a firmer edge, without this it has a tendency to curl*)
2nd row: K1, *P6, K2, rep fr. *to end
3rd row: *P2, K6, rep fr. *to last st., P1
4th row: As 2nd row
5th row: *P2, slip next 3 sts., on to cable needle and leave at back of work, K next 3 sts., bring forward slipped sts., and K these (this action will be referred to as C6), rep fr. *to last st., P1
6th row: K1, *P6, K2, rep fr. *to end
7th row: *P2, K6, rep fr. *to last st., P1
8th–10th rows: Rep 6th and 7th rows, then rep 6th row once again

Rows 5–10 inclusive form the cable.

Rep rows 5–10 inclusive 6 times more, then rep 5th row once again.

Proceed in pattern, increasing as follows:

1st row: K1, (P6, K18) twice, P6, K10
2nd row: P9, slip next st., onto cable needle and leave at back of work. K next 3 sts., bring forward slipped st. and P it (this action will be referred to as BC4 – Back Cable 4), slip next 3 sts. onto cable needle and bring to front of work, P following st., take back slipped sts., and K them (this action will be referred to as FC4 – Front Cable 4), P16, BC4, FC4, P16, BC4, FC4
3rd row: (P3, K2, P3, K16) twice, P3, K2, P3, K9
4th row: P7, slip next 2 sts. onto cable needle, leave at back of work, K next 3 sts., bring forward slipped sts., and P them (this action will be referred to as BC5 – Back Cable 5), P2, slip next 3 sts. on to cable needle and bring to front of work, P following 2 sts., take back slipped sts. and K them (this action will be referred to as FC5 – Front Cable 5), P12, BC5, P2, FC5, P12, BC5, P3, K1, inc. by working into front and back of last st.
5th row: P2, K6 (P3, K12, P3, K6) twice, P3, K7
6th row: P5, (BC5, P6, FC5, P8) twice, BC5, P7, K1
7th row: Inc. in 1st st., K9, (P3, K8, P3, K 10) twice, P3, K5
8th row: P3, (BC5, P10, FC5, P4) twice, BC5, P11
9th row: K13, (P3, K4, P3, K14) twice, P3, K3
10th row: P1, (BC5, P14, FC5) twice, BC5, P12, inc. in last st.
11th row: K16, (P6, K18) twice, P3, K1
12th row: P1, K3, (P18, C6) twice, P16
13th row: Inc. in 1st st., K15, (P6, K18) twice, P3, K1
14th row: P1, K3, (P18, K6) P17
15th row: K17, (P6, K18) twice, P3, K1
16th row: P1, K3, (P18, K6) twice, P16, inc. in last st.
17th row: K18, (P6, K18) twice, P3, K1
18th row: P1, K3, (P18, C6) twice, P18
19th row: Inc. in 1st st., K17, (P6, K18) twice, P3, K1
20th row: P1, K3, (P18, K6) twice, P19
21st row: K19, (P6, K18) twice, P3, K1
22nd row: P1, K3, (P18, K6) twice, P18, inc. in last st.
23rd row: K20, (P6, K18) twice, P3, K1
24th row: P1, K3, (P18, C6) twice, P20
25th row: Inc. in 1st st., K19, (P6, K18) twice, P3, K1
26th row: P1, (FC4, P16, BC4) twice, FC4, P17, K3
27th row: K1, (P3, K16, P3, K2) 3 times
28th row: (P2, FC5, P12, BC5) 3 times, inc. in last st.
29th row: K4, (P3, K12, P3, K6) twice, P3, K12, P3, K4
30th row: P4, (FC5, P8, BC5, P6) twice, FC5, P8, BC5, P4
31st row: Inc. in 1st st., K5, (P3, K8, P3, K10) twice, P3, K8, P3, K6
32nd row: P6, (FC5, P4, BC5, P10) twice, FC5, P4, BC5, P7
33rd row: K9, (P3, K4, P3, K14) twice, P3, K4, P3, K8
34th row: P8, (FC5, BC5, P14) twice, FC5, BC5, P8, inc. in last st.
35th row: K12, (P6, K18) twice, P6, K10
36th row: P10, (C6, P18) twice, C6, P12
37th row: Inc. in 1st., K11, (P6, K18) twice, P6, K10
38th row: P10, (K6, P18) twice, K6, P13
39th row: K13, (P6, K18) twice, P6, K10

40th row: P10, (K6, P18) twice, K6, P12, inc. in last st.
41st row: K14, (P6, K18) twice, P6, K10
42nd row: P10, (C6, P18) twice, C6, P14
43rd row: Inc. in 1st st., K133, (P6, K18) twice, P6, K10
44th row: P10, (K6, P18) twice, K6, P15
45th row: K15, (P6, K18) twice, P6, K10
46th row: P10, (K6, P18) twice, K6, P14, inc. in last st.
47th row: K16, (P6, K18) twice, P6, K10
48th row: P10, (C6, P18) twice, C6, P16
49th row: Inc. in 1st st., K15, (P6, K18) twice, P6, K10
50th row: P10, (K6, P18) twice, K6, P17
51st row: K17, (P6, K18) twice, P6, K10
52nd row: P10, (K6, P18) twice, K6, P16, inc. in last st.
53rd row: K18, (P6, K18) twice, P6, K10
54th row: P10, (C6, P18) twice, C6, P18
55th row: Inc. in 1st st., K 17, (P6, K18) twice, P6, K10
56th row: P10, (K 6, P18) twice, K6, P19
57th row: K19, (P6, K18) twice, P6, K10
58th row: P10, (K6, P18) 3 times, inc. in last st.
59th row: K20, (P6, K18) twice, P6, K10
60th row: P10, (C6, P18) twice, C6, P 19, K1
61st row: Inc. in 1st st., P1, (K 18, P 6) 3 times, K10
62nd row: P9, (BC4, FC4, P16) 3 times, BC4
63rd row: K1, (P3, K16, P3, K2) 3 times, P3, K9
64th row: P7, (BC5, P2, FC5, P12) 3 times, BC5, inc. in last st.
65th row: K4, (P3, K12, P3, K6) 3 times, P3, K7
66th row: P5, (BC5, P6, FC5, P8) 3 times, BC5, P4
67th row: Inc. in first st., K5, (P3, K8, P3, K10) 3 times, P3, K5 (87 sts.)
68th row: P3, (BC5, P10, FC5, P4) 3 times, BC5, P7
69th row: K9, (P3, K4, P3, K 14) 3 times, P3, K3
70th row: P1, (BC5, P14, FC5) 3 times, BC5, P9
71st row: K11, (P6, K18) 3 times, P3, K1
72nd row: P1, K3, (P18, C6) 3 times, P11
73rd row: K11, (P6, K18) 3 times, P3, K1
74th row: P1, K3, (P18, K6) 3 times, P11
75th–77th rows: Rep 73rd and 74th rows, then rep 73rd row again
78th row: P1, K3, (P18, C6) 3 times, P11

Shape armhole

1st row: Cast off 11 sts., P following 5 sts. (there are now 6 sts. on right-hand needle), (K18, P6) twice, K18, P3, K1
2nd row: P1, K3, (P18, K6) twice, P18, K4, sl.1, K1, psso
3rd row: P2tog tbs, P3, (K18, P6) twice, K18, P3, K1
4th row: P1, K3, (P18, K6) twice, P18, K2, sl.1, K1, psso
5th row: P2tog, tbs, P1, (K18, P6) twice, K18, P3, K1
6th row: P1, K3, (P18, C6) twice, P18, sl.1, K1, psso
7th row: K2tog, K17, (P6, K18) twice, P3, K1
8th row: P1, (FC4, P16, BC4) twice, FC4, P15, P2tog
9th row: K2tog, K14, P3, K2, (P3, K16, P3, K2) twice
10th row: (P2, FC5, P12, BC5) twice, P2, FC5, P11, P2tog
11th row: K2tog, K10, P3, (K6, P3, K12, P3) twice, K4
12th row: P4, (FC5, P8, BC5, P6) twice, FC5, P7, P2tog
13th row: K2tog, K6, P3, (K10, P3, K8, P3) twice, K6
14th row: P6, (FC5, P4, BC5, P10) twice, FC5, P3, P2tog
15th row: K2tog., K2, P3, (K14, P3, K4, P3) twice, K8
This completes the armhole shaping (62 sts.).

Proceed as follows:
*** **1st row:** P8, (FC5, BC5, P 14) twice, FC5, P1
2nd row: K1, P3, (K18, P6) twice, K10
3rd row: P10, (C6, P18) twice, K3, P1
4th row: K1, P 3, (K18, P6) twice, K10
5th row: P10, (K6, P18) twice, K3, P1
6th–8th rows: Rep 4th and 5th rows, then rep 4th row again
9th–28th rows: Rep 3rd to 8th rows inclusive 3 times, then rep 3rd and 4th rows again
29th row: P9, (BC4, FC4, P16) twice, BC4, P1
30th row: K2, (P3, K16, P3, K2) twice, P3, K9
31st row: P77, BC5, P2 (FC5, P12, BC5, P2) twice
32nd row: K4, (P3, K12, P3, K6) twice, P3, K7
33rd row: P5, BC5, (P6, FC5, P8, BC5) twice, P4
34th row: K6, (P3, K8, P3, K10) twice, P3, K5
35th row: P3, BC5, (P10, FC5, P4, BC5) twice, P6
36th row: K8, (P3, K4, P3, K14) twice, P3, K3
37th row: P1, BC5, (P14, FC5, BC5) twice, P8
38th row: K10, (P6, K18) twice, P8
39th row: K10, K3 (P18, C6) twice, P10
40th row: As 38th row ***

Shape neck

1st row: Cast off 12 sts., P following 9 sts. (10 sts. on right-hand needle), K6, P18, K6, P10
2nd row: K10, P6, K18, P6, K8, sl.1, K1, psso
3rd row: P9, K6, P18, K6, P10
4th row: K10, P6, K18, P6, K7, sl.1, K1, psso
5th row: P8, C6, P18, C6, P10
6th row: K10, P6, K18, P6, sl.1, K1, psso
7th row: P7, K6, P18, K6, P10
8th row: K10, P6, K18, P6, K5, sl.1, K1, psso
9th row: P6, K6, P18, K6, P10
10th row: K10, P6, K18, P6, K4, sl.1, K1, psso
11th row: P5, C6, P18, C6, P10
12th row: K10, P6, K18, P6, K3, sl.1, K1, psso
13th row: P4, K6, P18, K6, P10
14th row: K10, P6, K18, P6, K2, sl.1, K1, psso (43 sts.)
15th row: P3, K6, P18, K6, P10

16th row: K10, P6, K18, P6, K3
17th row: P3, C6, P18, C6, P10
18th row: K10, P6, K18, P6, K3
19th row: K10, P6, K18, P6, K3
20th–22nd rows: Rep 18th and 19th rows, then rep 18th row again
23rd–28th rows: As rows 17–22 inclusive

Shape shoulders

1st row: P3, C, P18, K2, turn
2nd row: P2, K18, P6, K3
3rd row: P3, K6, P6, turn
4th row: K6, P6, K3
Cast off.

Left Front

Cast on 65 sts.
1st row: Working into back of sts., P1, *K6, P2, rep fr. *end
2nd row: *K2, P6, rep fr. *to last st., K1
3rd row: P1, *K6, P2, rep fr. *to end
4th row: As 2nd row
5th row: *P1, C6, P2, rep fr. *to end
6th row: *K2, P6, rep fr. 8 to last st., K1
7th row: P1, *K6, P2, rep fr. *to end
8th–10th rows: Rep 6th and 7th rows, then rep 6th row again
Rows 5–10 inclusive form the cable.
Rep 5th to 10th rows inclusive 6 times more, then rep 5th row.

Proceed in pattern, increasing as follows:
1st row: K10, (P6, K18) twice, P6, K1
2nd row: (BC4, FC4, P16) twice, BC4, FC4, P9
3rd row: K9, (P3, K2, P3, K16), twice, P3, K2, P3
4th row: Inc. in first st., K1, P3, (FC5, P12, BC5, P2) twice, FC5, P7
Now rep rows 5–78 inclusive of the increase rows on right front, but reading the rows from the end to the beginning, also FC for BC and BC for FC, thus the 5th and 6th rows will read:
5th row: K7, P3, (K6, P3, K12, P3) twice, K6, P2
6th row: K1, P7, FC5, (P8, BC5, P6, FC5) twice, P5

Shape armhole

1st row: K1, P3, (K18, P6) 3 times, cast off remaining sts., break off wool
2nd row: Rejoin the wool, K2tog, K4, P18, (K6, P18) twice, K3, P1
3rd row: K1, P3, K18, (P6, K18) twice, P3, K2tog
4th row: K2tog, K2, P18, (K6, P18) twice K3, P1
5th row: K1, P3, K18, (P6, K18) twice P1, P2tog
6th row: K2tog, P18, (C6, P18) twice, K3, P1
7th row: K1, P3, (K18, P6) twice, K17, sl.1, K1, psso
8th row: P2tog tbs, P15, BC4, (FC4, P16, BC4) twice, P1
9th row: (K2, P3, K16, P3) twice, K2, P3, K14, sl.1, K1, psso
10th row: P2tog tbs, P11, BC5, P2, (FC5, P12, BC5, P2) twice
11th row: K4, (P3, K12, P3, K6) twice, P3, K10, sl.1, K1, psso
12th row: P2tog tbs, P7, BC5, (P6, FC5, P8, BC5) twice, P4
13th row: K6, (P3, K8, P3, K10) twice, P3, K6, sl.1, K1, psso
14th row: P2tog tbs, P3, BC5, (P10, FC5, P4, BC5) twice, P6
15th row: K8, (P3, K4, P3, K14) twice, P3, K2, sl.1, K1, psso
This completes the armhole shaping (62 sts.).
Now proceed as the instructions for the right front from ***to ***but reading the rows from the **end** to the **beginning** also BC for FC and FC for BC.

Shape neck

1st row: P10, K6, P18, K6, P10, cast off remaining sts. Break off wool
2nd row: Rejoin wool, K2tog, K8, P6, K18, P6, K10
3rd row: P10, K6, P18, K6, P9
4th row: K2tog, K7, P6, K18, P6, K10
5th row: P10, C6, P18, C6, P8
6th row: K2tog, K6, P6, K18, P6, K10
7th row: P10, K6, P18, K6, P7
8th row: K2tog, K5, P6, K18, P6, K10
9th row: P10, K6, P18, K6, P6
10th row: K2tog, K4, P6, K18, P6, K10
11th row: P10, C6, P18, C6, P5
12th row: K2tog, K3, P6, K18, P6, K10
13th row: P10, K6, P18, K6, P4
14th row: K2tog, K2, P6, K18, P6, K10 (43 sts.)
15th row: P10, K6, P18, K6, P3
16th row: K3, P6, K18, P6, K10
17th row: P10, C6, P18, C6, P3
18th row: K3, P6, K18, P6, K10
19th row: P10, K6, P18, K6, P3
20th–22nd rows: Rep 18th and 19th rows, then rep 18th row again
23rd–28th rows: As 17th to 22nd row inclusive
29th row: P10, K6, P18, C6, P3

Shape shoulder

1st row: K3, P6, K18, P2, turn
2nd row: K2, P18, K6, P3

3rd row: K3, P6, K6, turn
4th row: P6, K6, P3
Cast off.

Back

Cast on 128 sts.
1st row: Working into back of sts., *P1, K6, P1, rep fr. *to end
2nd row: *K1, P6, K1, rep fr. *to end
3rd row: *P1, K6, P1, rep fr. *to end
4th row: As 2nd row
5th row: *P1, C6, P1, rep fr. *to end
6th row: *K1, P6, K1, rep fr. *to end
7th row: *P1, K6, P1, rep fr. *to end
8th–10th rows: Rep 6th and 7th rows, then rep 6th row again
Rows 5–10 inclusive form the cable.
Rep rows 5–10 inclusive 6 times more, then rep 5th row again.

Proceed in pattern, increasing as follows:
1st row: K1, (P6, K18) 5 times, P6, K1
2nd row: (BC4, FC4, P16) 5 times, BC4, FC4
3rd row: (P3, K2, P3, K16) 5 times, P3, K2, P3
4th row: Inc. in 1st st., K1, P3, (FC5, P12, BC5, P2) 5 times, P1, K1, inc. in last st.
5th row: P2, K6, (P3, K12, P3, K6) 5 times, P2
6th row: K1, P7, (FC5, P8, BC5, P6) 5 times, P1, K1
7th row: Inc. in 1st st., K9, (P3, K8, P3, K10) 4 times, P3, K8, P3, K9, inc. in last st.
8th row: P11, (FC5, P4, BC5, P10) 4 times, FC5, P4, BC5, P11
9th row: K13, (P3, K4, P3, K14) 4 times, P3, K4, P3, K13
10th row: Inc. in 1st st., P12, (FC5, BC5, P14) 4 times, FC5, BC5, P12, inc. in last st.
11th row: K16, (P6, K18) 4 times, P6, K16
12th row: P16, (C6, P 18) 4 times, C6, P16
13th row: Inc. in 1st st., K15, (P6, K18) 4 times, P6, K15, inc. in last st.
14th row: P17, (K6, P18) 4 times, K6, P17
15th row: K17, (P6, K18) 4 times, P6, K17
16th row: Inc. in 1st st., P16, (K6, P18) 4 times, K6, P16, inc. in last st.
17th row: (K18, P6) 5 times, K18
18th row: (P18, K6) 5 times, P18
19th row: Inc. in 1st st., K17, (P6, K18) 4 times, P6, K17, inc. in last st.
20th row: P19, (K6, P18) 4 times, K6, P19
21st row: K19 (P6, K18) 4 times, P6, K19
22nd row: Inc. in 1st st., (P18, K6) 5 times, P18, inc. in last st.
23rd row: K20, (P6, K18) 4 times, P6, K20
24th row: K1, P1, (P18, C6) 5 times, P19, K1
25th row: Inc. in 1st st., P1, (K18, P6) 5 times, K18, P1, inc. in last st.
26th row: (FC4, P16, BC4) 6 times
27th row: K1, (P3, K16, P3, K2) 5 times, P3, K16, P3, K1
28th row: Inc. in 1st st., (FC5, P12, BC5, P2) 5 times, FC5, P12, BC5, inc. in last st.
29th row: K4, (P3, K12, P3, K6) 5 times, P3, K12, P3, K4
30th row: P4, (FC5, P8, BC5, P6) 5 times, FC5, P8, BC5, P4
31st row: Inc. in 1st st., K5, (P3, K8, P3, K10) 5 times, P3, K8, P3, K5, inc. in last st.
32nd row: P7, (FC5, P4, BC5, P10) 5 times, FC5, P4, BC5, P7
33rd row: K9, (P3, K4, P3, K14) 5 times, P3, K4, P3, K9
34th row: Inc. in 1st st., P8, (FC5, BC5, P14) 5 times, FC5, BC5, P8, inc. in last st.
35th row: K12, (P 6, K18) 5 times, P6, K12
36th row: P12, (C6, P18) 5 times, C6, P12
37th row: Inc. in 1st st., K11, (P6, K18) 5 times, P6, K11, inc. in last st.
38th row: P13, (K6, P18) times, K6, P13
39th row: K13, (P6, K18) 5 times, P6, K13
40th row: Inc. in 1st st., P12, (K6, P18) 5 times, K6, P12, inc. in last st.
41st row: K14, (P6, K18) 5 times, P6, K14
42nd row: P14, (C6, P18) 5 times, C6, P14
43rd row: Inc. in 1st st., K13, (P6, K18) 5 times, P6, K13, inc. in last st.
44th row: P1, (K6, P18) 5 times, K6, P15
45th row: K15, (P6, P18) 5 times, P6, K15
46th row: Inc. in 1st st., P14, (K6, P18) 5 times, K6, P14, inc. in last st.
47th row: K16, (P6, K18) 5 times, P6, K16
48th row: P16, (C6, P18) 5 times, C6, P16
49th row: Inc. in 1st st., K15, (P6, K18) 5 times, P6, K15, inc. in last st.
50th row: P17, (K6, P18) 5 times, K6, P17
51st row: K17, (P6, K18) 5 times, P6, K17
52nd row: Inc. in 1st st., P16, (K6, P18) 5 times, K6, P16, inc. in last st.
53rd row: (K18, P6) 6 times, K18
54th row: (P18, C6) 6 times, P18
55th row: Inc. in 1st st., K17, (P6, K18) 5 times, P6, K17, inc. in last st.
56th row: P1, (P18, K6) 6 times, P19
57th row: K1, (K18, P6) 6 times, K19
58th row: Inc. in 1st st., (P18, K6) 6 times, P18, inc. in last st.
59th row: K2, (K18, P6) 6 times, K20
60th row: K1, P19, (C6, P18) 5 times, C6, P19, K1
61st row: Inc. in 1st st., P1, (K18, P6) 6 times, K18, P1, inc. in last st.
62nd row: (FC4, P 16, BC4) 7 times
63rd row: K1, (P3, K16, P3, K2) 6 times, P3, K16, P3, K1

64th row: Inc. in 1st st., (FC5, P12, BC5, P2) 6 times, FC5, P12, BC5, inc. in last st.
65th row: K4, (P3, K12, P3, K6) 6 times, P3, K12, P3, K4
66th row: P4, (FC5, P8, BC5, P6) 6 times, FC5, P8, BC5, P4
67th row: Inc. in 1st st., K5, (P3, K8, P3, K10) 6 times, P3, K8, P3, K5, inc. in last st. (172 sts.)
68th row: P7, (FC5, P4, BC5, P10) 6 times, FC5, P4, BC5, P7
69th row: K9, (P3, K4, P3, K14) 6 times, P3, K4, P3, K9
70th row: P9, (FC5, BC5, P14) 6 times, FC5, BC5, P9
71st row: K11, (P6, K18) 6 times, K11
72nd row: P11, (C6, P18) 6 times, C6, P11
73rd row: K11, (P6, K18) 6 times, P6, K11
74th row: P11, (K6, P18) 6 times, K6, P11
75th–77th rows: Rep 73rd and 74th rows, then rep 73rd row again
78th row: As 72nd row

Shape armhole

1st row: Cast off 11 sts., P following 5 sts., there now being 6 sts. on right-hand needle after casting off, (K18, P6) 6 times, cast off remaining sts., break off wool
2nd row: Rejoin wool, K2tog, K4, (P18, K6) 5 times, P18, K4, sl.1, K1, psso
3rd row: P2tog tbs, P3, (K18, P6) 5 times, K18, P3, P2tog
4th row: K2tog, K2, (P18, K6) 5 times, P18, K2, sl.1, K1, psso
5th row: P2tog tbs, P1, (K18, P6) 5 times, K18, P1, P2tog
6th row: K2tog, (P18, C6) 5 times, P18, sl.1, K1, psso
7th row: K2tog, K17, (P6, K18) 4 times, P6, K 7, sl.1, K1, psso
8th row: P2tog tbs, P15, (BC4, FC4, P16) 4 times, BC4, FC4, P15, P2tog
9th row: K2tog, K14, (P3, K2, P3, K16) 4 times, P3, K2, P3, K14, sl.1, K1, psso
10th row: P2tog tbs, P11, (BC5, P2, FC5, P12) 4 times, BC5, P2, FC5, P11, P2tog
11th row: K2tog, K10, (P3, K6, P3, K12) 4 times, P3, K6, P3, K10, sl.1, K1, psso
12th row: P2tog tbs, P7, (BC5, P6, FC5, P8) 4 times, BC5, P6, FC5, P7, P2tog
13th row: K2tog, K6, (P3, K10, P3, K8) 4 times, P3, K10, P3, K6, sl.1, K1, psso
14th row: P2tog tbs, P3, (BC5, P10, FC5, P4) 4 times, BC5, P10, FC5, P3, P2tog
15th row: K2tog, K2, (P3, K14, P3, K4) 4 times, P3, K14, P3, K2, sl.1, K1, psso
This completes the armhole shaping (122 sts.).

Proceed as follows:
1st row: P1, (BC5, P14, FC5) 5 times, P1
2nd row: K1, P3, (K18, P6) 4 times, K18, P3, K1
3rd row: P1, K3, (P18, C6) 4 times, P18, K3, P1
4th row: K1, P3, (K18, P6) 4 times, K18, P3, K1
5th row: P1, K3, (P18, K6) 4 times, P18, K3, P1
6th–8th rows: Rep 4th and 5th rows. Then rep 4th row again
9th–28th rows: Rep 3rd to 8th rows inclusive 3 times, then rep 3rd and 4th rows again
29th row: P1, (FC4, P16, BC4) 5 times, P1
30th row: (K2, P3, K16, P3) 5 times, P1
31st row: (P2, FC5, P12, BC) 5 times, P2
32nd row: K4, (P3, K12, P3, K6) 4 times, P3, K12, P3, K4
33rd row: P4, (FC5, P8, BC5, P6) 4 times, FC5, P8, BC5, P4
34th row: K6, (P3, K8, P3, K10) 4 times, P3, K8, P3, K6
35th row: P6, (FC5, P4, BC5, P10) 4 times, FC5, P4, BC5, P6
36th row: K8, (P3, K4, P3, K14) 4 times, P3, K4, P3, K8
37th row: P8, (FC5, BC5, P14) 4 times, FC5, BC5, P8
38th row: K10, (P6, K18) 4 times, P6, K10
39th row: P10, (C6, P18) 4 times, C6, P10
40th row: K10, (P6, K18) 4 times, P6, K10
41st row: P10, (K6, P18) 4 times, K6, P10
42nd–44th rows: Rep 40th and 41st rows, then rep 40th row again
45th–59th row: rep rows 39–44 inclusive twice, the rep rows 39–41 inclusive
60th row: As 40th row

Shape shoulders

1st row: P10, (K6, P18) 4 times, K2, turn
2nd row: P2, (K18, P6) 3 times, K18, P2, turn
3rd row: K2, (P18, C6) 3 times, P6, turn
4th row: K6, (P6, K18) twice, P6, K6, turn
5th row: P6, K6, P18, K6, P15, turn
6th row: K15, P6, K15. Break off wool
Slip all the sts. onto one needle, rejoin wool and, with right side facing, cast off across all stitches.

Sleeves (Both Alike)

Cast on 58 sts.
1st row: Working into the back of the sts., *P2, K6, rep fr. *to last 2 sts., P2
2nd row: *K2, P6, rep fr. *to last 2 sts., K2
3rd row: *P2, K6, rep fr. *to last 2 sts., P2
4th row: As 2nd row
5th row: *P2, C6, rep fr. *to last 2 sts., P2
6th row: *K2, P6, rep fr. *to lats 2 sts., K2
7th row: *P2, K6, rep fr. *to last 2 sts., P2

8th–10th rows: Rep 6th and 7th rows, then rep 6th row again
11th–23rd rows: Rep rows 5–10 inclusive twice, then rep 5th row again

Proceed as follows:
1st row: K2, (P6, K18) twice, K6, P2
3rd–5th rows: Rep 1st and 2nd rows, then rep 1st row again
6th row: Inc. in 1st st., P1, (C6, P18) twice, C6, P1, inc. in last st.

Keeping the cables correct and working the increased sts. in *reversed* stocking stitch, continue increasing 1 st. at both ends of every following 4th row until 15 more sets of increases have been worked and there are 90 sts. on the needle.

Keeping the cables correct and working the increased sts. in stocking st. (*not reversed, as these will form the next cables*), inc. at both ends of every following 4th row until 6 more sets of increases have been worked and there are 102 sts. on the needle.

Keeping the cables correct, cont. inc. 1 st. at both end of every foll. 4th row, working increased sts. in *reversed* st.st, until 5 more sets of increases have been worked and there are 112 sts. on the needle.

Keeping the cables correct, proceed without further shaping until work measures 40.5 cm/16" from the commencement, finishing at the end of a cable row.

Proceed as follows:
1st row: K5, (P6, K18) 4 times, P6, K5
2nd row: P4, (BC4, FC4, P16) 4 times, BC4, FC4, P4
3rd row: K4, (P3, K2, P3, K16) 4 times, P3, K2, P3, K4
4th row: P2, (BC5, P2, FC5, P12) 4 times, BC5, P2, FC5, P2
5th row: K2, (P3, K6, P3, K12) 4 times, P3, K6, P3, K2
6th row: (BC5, P 66, FC5, P8) 4 times, BC5, P6, FC5
7th row: P3, K10, (P3, K8), P3, K10) 4 times, P3
8th row: K2, P11, (FC5, P4, BC5, P10) 4 times, P1, K2
9th row: P1, K14, (P3, K4, P3, K14) 4 times, P1
10th row: P15, (FC5, BC5, P14) 4 times, P1
11th row: K17, (P6, K18) 3 times, P6, K17
12th row: P17, (C6, P18) 3 times, C6, P17
13th row: K17, (P6, K18) 3 times, P6, K17
14th row: P17, (K6, P18) 3 times, K6, P17
15th–17th rows: Rep 13th and 14th rows, then rep 13th row again
18th row: As 12th row

Shape top

1st row: Cast off 7 sts., K following 9 sts., (10 sts. on right-hand needle), (P6, K18) 3 times, P6, K10, cast off remaining sts. Break off wool
2nd row: Rejoin wool, P10, (K6, P18) 3 times, K6, P10
3rd row: K2tog, K8, (P6, K18) 3 times, P6, K8, sl.1, K1, psso
4th row: P9, (K6, P18) 3 times, K6, P9
5th row: K2tog, K7, (P6, K18) 3 times, P6, K7, sl.1, K1, psso
6th row: P8, (C6, P18) 3 times, C6, P8
7th row: K2tog, K6, (P6, K18) 3 times, P6, K6, sl.1, K1, psso
8th row: P6, BC4, (FC4, P16, BC4) 3 times, FC4, P6
9th row: K2tog, K4, P3, K2, (P3, K16, P3, K2) 3 times, P3, K4, sl.1, K1, psso
10th row: P3, BC5, P2, (FC5, P12, BC5, P2) 3 times, FC5, P3
11th row: K2tog, K1, P3, K6, (P3, K12, P3, K6) 3 times, P3, K1, sl.1, K1, psso
12th row: BC5, P6, (FC5, P8, BC5, P6) 3 times, FC5
13th row: P2tog, P1, K10, (P3, K8, P3, K10) 3 times, P1, P2tog tbs
14th row: K1, P11, (FC5, P4, BC5, P10) 3 times, P1, K1
15th row: K2tog, K12, (P3, K4, P3, K14) twice, P3, K4, P3, K12, sl.1, K1, psso
16th row: P13, (FC5, BC5, P14) twice, FC5, BC5, P13
17th row: K2tog, K13, (P6, K18) twice, P6, K13, sl.1, K1, psso
18th row: P14, (C6, P18) twice, C6, P14
19th row: K2tog, K12, (P6, K18) twice, P6, K12, sl.1, K1, psso
20th row: P13, (K6, P18) twice, K6, P13
Keeping the cables correct, cont. decreasing 1 st. at both ends of next and every alternate row, until 68 sts. remain.
Work 1 row.
Now dec. at both ends of every row, until 26 sts. remain.
Cast off.
Work a second sleeve in the same manner.

Making Up

Pressing is not recommended as this will flatten all cabling, and lose elasticity.

Embroider each diamond-shaped portion of the work with a flower spray, placing these as in the original or the recreated model, as preferred. The flower sprays are worked as in the diagram.

Join shoulders of back and fronts together.

Borders

Using the crochet hook and with right side of work facing, join wool to lower edge and work 1 row dc. up the edge of right front, missing the edge st. of every 3rd row, finishing at neck edge (around 120 sts.). Now work in dc. around neck, working into every st. and working 3 dc. into the corner sts.

Finally, work in dc. down left front, missing the edge st. of every 3rd row down to lower edge, 1 ch., turn. Working through both top loops of the sts. of the previous row and working 3 dc.

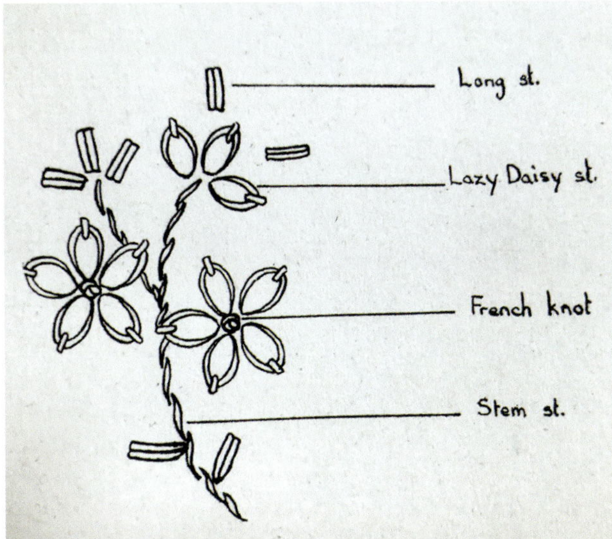

The original Copley's pattern includes a diagram of the embroidery motifs repeated in each of the smaller shapes framed by cables.

The embroidery is executed in simple stitches and the colours used in the recreated model are as close as possible to the original pattern and photograph for authenticity.

into each corner st., work 3 more rows in dc., turning at the end of each row with 1 ch.

Next row: Work 7 dc., *4 ch., miss the foll. 4 sts., 1 dc. into foll. 10 sts., rep fr. *7 times more, 4 ch., miss foll. 4 sts., working 3 dc. into corner sts., cont. in dc. to the end of the row at lower edge of left front, 1 ch., turn.

Work 3 more rows in dc. Fasten off.

Join side and sleeve seams.
Stitch sleeves into position, matching the pattern as far as possible.

Attach buttons to left front to correspond to buttonholes.

Crochet borders create a neat finish to the front and neck edges of the cardigan.

Cosy for Cold Days Cardigan

Stitchcraft, *December 1951.*

The December 1951 issue of *Stitchcraft* offers some very festive knitting in seasonal colours of red, white and green. Every pattern is all about staying warm, and using thick wool to keep out the cold. The high buttoned neckline adds to the feeling of cosiness in this warming cardigan.

This neatly buttoned pattern has the distinctive high shaped ribbing at the waist, longer line and softer rounded shoulders of early 1950s style. An all-over grid made of bobbles frames the embroidered flowers, which are cleverly placed to accentuate the flattering lines of the ribbed bodice shaping. The bobbles are easy to create over three rows as part of the main knitting, with no additional turning of the work. You may choose to make the back without the bobbles, as in the recreated model, or continue the bobble pattern as in the original.

There are no guidelines at all in the original for the floral embroidery, neither for the colours nor the placing, only 'embroider lazy-daisies and leaves as shown in photograph', but both of the photos are not very clear, and there is no mention of embroidering the back, nor apparently the sleeves. Therefore, in recreating the model for this book, the pattern is adapted to omit the bobbles on the reverse stocking-stitch back. This makes the cardigan quicker and more economical to knit, but the bobbles can easily be included if preferred. The embroidery is an interpretation from the pattern's photographs to create a similar effect close to the original images, but this can be varied as desired.

The original Patons wool recommended is 'Glengarry', declared to be a 'thick wool' with a tension of 26 stitches to 10 cm/4″ knitted on 3.7 mm/9 needles. This is less thick than a modern double knitting (which averages 22–24 stitches to 10 cm/4″ on 4 mm/8 needles), and by using a modern double knitting yarn the finished cardigan fits a 36–38″ bust with generous stretch at the waist ribbing for a flattering shape. As double knitting is a slightly thicker yarn than the original, the pattern knits up with fewer squares made along the upper front, and consequently the embroidery is placed slightly differently in order to achieve the closest possible effect. For a smaller size, a finer yarn is suggested with smaller needles.

Materials

400 g of double knitting
For an economical project, the recreated model omitted the bobbles on the back of the garment and used 4 x 100 g of Stylecraft Life DK in Cardinal, a soft pliable yarn with 25% wool.
If preferred, Cygnet 100% Pure Wool Superwash DK has the same rich red, Cranberry, which knits up a little thicker.
1 x pair 3.25 mm/10 needles
1 x pair 4 mm/8 needles
10 buttons
2 safety pins (for front bands)

Measurements

36–38" bust
(For 34" bust use a yarn with tension of around 26 sts. to 10 cm/4" on 3.75 mm/9 needles, such as Rowan Pure Wool 4 ply or Drops Flora Wool/Alpaca mix, which match the tension if worked on 3.75 mm needles, but please check your own tension and adjust the needle size you use accordingly. You will need 9 x 50 g balls of either of these)
Length at centre back 51 cm/20"
Sleeve seam length 45.5 cm/18"

Tension

22 sts. to 10 cm/4"

The Bobble Pattern

1st row (right side facing): *P2, (P1, K1, P1, K1, P1) all into next stitch, rep from *to last 2 sts., P2
2nd row: Knit
3rd row: *P2, wool back, slip 4 purlways, P1, pass slipped stitches over, rep fr. *to last 2 sts., P2
4th row: Knit
5th row: P8, *(P1, K1, P1, K1, P1) all into next stitch, P11, rep fr. *to last 9 sts., (P1, K1, P1, K1, P1) all into next stitch, P8
6th row: Knit
7th row: P8, *wool back, slip 4 purlways, P1, psso, P11; rep fr. *to last 13 sts., wool back, slip 4 purlways, P1, psso, P8
8th row: Knit
Rep the last 4 rows 3 times more. These 20 rows form the pattern.

Left Front

With 3.25 mm/10 needles, cast on 54 sts. and work 10 cm/4″ K2, P2 rib as before, decreasing 1 st. at end of last row (53 sts.).
Change to 4 mm/8 needles and start introducing the bobble pattern in steps as follows:
1st row: Pattern 19 from bobble pattern, rib 34
2nd row: Rib 34, pattern 19
Rep these 2 rows 9 times more.
21st row: Pattern 33, rib 20
22nd row: Rib 20, pattern 33
Rep these 2 rows 9 times more.
Now continue over all sts. in pattern until front measures 30.5 cm/12″.

Shape armhole

With right side of work facing, cast off 6 sts. at beg. of next row then K2tog at beg. of every
alternate row 6 times in all (41 sts.).
Work straight until front measures 44.5 cm/17.5″, ending with wrong side of work facing for next row.

Shape neckline

Cast off 10 sts. at beg. of next row, then K2tog at neck edge on every row until 24 sts. remain.
Work straight until front measures 49.5 cm/19.5″ ending with right side facing for next row.

Shape shoulder

Cast off 8 sts. at beg. of next and following 2 alternate rows on armhole edge.

Right Front

Work to correspond with left front, decreasing 1 st. at beginning of last row on ribbing (instead of at the end of the row) and reverse the pattern as follows:
1st row: Rib 34, P1 *(P1, K1, P1, K1, P1) all into next st., P2, rep fr. *to end
This places the pattern; now continue as for left front but reversing all shaping.

Back

With 3.25 mm/10 needles cast on 102 sts. and work 10 cm/4" K2, P2 rib (rows on right side have K2 at each end) and decreasing 1 st. at end of last row (101 sts.).
Change to 4 mm/8 needles, and starting with a purl row on right side facing, continue straight in reverse st.st.
If bobble pattern is desired on the back, follow the 20 pattern rows as given and continue the pattern to complete the back.
Continue until work measures 30.5 cm/12", ending with right side facing for start of next row.

Shape armholes

Cast off 6 sts. at beg. of next 2 rows, then K2tog at each end of next and every alternate row until 77 sts. remain.
Continue straight until back measures 49cm/19.5".

Shape shoulders

With right side facing, cast off 8 sts. at beginning of next 6 rows.
Cast off.

Sleeves (Both Alike)

With 3.2 mm/10 needles cast on 42 sts. and work 7.5 cm/3" K2, P2, rib, decreasing 1 st. at end of last row (41 sts.).

Change to 4 mm/8 needles and start bobble pattern, increasing 1 st. at each end of 7th and every following 6th row until there are 73 sts., taking increased sts. into pattern as they are made.

Work in pattern without further shaping until sleeve measures 45.5 cm/18" ending with right side facing for next row.

Shape top

Cast off 4 sts. at beg. of next 2 rows, then K2tog at each end of next and every alternate row until 25 sts. remain. Cast off.

Front Bands

Left button band

With 3.25 mm/10 needles cast on 8 sts. and work a strip in K1, P1 rib to fit up left front edge when slightly stretched, having a knit st. at front edge. Sew in position and leave sts. on safety pin at top.

Right buttonhole band

Work a similar strip for right front with the addition of buttonholes. The first buttonhole is worked 16 mm/0.75" from lower edge and the last about 2.5 cm/1" from the top, allowing for an additional buttonhole to be worked into the neckband later. Mark out the remaining spaces for the number of buttons you wish to use along the left front band and make the buttonholes at equal intervals.
The model used 10 buttons in all, so 7 further buttonholes were needed between the top and bottom placings, which worked out at 14 rows between each buttonhole, which is worked over 2 rows as follows:
Buttonhole row 1: Rib 3, cast off 2, rib 3
Row 2: Rib 3, cast on 2, rib 3
Complete and leave sts. on safety pin at top. Sew in position.

Embroidery

The fronts are very much the focus of this cardigan, as with so many Tyrolean designs, and the recreated model has kept the embellishments to the front. It is suggested that the embroidery is worked before joining the pieces together for easier handling, especially if you choose to embroider the sleeves and back in addition to the fronts.

As there are no instructions given in the original pattern on how to execute the embroidery, the recreated model interpreted the two photographs from the original publication, working as follows:
Wool used was 4 ply in gold, green, cream, violet and pale blue.

The original Stitchcraft *pattern only gives the front cover and this black and white illustration as a guide to the embroidered details, so these can be interpreted individually.*

The placement of the embroidery followed the 3 squares along the front rib shaping, with additional leaves in adjoining squares, as shown in the photograph of the finished cardigan. The larger daisies were made with lazy daisy stitch using a single strand of violet, each petal filled with double strand of pale blue. A French knot in single strand of cream completes the centres. The smaller cream flowers are made with single strand of cream in lazy daisy for the petals, filled in with double strand, and a French knot in violet at the centre.
The stems are in single strand gold using stem stitch.
The leaves are in single strand green using lazy daisy stitch.

Join shoulder seams.

Neckband

With 3.25 mm/10 needles, rib the 8 sts. from the right front band, then pick up and knit 76 sts. all around the neck (23 sts. along right front neckline, 30 across back neck, 23 across left front neckline), then rib across the 8 sts. of the left front band.

Work 2.5 cm/1″ in K1, P1 rib, making last buttonhole on right front edge after 1.5 cm/0.5″ has been worked. Cast off loosely in rib (it helps to use a needle one size larger – 3.75 mm/9 – to achieve this easily and with regular stitches).

Making Up

Do not press.
Join side and sleeve seams and insert sleeves.
Sew on buttons.

Embroidered flowers in the recreated model have been worked in lazy daisy stitch, stem stitch and French knots.

CHAPTER 5

CREATING YOUR OWN TYROLEAN KNITWEAR

Creating your own Tyrolean vintage-style knitwear is a greatly rewarding opportunity to practise your skills and find new effects to enjoy. You can make your design into something authentically vintage by incorporating the features and techniques of the glory days of vintage knitting, combining your favourite elements from different patterns or creating something unique and modern as a contemporary statement of this enduring style.

The exclusive pattern created for this book offers a 'menu' of Tyrolean features and shapes, drawn entirely from vintage patterns and techniques. You can combine the elements as given, or use them as a starting point for your own inspiration. The intention is for this to inspire you to make your own individual creation where you can use your favourite elements (and of course avoid the ones you don't enjoy!), adding in or leaving out just as you wish. At each stage, knitted options are offered as alternatives where crochet is suggested, and similarly, alternative methods are described to replace intricate stitches and cables, substituting simpler knitting techniques.

The following pattern combines some of the distinctive features of 1930s and 1940s designs with some of the familiar details which celebrate Tyrolean style from every era. Notes are given to modify the shapes to suit different decades, and all techniques used here can be easily modified by using some of those suggested in the 'Texture through Stitches' section of Chapter 3.

Flowers for Laura: Design Decisions and Options

The Flowers for Laura pattern starts with a waistcoat version, offering optional sleeves, short or long, and a peplum which can be added separately or integrated into the body. Knit this to look more 1930s in style with softer gathered sleeves, or with even more pronounced shoulders and higher ribbing for a more dramatic 1940s look; all these options are here for you to enjoy making your own vintage-style Tyrolean knitwear.

The Colours

There is no doubt that the most popular colour combination for Tyrolean knitwear is for a cream background with coloured details. Classically, red is a favourite combination with the cream, reflecting the Tyrolean flag, with dark green and yellow also frequently appearing as accents in edgings, adding blue to these for embroidered details.

Some of the earliest Tyrolean patterns of the 1930s reveal that many surprisingly varied colourways were suggested and light pink, dark green or navy blue backgrounds were all favoured, with pastel or dark embroidery contrasts.

Flowers for Laura version without the peplum.

If you like the colour accent at the edges, but prefer not to crochet, you can create this by casting on with the contrast colour and changing to the main colour for the remaining rows of ribbing. You can introduce as many colours as you like to accentuate a Tyrolean-style border – red, green and yellow being the most typical in Tyrolean knitwear.

Contrast coloured edgings for highlighting the lines of a design.

The colours suggested in the original 1930s Copley's pattern for Annie's Jacket, included in the Pattern Collection, are an inspiration. Some colours will be more effective than others as backgrounds, and the 1960s and early 1970s taught us that excessive brightness and synthetic colours may be limited in their appeal in this context, but the message is to enjoy your own choice and not feel restricted to the more typical colour palette of cream background associated with Tyrolean knitwear through the decades. It has certainly left its mark, but it is not by any means exclusive.

The Ribbed Edge

One of the key features of 1940s knitted garments is the shorter body length, and typically with 3.5″ (9 cm) of ribbing, which is not only a flattering shape but also helps a shorter garment stay in place with a closer fit. The instructions given below for the Flowers for Laura cardigan give a shorter rib to allow for the separate peplum to be attached, but if you prefer a longer body (the finished design measures 47 cm/18.5″ as a standard length for knitwear at the time) you can add as many extra rib rows as desired. On average 10 rows give an extra 2.5 cm/1″ using 4 ply on 2.75 mm/12 needles, but check your tension with the yarn you are using.

The Stitches

The foundation for the distinctive style of so many Tyrolean vintage garments is to create textures and a 'grid' to frame embroidery work. There is such a variety of pattern, colour and stitches to choose from, you can make this very much your own. To create a full Tyrolean effect a combination of textured stitches and colour accents achieves the most effective design, but these can be interpreted in an infinite number of ways according to your preferences. The only note would be that texture alone isn't as striking at conveying the full Tyrolean effect as when there are touches of added colour. This can be minimal, such as one row of contrast colour on edgings, but it makes all the difference in making the Tyrolean statement.

The basic Tyrolean-style application of textured stitches has evolved to be very close to our own traditional Aran knitwear, and some characteristic touches are needed to be recognizably 'Tyrolean', whether with colour or other details, such as those in the designs chosen for the Pattern Collection.

If you prefer not to embellish with floral embroidery, there are alternative motifs offered in the 'Embroidery' section of Chapter 3, and more ideas in the 'Trimmings' section of Chapter 2. These are all taken from the original vintage patterns featured in the Pattern Collection, adding contrast coloured edgings, for example, to give the Tyrolean touch instead of floral motifs.

> Textured stitches don't have to be complicated to create an authentic effect. Alternative stitches for cables, bobbles and grids, which avoid using extra cable needles or demanding work, are given in the 'Stitches' section of Chapter 3. You can make this part as challenging or as simple as you wish.

The waistcoat version of the Flowers for Laura design.

Tyrolean-style waistcoats

Waistcoats rose in popularity during the 1940s, maybe for their additional promise of warmth, or to use less of the rationed wool. Whatever the reason, along with its close cousin, the sleeveless top, (which was favoured by the forces for insulation under uniforms but which doesn't really fit in here with Tyrolean styles) there were many more patterns available for waistcoats during this decade. Also included in the Pattern Collection are the very Tyrolean examples of Hollywood comes to Broadway and Heartfelt Waistcoat.

The Back

The back of the Flowers for Laura design can be worked plain to the yoke, where the textured double moss stitch is used to finish, tying in with the fronts. If preferred, the textured stitch panel can also be worked in to match the fronts, with or without the same embroidery details. A line of coloured stitching (embroidered in chain or running stitch) gives added accent to a plain back as seen in the Forties Favourite cardigan.

The Button Bands

You can work these in a number of different ways to create different effects and the options for the Flowers for Laura pattern are noted as part of the instructions for reference. Your choice may be determined by whether you like to work these

The back of the Flowers for Laura design can be left as plain stocking stitch, worked with the stitch textures, and embroidered as the front panels.

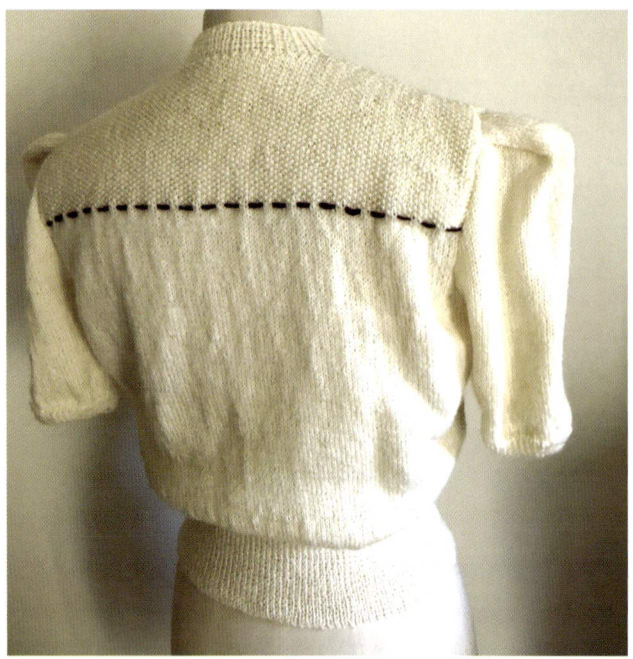

A line of contrast stitching defines the yoke as in the Forties Favourite pattern.

at the same time as the main knitting, or after the fronts are completed. If you like the vertical striped effect, these have to be worked afterwards, as with a contrast edging which will need to be knitted or crocheted after finishing the bands.

The Sleeves

Instructions are given for short or long sleeves, with two different sleeve headings to create either gathered or darted tops. Both are taken from original vintage patterns for authenticity and to emphasize the features of your favourite decade. Again, the edges can be accented with colour, by casting on and working the ribbing in your choice of contrasts, or added later after knitting is complete.

The Peplum

A delightful feature which appeared in many 1930s knitted patterns and never lost its charm, the peplum has remained especially popular in the realm of Tyrolean knitwear. There are many varieties of peplum shapes for knitting, and this design uses 'godets' to echo the textured detail, highlighted with the same contrast edging to accentuate the shape. Instructions for this are given both as a separate piece that can be tied on for the effect, or knitted integrally, with or without eyelet spaces through which to thread a tie cord, as desired. This feature was inspired by the details seen on the back of a jacket in one of the charming illustrations in the 1937 book *Original Tyrolean Costumes*[1].

Running contrast lines along the 'folds' of the peplum adds definition and impact to the godet shapes.

The inspiration for the peplum came from one of the illustrations found in the 1937 publication of traditional Tyrolean dress.

The Tie Cord

These have been a most popular feature of Tyrolean knitwear since the 1930s, adorning waists and neckbands. The earlier 1930s garments tend to place the waist cords relatively low, sitting on the hips, and though they do not often appear in 1940s patterns until after the war, they returned as a key feature in the 1950s, emphasizing a fashionably small waist.

Copley's reprinted their mid-1930s pattern for the Viennese Jacket, updating it to better suit the early 1950s style, and this illustrates how the longer peplum (and softer shoulder line) was preferred over the decades.

For the neckbands, tie cords can be threaded through eyelets knitted into the work, or through added crocheted loops. Bows fashioned of crocheted wool chains were also tied at the neck performing no function, but just as a decorative detail, as seen on the Forties Favourite cardigan.

Tie cords can be made up of one or many colours, finished by simply neatening the ends, adding tassels or cheerful pompoms of plain or mixed colours. Details on making these are given in Chapter 3 in the section on 'Finishing Touches'.

Copley's pattern 794 for a Lady's Viennese Coat, their first version from the 1930s with sharper shoulders and a shorter peplum.

Copley's later reprinted version of the Viennese Coat, renumbered 1890 and updated for the 1950s with softer shoulders and a longer peplum.

Embroidery

The pattern as given sets out four diamond-shaped spaces to embroider on each front and the back, offering a blank canvas for individual creativity. Any flowers or other motifs can be worked here – or into your own choice of grid or frame – in entirely your choice of colours and stitches. The stitch pattern is broken down into groups of stitches so that you can interchange with different ones of the same number. The 'Stitches' section of Chapter 3 offers a range of suggestions.

The spaces created by the textured stitch shapes in the Flowers for Laura cardigan can be embellished in an infinite number of ways. The original is embroidered with flowers in the diamond panels and contrast coloured lines to define the panels.

Edgings

In most vintage Tyrolean patterns, edgings are achieved by a variety of crochet stitches in contrasting colours, but if you prefer not to crochet, the contrast edgings can be worked by knitting with a contrasting colour and using this to cast on or cast off, as appropriate (this is noted in the pattern's instructions).

The arrangement of the textured stitches used in the Flowers for Laura pattern offers flexibility for substituting combinations and individual creativity.

If knitted edges are preferred to crochet, contrast colours are effectively introduced as in the Lilli Bolero pattern.

Buttons and Trimmings

These are often the reward for the work completed, adding the essential finishing touches and satisfying details to the garment. One of the distinctive elements of Tyrolean style until later in the 1950s is that all the garments were fastened down the front. Be they cardigans, jackets or waistcoats, Tyrolean style meant buttons, hooks or even zips, but there was always a fastened edge at the front.

Of all the elements of recreating vintage knitwear, buttons and trims are among the only haberdashery that are still available relatively easily. Novelty buttons have always been popular and are still made, so if the ideal match in original vintage is hard to come by then there will always be a modern style that will fit well.

If you find the perfect vintage buttons there may not always be the necessary number mentioned in the pattern, but as long as you have enough to effectively close the garment, you can re-adjust the spacing for the buttonholes to fit. (Guidance for this is given in the pattern.)

Hand-crocheted buttons were extremely popular through the decades, especially before the advent of cheaper plastic materials, and these work very effectively to complete any garment. Ironically, it is harder today to source the button moulds which were used then for covering with yarn, but they can be created without moulds, or using plain buttons which can be covered. (Instructions for making crochet buttons are included in the pattern for the Heartfelt Waistcoat.)

Very often, the details such as buttons will be the inspiration for colours or motifs to use, as with the Hollywood Comes to Broadway waistcoat, and can create the whole character of a garment.

Crochet buttons add a distinctly vintage touch, and are the ideal way to match the colour of buttons to the garment. The Heartfelt Waistcoat has its own buttons made in this way and the instructions on how to make them.

Flowers for Laura

Materials

The original design uses Cygnet Truly Wool Rich 4 ply in Cream (2614)
7 (8) × 50 g balls are needed in total for the short-sleeved version with peplum, as the original
For the waistcoat: 4 (5) × 50 g balls (plus 1 x 50g ball if adding the peplum)
For the short-sleeved cardigan without peplum:
6 (7) × 50 g balls
For the long-sleeved cardigan without peplum:
8 (9) x 50 g balls
For the cardigan with peplum: 7 (8) x 50 g balls for short sleeves and 9 (10) × 50 g balls for long sleeves

For all styles

1 × 50 g ball 4 ply contrast (and the same amount in each additional colour if desired)
1 pair 2.75 mm/12 needles (3 mm/11)
1 pair 3.25/10 needles (3.75 mm/9)
1 pair 3 mm needles (for larger size)
1 × 3.25 mm/10 double-pointed cable needle (3.75 mm/9)
1 × 3 mm crochet hook (3.25 mm/10)
1 × 3.5 mm crochet hook (for larger size)
6 × buttons (can be adjusted)
Optional shoulder pads

Measurements

To fit a size 86.5 cm/34" bust (instructions in brackets for 36–38")
Finished length centre back from neck to bottom edge 47 cm/18.5" without peplum
Finished length with peplum 51.5 cm/20.25"
Short sleeves seam length 11.5 cm /4.5"
Long sleeves seam length 46 cm/18"
Peplum height 10 cm/4"

Tension

28 sts. to 10 cm/4" on 3.25 mm/10 needles.

Left Front

If you wish to knit the peplum as an integral part of the design, please start at the peplum instructions given below.

A note on working the button band integrally if wished: Instructions are given without an integral button band but if you wish to knit this as you go, cast on 69 sts. and work the additional 10 sts. at the front edge of each row in K1, P1 rib throughout (please note this is not given in the main instructions).

You can also work these extra stitches until the ribbed section is complete, and leave the 10 extra stitches on a safety pin. You can then pick them up again when the front piece is finished and work the remaining bands on the smaller needles, as used for the main ribbing, which will ensure the regularity of the stitches.

Remember to make the buttonholes on the right front as you go if you are working the band integrally, following the instructions given for the separate buttonhole band for spacings and buttonholes, which are given below.

For a knitted contrast coloured edge, cast on with C then change to M after ribbing is complete.

With main colour M and 2.75 mm (3 mm) needles, cast on 59 sts. and work in K1, P1, rib until work measures 5 cm/2", or to desired length to make finished garment longer than 47 cm/18.5". Allow about 10 rows per additional 2.5 cm/1" required but check your tension and the yarn used.

If you prefer to alter the choice of textured sts: the groups of stitches forming the panels are set out as 11, 10, 14, 10, 14 (st. st at side, cable, grid, cable, double moss st. at front edge) and in reverse order for the right front. You can substitute other pattern sts. in each of these groups (for example, for a mock cable that doesn't use a separate cable needle but noting that the cable is worked over two rows) for the same number of sts. – please see instructions in the 'Stitches' section of Chapter 3.

Change to 3.25 mm (3.75 mm) needles and set the pattern as follows – every row is given for guidance.

**(continue with work from here if knitting the integral peplum, with or without line of eyelet holes for threading a cord).

1st row: K11, P1 K8 P1, then P6 T2B P6, then P1 K8 P1, (K2, P2) 3 times, K2

The groups of stitches for the pattern sections will be marked in this way throughout, separated by commas, to help if substituting alternative groups of stitches if desired, as indicated above.

2nd row: P2 (K2 P2) 3 times, K1 P8 K1, K6 P2 K6, K1 P8 K1, P11

3rd row: K11, P1 K8 P1, P5 T2F T2B P5, P1 K8 P1, (P2 K2) 3 times P2

4th row: K2 (P2 K2) 3 times, K1 P8, K1, K5 P4 K5, K1 P8 K1, P11

5th row: Inc. in 1st st. K10, P1 C8B P1, P4 T2F K2 T2B P4, P1 C8B P1, (K2 P2) 3 times K2

6th row: P2 (K2 P2) 3 times, K1 P8 K1, K4 P6 K4, K1 P8 K1, P12

7th row: K12, P1 K8 P1, P3 T2F K4 T2B P3, P1 K8 P1, (P2 K2) 3 times P2

8th row: K2 (P2 K2) 3 times, K1 P8 K1, K3 P8 K3, K1 P8 K1, P12

9th row: K12, P1 K8 P1, P2 T2F K6 T2B P2, P1 K8 P1, (K2 P2) 3 times K2

10th row: P2 (K2 P2) 3 times, K1 P8 K1, K2 P10 K2, K1 P8 K1, P12

11th row: Inc. in 1st st. K11, P1 K8 P1, P1 T2F K8 T2B P1, P1 K8 P1, (P2 K2) 3 times P2

12th row: K2 (P2 K2) 3 times, K1 P8 K1, K1 P12 K1, K1 P8 K1, P13

13th row: K13, P1 K8 P1, T2F K10 T2B, P1 K8 P1, (K2 P2) 3times K2

14th row: P2 (K2 P2) 3 times, K1 P8 K1, P14, K1 P8 K1, P13

15th row: K13, P1 C8B P1, T2B K10 T2F, P1 C8B P1, (P2 K2) 3 times P2

16th row: K2 (P2 K2) 3 times, K1 P8 K1, K1 P12 K1, K1 P8 K1, P13

17th row: Inc. in 1st st. K12, P1 K8 P1, P1 T2B K8 T2F P1, P1 K8 P1, (K2 P2) 3 times K2

18th row: P2 (K2 P2) 3 times, K1 P8 K1, K2 P10 K2, K1 P8 K1, P14

19th row: K14, P1 K8 P1, P2 T2B K6 T2F P2, P1 K8 P1, (P2 K2) 3 times P2

20th row: K2 (P2 K2) 3 times, K1 P8 K1, K3 P8 K3, K1 P8 K1, P14

21st row: K14, P1 K8 P1, P3 T2B K4 T2F P3, P1 K8 P1, (K2 P2) 3 times K2

22nd row: P2 (K2 P2) 3 times, K1 P8 K1, K4 P6 K4, K1 P8 K1, P14

23rd row: Inc. in 1st st. K13, P1 K8 P1, P4 T2B K2 T2F P4, P1 K8 P1, (P2 K2) 3 times P2

24th row: K2 (P2 K2) 3 times, K1 P8 K1, K5 P4 K5, K1 P8 K1, P15

25th row: K15, P1 C8B P1, K5 T2B T2F K5, P1 C8B P1, (K2 P2) 3 times K2

26th row: P2 (K2 P2) 3 times, K1 P8 K1, K5 P4 K5, K1 P8 K1, P15

27th row: K15, P1 K8 P1, P6 T2B P6, P1 K8 P1, (P2 K2) 3 times P2

28th row: K2 (P2 K2) 3 times, K1 P8 K1, K6 P2 K6, K1 P8 K1, P15

29th row: Inc. in 1st st. K 14, P1 K8 P1, P6 T2B T2F P6, P1 K8 P1, (K2 P2) 3 times, K2

30th row: P2 (K2 P2) 3 times, K1 P8 K1, K5 P4, K5, K1 P8 K1, P16

31st row: K 16, P1 K8 P1, P4 T2F K2 T2B P4, P1 K8 P1, (P2 K2) 3 times P2

32nd row: K2 (P2 K2) 3 times, K1 P8 K1, K4 P6 K4, K1 P8 K1, P16

33rd row: K16, P1 K8 P1, P3 T2F K4 T2B P3, P1 K8 P1, (K2 P2) 3 times K2

34th row: P2 (K2 P2) 3 times, K1 P8 K1, K3 P8 K3, K1 P8 K1, P16

35th row: Inc. in 1st st. K15, P1 C8B P1, P2 T2F K6 T2B P2, P1 C8B P1, (P2 K2) 3 times P2 (65 sts.)

36th row: K2 (P2 K2) 3 times, K1 P8 K1, K2 P10 K2, K1 P8 K1, P17

37th row: K17, P1 K8 P1, P1 T2F K8 T2B P1, P1 K8 P1, (K2 P2) 3 times K2

38th row: P2 (K2 P2) 3 times, K1 P8 K1, K1 P12 K1, K1 P8 K1, P17

39th row: K17, P1 K8 P1, T2F K10 T2B, P1 K8 P1, (P2 K2) 3 times P2

40th row: K2 (P2 K2) 3 times, K1 P8 K1, P14, K1 P8 K1, P17

41st row: K17, P1 K8 P1, T2B K10 T2F, P1 K8 P1, (K2 P2) 3 times K2

42nd row: P2 (K2 P2) 3 times, K1 P8 K1, K1 P12 K1, P17
43rd row: K17, P1 K8 P1, P1 T2B K8 T2F P1, P1 K8 P1, (P2 K2) 3 times P2
44th row: K2 (P2 K2) 3 times, K1 P8 K1, K2 P10 K2, K1 P8 K1, P17
45th row: K17, P1 C8B P1, P2 T2B K6 T2F P2, P1 C8B P1, (K2 P2) 3 times K2
46th row: P2 (K2 P2) 3 times, K1 P8 K1, K3 P8 K3, K1 P8 K1, P17
47th row: K17, P1 K8 P1, P3 T2B K4 T2F P3, P1 K8 P1, (P2 K2) 3 times P2
48th row: K2 (P2 K2) 3 times, K1 P8 K1, K4 P6 K4, K1 P8 K1, P17
49th row: K17, P1 K8 P1, P4 T2B K2 T2F P4, P1 K8 P1, (K2 P2) 3 times K2
50th row: P2 (K2 P2) 3 times, K1 P8 K1, K5 P4 K5, K1 P8 K1, P17
51st row: K17, P1 K8 P1, P5 T2B T2F K5, P1 K8 P1, (P2 K2) 3 times P2
52nd row: K2 (P2 K2) 3 times, K1 P8 K1, K6 P2 K6, K1 P8 K1, P17
53rd row: K17, P1 K8 P1, P6 T2B P6, P1 K8 P1, (K2 P2) 3 times K2
54th row: P2 (P2 K2) 3 times, K1 P8 K1, K6 P2, K6, K1 P8 K1, P17
55th row: K17, P1 C8B P1, P5 T2F T2B P5, P1 C8B P1, (P2 K2) 3 times P2
56th row: K2 (P2 K2) 3 times, K1 P8 K1, K5 P4 K5, K1 P8 K1, P17
57th row: K17, P1 K8 P1, P4 T2F K2 T2B P4, K1 P8 K1, (K2 P2) 3 times K2
58th row: P2 (K2 P2) 3 times, K1 P8 K1, K4 P6 K4, K1 P8 K1, P17
59th row: K17, P1 K8 P1, P3 T2F K4 T2B P3, P1 K8 P1, (P2 K2) 3 times P2
60th row: P2 (K2 P2) 3 times, K1 P8 K1, K3 P8 K3, K1 P8 K1, P17
61st row: K17, P1 K8 P1, P2 T2F K6 T2B P2, P1 K8 P1, (K2 P2) 3 times K2
62nd row: (P2 (K2 P2) 3 times, K1 P8 K1, K2 P10 K2, K1 P8 K1, P17
63rd row: K17, P1 K8 P1, P1 T2F K8 T2B P1, P1 K8 P1, (P2 K2) 3 times P2
64th row: K2 (P2 K2) 3 times, K1 P8 K1, K1 P12 K1, K1 P8 K1, P17
65th row: K17, P1 C8B P1, T2F K10 T2B, P1 C8B P1, (K2 P2) 3 times K2
66th row: P2 (K2 P2) 3 times, K1 P8 K1, P14, K1 P8 K1, P17
67th row: K17, P1 K8 P1, T2B P10 T2F, P1 K8 P1, (P2 K2) 3 times P2
68th row: K2 (P2 K2) 3 times, K1 P8 K1, K1 P12 K1, K1 P8 K1, P17
69th row: K17, P1 K8 P1, P1 T2B K8 T2F P1, P1 K8 P1, (K2 P2) 3 times K2
70th row: P2 (K2 P2) 3 times, K1 P8 K1, K2 P10 K2, K1 P8 K1, P17
71st row: K17, P1 K8 P1, P2 T2B K6 T2F P2, P1 K8 P1, (P2 K2) 3 times P2
72nd row: K2 (P2 K2) 3 times, K1 P8 K1, K3 P8 K3, K1 P8 K1, P17
73rd row: K177, P1 K8 P1, P3 T2B K4 T2F P3, P1 K8 P1, (K2 P2) 3 times K2
74th row: K2 (P2 K2) 3 times, K1 P8 K1, K4 P6 K4, K1 P8 K1, P17
75th row: K17, P1 C8B P1, P4 T2B K2 T2F P4, P1 C8B P1, (P2 K2) 3 times P2
76th row: K2 (P2 K2) 3 times, K1 P8 K1, K5 P4 K5, K1 P8 K1, P17
77th row: K17, P1 K8 P1, P5 T2B T2F P5, P1 K8 P1, (K2 P2) 3 times K2
78th row: P2 (K2 P2) 3 times, K1 P8 K1, K6 p2 K6, K1 P8 K1, P17
79th row: K177, P1 K8 P1, P6 T2B P6, P1 K8 P1, (P2 K2) 3 times P2
80th row: K2 (P2 K2) 3 times, K1 P8 K1, K6 P2 K6, K1 P8 K1, P17
81st row: K17, P1 K8 P1, P5 T2F T2B P5, P1 K8 P1, (K2 P2) 3 times K2
82nd row: P2 (K2 P2) 3 times, K1 P8 K1, K5 P4 K5, K1 P8 K1, P17
83rd row: K17, P1 K8 P1, P4 T2F K2 T2B P4, P1 K8 P1, (P2 K2) 3 times P2
84th row: K2 (P2 K2) 3 times, K1 P8 K1, K4 P6 K4, K1 P8 K1, P17

Shape armhole

85th row: Cast off 8 sts., K8, P1 C8B P1, P3 T2F K4 T2B P3, P1 C8B P1, (K2 P2) 3 times K2
86th row: P2 (K2 P2) 3 times, K1 P8 K1, K3 P8 K3, K1 P8 K1, P9
87th row: K2tog, K7, P1 K8 P1, P2 T2F K6 T2B P2, P1 K8 P1, (P2 K2) 3 times P2
88th row: K2 (P2 K2) 3 times, K1 P8 K1, K2 P10 K2, K1 p8 K1, P8
89th row: K2tog, K6, P1 K8 P1, P1 T2F K8 T2B P1, P1 K8 P1, (K2 P2) 3 times K2
90th row: P2 (K2 P2) 3 times, K1 P8 K1, K1 P12 K1, K1 P8 K1, P7
91st row: K2tog, K5, P1 K8 P1, T2F K10 T2B, P1 K8 P1, (P2 K2) 3 times P2
92nd row: K2 (P2 K2) 3 times, K 1 P8 K1, P14, K1 P8 K1, P6
93rd row: K2tog, K4, P1 K8 P1, T2B K10 T2F, P1 K8 P1, (K2 P2) 3 times K2

94th row: P2 K2 P2) 3 times, K1 P8 K1, K1 P12 K1, K1 P8 K1, P5
95th row: K2tog, K3, P1 C8B P1, P1 T2B K8 T2F P1, P1 C8B P1, (P2 K2) 3 times P2
96th row: K2 (P2 K2) 3 times, K1 P8 K1, K2 P10 K2, K1 P8 K1, P4
97th row: K2tog, K2, P1 K8 P1, P2 T2B K6 T2F P2, P1 K8 P1, (K2 P2) 3 times K2 (51 sts.)
98th row: P2 (K2 P2) 3 times, K1 P8 K1, K3 P8 K3, K1 P8 K1, P3
99th row: K3, P1 K8 P1, P3 T2B K4 T2F P3, P1 K8 P1, (P2 K2) 3 times P2
100th row: K2 (P2 K2) 3 times, K1 P8 K1, K4 P6 K4, K1 P8 K1, P3
101st row: K3, P1 K8 P1, P4 T2B K2 T2F P4, P1 K8 P1, (K2 P2) 3 times K2
102nd row: P2 (K2 P2) 3 times, K1 P8 K1, K5 P4 K5, K1 P8 K1, P3
103rd row: K3, P1 K8 P1, P5 T2B T2F P5, P1 K8 P1, (P2 K2) 3 times P2
104th row: K2 (P2 K2) 3 times, K1 P8 K1, K6 P2 K6, K1 P8 K1, P3
105th row: K3, P1 C8B P1, P6 T2B P6, P1 C8B P1, (K2 P2) 3 times K2 (this completes the last diamond grid)
106th row: P2 (K2 P2) 3 times, K1 P8 K1, K14, K1 P8 K1, P3
107th row: K3, P1 K8 P1, P14, P1 K8 P1, (P2 K2) 3 times, P2
108th row: K2 (P2 K2) 3 times, K1 P8 K1, K14, K1 P8 K1, P3
Change to 3 mm (3.25 mm) needles.
109th row: P1, then (K2 P2) to end of row
This sets the pattern for double moss st. to be continued for further 20 rows ending row 130.
131st row: K1, (P2 K2) to last 2 sts., P2

Shape neckline

132nd row: Cast off 6 sts., patt. to end
Then dec. 1 st. at neck edge on every row until 35 sts. remain.
Cont. in patt. as set for a further 24 rows without further shaping.
Next row: Cast off 9 sts. at side edge at beg.of next 3 rows alt
Work 1 row.
Cast off remaining 8 sts.

Right Front

For a knitted contrast edge, cast on with C then change to M after ribbing is complete.

If working with integral button bands, buttonhole placement is worked out as follows:

The buttonholes should be spaced equally and the easiest way to achieve this is by placing the buttons along the button band of the completed left front. If you plan to include a button at the neckband, remember to include this in allowing for the spacing.

Place pin to mark the first buttonhole 1 cm/0.5" from the bottom edge and mark for the top buttonhole 1 cm/0.5" from top edge.

If you plan to include a buttonhole and button in the neckband, remember to include this in allowing for the spacing.

Space the buttons equally along the left front button band and mark each place with a pin. Measure and adjust spacings to correct. If you can count the number of rows between markings, note this and use to guide the intervals for the buttonholes to be worked on the right front band.

If not, keep a count of the number of rows worked on right front section which matches the space between the first two markings made on left front band, and make a buttonhole accordingly, repeating at the same intervals along the front band as you go.

With main colour M and 2.75 mm (3 mm) needles, cast on 59 sts. and work in K1, P1, rib until work measures 5 cm/2", or to desired length as explained above for left front – remembering to make buttonholes if working the front bands integrally, as for left front.

Change to 3.25 mm/10 (3.75 mm/9) needles and working with M, set the pattern as follows:
**(continue with work from here if knitting the integral peplum, with or without line of eyelet holes for threading a cord).

1st row: K2 (P2, K2) 3 times, P1 K8 P1, P6 T2F P6, P1 K8 P1, K11 to end of row
This sets the pattern and stitch sequence. Work as for left front, reversing the sequence and increases on the opposite (underarm side) edge, and work C8F instead of C8B for cables so that the twist is in mirror image to the left front, for symmetry. Similarly, the twist stitches where the diamond grid lines cross together as set in row 1 are worked **T2F in place of T2B** (as marked in left front instructions).
Now you have completed the left front, the patterns will seem logical.
Work until 84th row is complete.
85th row: K2 (P2 K2) 3 times, P1 C8F P1, P3 T2F K4 T2B P3, P1 C8F P1, K to end of row
86th row: Cast off 8 sts. P8, K1 P8 K1, K3 P8 K3, K1 P8 K1, (P2 K2) 3 times P2
87th row: P2 (K2 P2) 3 times, P1 K8 P1, P2 T2F K6 T2B P2, K to end

88th row: P2tog, P7, K1 P8 K1, K2 P10 K2, K1 P8 K1, (K2 P2) 3 times K2
89th row: K2 (P2 K2) 3 times, P1 K8 P1, P1 T2F K8 T2B P1, P1 K8 P1, K to end
90th row: P2tog P6, K1 P8 K1, K1 P12 K1
91st row: P2 (K2 P2) 3 times, P1 K8 P1, T2F K10 T2B, P1 K8 P1, K to end
92nd row: P2tog P5, K1 P8 K1, P14, K1 P8 K1, (K2 P2) 3 times K2
93rd row: K2 (P2 K2) 3 times, P1 K8 P1, T2B K10 T2F, P1 K8 P1, K to end
94th row: P2tog P4, K1 P8 K1, K1 P12 K1, (P2 K2) 3 times P2
95th row: P2 (K2 P2) 3 times, P1 C8F P1, P1 T2B P8 T2F P1, P1 C8F P1, K to end
96th row: P2tog P3, K1 P8 K1, K2 P10 K2, K1 P8 K1, (K2 P2) 3 times K2
97th row: K2 (P2 K2) 3 times, P1 K8 P1, P2 T2B K6 T2F P2, P1 K8 P1, K to end
98th row: P2tog P2, K1 P8 K1, K3 P8 K3, K1 P8 K1, (P2 K2) 3 times P2 (51 sts.)
99th row: P2 (K2 P2) 3 times, P1 K8 P1, P3 T2B K4 T2F P3, P1 K8 P1, K3 to end
100th row: P3, K1 P8 K1, K4 P6 K4, K1 P8 K1, (K2 P2) 3 times K2
Continue as set until 108th row has been completed, remembering the last cables in row 105.
Change to 3 mm (3.25 mm) needles and work in double moss st. for yoke as follows:
109th row: (K2 P2) to last 3 sts., K2 P1
Continue straight as set until 132nd row has been completed.

Shape neckline

133rd row: Cast off 6 sts., continue in patt. to end of row
Dec. 1 st. at neck edge on every row until 35 sts. remain.
Work 24 more rows in pattern without further decreasing.
Cast off 9 sts. at the beg. of next 3 rows at side edge.
Work 2 more row.
Cast off rem. 8 sts.

Back

Plain and pattern panel versions begin alike:
With 2.75 mm (3 mm) needles and M (or C if chosen) cast on 118 sts.
Work 5 cm/2" (or desired length) in K1 P1 rib, as for fronts.
Change to 3.25 mm (3.75 mm) needles and M.

***continue from here if working the integral peplum back, with or without line of eyelet holes for threading a cord.

The instructions that follow are for the version with the patterned panel. For the plain stocking stitch version omitting the pattern panel, please see below from *continuing in stocking stitch throughout to the beginning of the yoke.

Patterned panel version

The centre pattern panel of 34 sts. is worked as for each of the front pieces (10 sts. cable, 14 sts., diamond grid, 10 sts. cable).
Place this as follows:
1st row: K 42, P1 K8 P1, P6 T2B P6, P1 K8 P1, K42
Now continue the pattern panel as given for left front.
Remember to increase at each end of 5th and every following 6th row until there are 126 sts.
Continue in pattern as set until 84 rows have been completed.

Armhole shaping
85th row: Continuing in pattern, cast off 8 sts. at beg. of each of the next 2 rows
Continuing in pattern, cast off 1 st. at beginning of next 8 rows until 102 sts. remain.
Cont. working in pattern until 108 rows have been completed.
Change to smaller needles and begin working yoke, as given below.

Stocking stitch version*

Work 4 rows.
5th row: Inc. at each end of K row
Continue in st.st increasing at each end of every following 6th row until there are 126 sts.
Continue working straight in st.st until 84 rows have been completed.

Armhole shaping
Cast off 8 sts. at beg. of each of the next 2 rows.
Cast off 1 st. at beginning of next 8 rows until 102 sts. remain.
Cont. working straight in st.st. until 108 rows have been completed.

Yoke

(Both versions.)
Change to 3 mm (3.25 mm) needles and continue in double moss st. as previously set (K2 P2 alternating) for a further 58 rows.
(*Using the smaller needles maintains a better shape for the yoke.*)

Shape the shoulders

Cast off 9 sts. at beg. of next 2 rows.
Then cast off 8 sts. at beg of next 6 rows (36 sts.).
Cast off remaining sts.

Button Bands

(If making separately.)
Work button band for left front first so that you can space the buttons (this is explained for integral button and buttonhole bands).

For separate bands: Remember to cast on in C if you have done this for the other parts.

Left front button band

Using 2.75 mm (3 mm) needles and M, cast on 10 sts. and work in K1 P1 rib so that this will fit along the inner edge of the left front, slightly stretched (*if you knit exactly the same length this has a tendency to ripple*). Keep a note of the number of rows worked to replicate for the right front buttonhole band, and to help with spacing the buttons at regular intervals. If you prefer a knitted neck band to be added (rather than crocheted), do not cast off the sts. of the completed button band but keep these on a safety pin to pick up later.

Sew the button band to the left front and mark out the spacings for the buttons (this will also act as your guide for placing the buttonholes when working the right front band), as given in the instructions for the right front integral button bands.

If you have kept note of the number of rows of rib worked to make the left front band, you can calculate the spacings mathematically.

If you are picking up the 10 sts. left on the safety pin after working the ribbing for each front: continue in ribbing on these 10 sts. with the smaller needles used, and complete as for instructions for the separate bands, as above.

Right front buttonhole band

Firstly follow the instructions above for marking button spacings on left front band, and make buttonholes at the regular marked/counted intervals as follows:
First buttonhole row: Rib 4, cast off 3 (or enough sts. to slide over buttons without over-stretching), rib 3
Second buttonhole row: Rib 3, cast on 3 sts. (or required number) over the cast-off sts. of previous row, rib 4
Repeat these 2 buttonhole rows for each of the number of buttons, keeping the same number of rows between each, and allowing for a buttonhole at the neckband if desired. Leave the sts. on a safety pin as with left front band to pick up later if you are adding a knitted neckband.

Working button bands along the whole edge

This method ensures the same number of rows are worked and an even spacing between buttonholes. It also allows for colours to be used to great effect in sequences to create vertical stripes, or as final row edging, as preferred. These bands are worked as follows:

Left front button band (horizontally knitted version)
Using 2.75 mm (3 mm) needles and chosen colour, with right side of work facing, pick up and knit stitches evenly all along the edge, without leaving gaps as much as possible, keeping a note of the number of stitches made (to replicate for right front band). Work in K1 P1 rib for 9 rows or more, depending on preferred width of band (and size of buttons), remembering to allow for the 2 rows needed to make each of the buttonholes, and finishing with right side facing. Cast off all along the row – this is effective if changed to a contrast colour to cast off.

Right front buttonhole band (horizontally knitted version)
With 2.75 mm (3 mm) needles and right side of work facing, using chosen colour, pick up and knit the same number of stitches as with the left front band. Work in K1 P1 rib for 5 rows. With right side of work facing, and in line with the markings on the left front button band, make buttonholes evenly spaced with the same number of stitches between

them, all along the row. You will need to adjust the number of stitches cast off to create a buttonhole to fit over the buttons you have chosen.

Place a marker pin along the rows you have already completed to mark the centre for each buttonhole, in line with the markings on the left front band.

First buttonhole row: Rib to within one st. (or more sts. as needed for larger buttons) of the first marker pin, cast off 3 (or enough sts. to slide over buttons without over-stretching). Rib to next marker and repeat the buttonholes along the row, casting off the same number of stitches and ribbing the same number between each.

Second buttonhole row: Rib to cast-off sts. of previous row, cast on 3 sts. (or same number of sts. as cast off in previous row) over the cast-off sts. of previous row. Rib to next group of cast-off sts. and repeat to complete the row. (This has the advantage of making all the buttonholes evenly in one row.)

Complete in ribbing to the same number of rows as worked for left front band, then cast off (using contrast colour as before, if chosen).

For a knitted neckband

Join the shoulder seams.

With right side of work facing, using 2.75 mm (3 mm) needles and M (for a neat foundation line), pick up and work the 10 rib sts. left on the safety pin, then pick up and K even number of sts. (38–40 sts.) along right side of neck edge up to shoulder seam. Then pick up and K 35 sts. along back neck edge, then pick up and K same number of sts. along the left neck edge as on right neck edge and finish with the 10 sts. from the safety pin at the top of the left button band. Now work 11 rows in K1 P1 rib (or desired number) using chosen colour(s) and making a buttonhole as before in the 6th and 7th rows at right front edge. Cast off.

Crochet neck edging and button bands

Join the shoulder seams together.

Start at bottom corner of right front edge, with right side facing.

With the 3 mm crochet hook and using M (*this ensures a neat foundation edge with which to continue, even if you then wish to vary the colours to complete the edging*).

Join the yarn to the work and ch.1. Then work a row of dc. along the front edge to the last st. at the top corner – 85 dc. were

A knitted neckband can be worked rather than a crochet edge, as seen in the Forties Favourite cardigan (instructions are also included as an option in the Flowers for Laura pattern).

The crochet neckband version, as it has been worked on the Flowers for Laura pattern, with contrast coloured finish.

worked in the original, but adjust this as needed (*keep a note of how many dc. stitches are worked so that this can be repeated on the left front edge*).

For the corner: Work 1 dc., ch.1, and a further dc. into the same stitch – this gives a neat corner.

Continue working a line of dc. along the neck edge to the shoulder seam – 32 dc. were worked in the original (again noting the number of dc. sts.); dc. across the back cast-off edge and down the second side of the neck to the top of the left front edge (32 dc.), ch.1 and work a second dc. in the same stitch for the corner, then continue working dc. along left front edge (85 dc.) This brings you back to the bottom corner of the left front. Ch.1 and turn, and work 1 dc. into each dc. of the previous round, working the corners as before.

You can work the buttonholes along the right front on any following row starting at this corner (these were worked in 3rd row of dc. in the original) as follows:

Buttonhole shaping in right front edge

In the original these were worked to fit 13 mm buttons:
Start row at bottom corner of right front: 2 dc., *ch.3, skip 3, 17 dc., rep fr. *to complete 6 buttonholes in total, ending last rep dc. to end of row. Turn corner as before.
In the next round, work dc. into the ch. sts. made to close the buttonholes, keeping the same number of original sts.

The original worked 4 rounds of dc. with the buttonholes in the third round. The 5th (last) round was worked in the contrast colour (red) for definition.
More rounds can be worked if a wider band is preferred, and if larger buttons require a wider backing. Other colours can be introduced very effectively and detailed edging stitches can be worked, such as the shell stitch of the 1940s Warm Red Cardigan (the pattern includes instructions for this).

The buttonholes worked into the crochet rows of the borders of Flowers for Laura.

The crochet shell stitch edging along the right border of the Warm Red Cardigan gives a pretty detail against the contrast of the main colour.

> You can repeat as many rounds as you wish to create the width of band preferred, but always finish with an even number if you wish to make one or more rounds in a different colour. This creates a neater finish due to the direction of the stitches.

Crochet sleeve edging

This is worked as 1 row of dc. into the cast-on row of the ribbing on the finished sleeves, making sure the stitches are eased to retain some stretch.

Sleeves

There are instructions given here for two styles of sleeve top, and for long and short versions.

Short sleeves: both versions, knit 2 alike

With 2.75 mm (3 mm) needles and M cast on 81 sts. (use C if preferred for cast-on row).
Work K1 P1 rib for 2.5 cm/1" (or more if a longer sleeve is required – the original length is 11.5 cm/4.5").
Change to 3.25 mm (3.75 mm) and work in st.st, increasing at each end of 3rd and every following 4th row, until there are 97 sts.
Work 3 more rows straight.

Shape top: gathered version

Cast off 5 sts. at beg of next 2 rows.
3rd row: K2tog at each end of row (85 sts.)
4th row and each alt. wrong side row: P
5th, 7th, 9th, 11th rows: K2tog at each end (77 sts.)
12th row: P
Now work 12 rows straight without shaping.
Next row: Dec 1 st. at each end of next 15 rows
Work 1 row straight.
Dec. 1 st. at each end of next 10 rows (27 sts.).
Next row: K1, K2tog across row
Cast off remaining sts.

Shape top: pleated version (emphasized 1940s shaping)

Cast off 5 sts. at beg. of next 2 rows.
Dec. 1 st. at beg. of every row until 45 sts. remain.

The darted sleeve top lends an unmistakeable 1940s flair, given as an optional sleeve in the instructions, as adapted from the original Forties Favourite pattern.

Cast off 15 sts. at beg. of next 2 rows then work 18 rows straight on remaining 15 sts.
Cast off.

Long sleeves

With 2.75 mm (3 mm) needles and M (or C if preferred) cast on 57 sts.
Work in K1 P1 rib for 29 rows.
30th row: Rib 7, (inc. 1 in next st., rib 5) rep to last 9 sts., inc. in next st., rib 8 (65 sts.)
Change to 3.25 mm (3.75 mm) needles and cont. in st.st., increasing at each end of 5th and every following 4th row until there are 97 sts.
Cont. straight without further shaping until work measures 46 cm/18" or desired length.

Shape top as preferred, as given above for short sleeves.

Peplum

A favourite of the 1930s and late 1940s.

The peplum of the Flowers for Laura cardigan is a distinctive vintage and Tyrolean feature, designed to be worked into the main knitting or as a detachable addition.

Peplum back

With 2.75 mm (3 mm) needles and M, cast on 226 sts.
K2 rows.
Change to 3.25 mm (3.75 mm) needles.
1st row: K18 *(P2 K2) 3 times P3, K20 rep fr. *ending last rep K18
2nd row: P18 *K1 (K2 P2) 3 times K2, P20 rep fr. *ending last rep P18
3rd row: K18 *(K2 P2) 3 times K2 P1, K20 rep fr. *ending last rep K18
4th row: P18 *K1 (P2 K2) 3 times P2, P20 rep fr. *ending last rep P20
5th row: K16 *sl.1, K1 psso (P2 K2) 3 times P3, K2tog, K16 rep fr. *
6th row: P17 *K3 (P2 K2) 3 times, P18 rep fr. *ending last rep P17
7th row: K17 *(K2 P2) 3 times K2 P1, K18 rep fr. *ending last rep K17
8th row: P17 *K1 (P2 K2) 3 times P2, P18 rep fr. *ending last rep P17
9th row: K16 *sl.1, K1, psso, P1 (K2 P2) 3 times, K2tog, K16 rep fr.*
10th row: P17 *(K2 P2) 3 times K1, P18 rep fr. *ending last rep P17
11th row: K17 *K1 (P2 K2) 3 times K18 rep fr. *ending last rep K17
12th row: P17 *(P2 K2) 3 times P1, P14 rep fr. *ending last rep P17
13th row: K16 *sl.1, K1, psso (K2 P2) twice K2 P1, K2tog, K16 rep fr. *
14th row: P17 *K1 (P2 K2) P2, P18 rep fr. *ending last rep P17
15th row: K17 *(P2 K2) twice P2 K1, K18 rep fr. *ending last rep K17
16th row: P17 *P1 (K2 P2) twice K2 P1, P18 rep fr. *ending last rep P17
17th row: K16 *sl.1, K1, psso K1(P2 K2) twice K2tog, K16 rep fr. *
18th row: P17 *(P2 K2) twice P1, P18 rep fr. *ending last rep P17
19th row: K17 *P1 (K2 P2) twice, K18 rep fr. *ending last rep K17
20th row: P17 *(K2 P2) K1, P18 rep fr. *ending last rep P17
21st row: K16 *sl.1, K1, psso P2 K2 P2 K1, K2tog, K16 rep fr. *
22nd row: P17 *P1 K2 P2 K2, P18 rep fr. *ending last rep P17
23rd row: K17 *K2 P2 K2 P1, K18 rep fr. *ending last rep K17
24th row: P17 *K1 P2 K2 P2, P18 rep fr. *ending last rep P17
25th row: K16 *sl.1, K1, psso P1 K2 P2, K2tog, K16 rep fr. *
26th row: P17 *K2 P2 K1, P18 rep fr.*ending last rep P17
27th row: K17 *K1 P2 K2, K18 rep fr. *ending last rep K17
28th row: P17 *P2 K2 P1, P18 rep fr. *ending last rep P17
29th row: K16 *sl.1, K1, psso K2 P1, K2tog, K16 rep fr. *
30th row: P17 *K1 P2, P18 rep fr. *ending last rep P17
31st row: K17 *P2 K1, K18 rep fr. *ending last rep K17
32nd row: P17 *P1 K2, P18 rep fr. *ending last rep P17
33rd row: K16 *sl.1, K1, psso P1, K2tog, K16 rep fr.*
34th row: P17 *K1, P18 rep fr. *ending last rep P17
35th row: K16 *sl.1, K2tog psso, K16 rep fr.*
36th row: P (118 sts.)

For a detachable peplum, cast off the remaining 118 sts.
For an integral peplum, proceed as follows:

Integral peplum (back)

For an integral peplum with no line of holes for threading a cord: continue working the pattern as given for the back from ***in the main instructions.

For an integral peplum with eyelets through which to guide a cord tie at the waist, proceed as follows:
Next row: K1, *w.f., K2tog, K1 rep fr. *to end
Next row: P (118 sts.)
Now work as 'back' from***.

Left and right peplum fronts (both knitted alike)

With 2.75 mm (3 mm) needles and M, cast on 113 sts.
K2 rows.
Change to 3.25 mm (3.75 mm) needles.
1st row: K14 *(P2 K2) 3 times, P3, K20, rep fr. *then rep to last 14 sts., K14
2nd row: P14 *K3 (P2 K2) 3 times, P20, rep fr. *ending last rep P14
3rd row: K14 *(K2 P2) 3 times K2, P1, K20, rep fr. *ending last rep K14
4th row: P14 *K1 (P2 K2) 3 times, P2, P20 rep fr.*ending last rep P14
5th row: K12 *sl.1, K1, psso, (P2 K2) 3 times P2, P1 K2tog, K16 rep fr. * ending last rep K12
6th row: P13 *K1 (K2 P2) 3 times, K2, P18, rep fr.*ending last rep P13
7th row: K13 *(K2 P2) 3 times, K2, P1, K18, rep fr.*ending last rep K13
8th row: P13 *(P2 K2) 3 times P2, P18, rep fr. *ending last rep P13

9th row: K12 *sl.1, K1, psso, P1 (K2 P2) 3 times, K2tog, K16, rep fr. *ending last rep K12
10th row: P13 *(K2 P2) 3 times K1, P18, rep fr. *ending last rep P13
11th row: K13 *K1 (P2 K2) 3 times, K18, rep fr.*ending last rep K13
12th row: P13 *(P2 K2) 3 times P1, P18 rep fr.*ending last rep P13
13th row: K12 *sl. 1, K1, psso, (K2 P2) twice K2, P1, K2tog, K16, rep fr.*ending last rep K12
14th row: P13 *K1 (P2 K2) twice P2, P18, rep fr. *ending last rep P13
15th row: K13 *(P2 K2) twice P3, K18, rep fr. *ending last rep K13
16th row: P13 * K1 (K2 P2) twice K2, P18, rep fr. *ending last rep P13
17th row: K12 *sl.1, K1, psso, K1 (P2 K2) twice, K2tog, K16 rep fr. *ending last rep K12
18th row: P13 *(P2 K2) twice P1, P18 rep fr. *ending last rep P13
19th row: K13 *P1 (K2 P2) twice, K18 rep fr. *ending last rep K13
20th row: P13 *(K2 P2) twice K1, P18 rep fr. *ending last rep P13
21st row: K12 *sl.1, K1, psso, P2 K2 P2 K1, K2tog, K16 rep fr.*ending last rep K12
22nd row: P13 *P1 K2 P2 K2, P18 rep fr. *ending last rep P13
23rd row: K13 *K2 P2 K2 P1, K18 rep fr.*ending last rep K13
24th row: P13 *K1 P2 K2 P2, P18 rep fr. *ending last rep P13
25th row: K12 *sl.1, K1, psso, P1 K2 P2, K2tog, K16 rep fr. *ending last rep K12
26th row: P13 *K2 P2 K1, P18 rep fr. * ending last rep P13
27th row: K13 *K1 P2 K2, K18 rep fr. * ending last rep K13
28th row: P13 *P2 K2 P1, P18 rep fr. * ending lat rep P13
29th row: K12 *sl.1, K1, psso, K2 P1, K2tog, K16 rep fr. *ending last rep K12
30th row: P13 *K1 P2, P18 rep fr. * ending last rep P13
31st row: K13 *P2 K1, K18 rep fr. * ending last rep K13
32nd row: P13 *P1 K2, P18 rep fr. * ending last rep P13
33rd row: K12 * sl.1, K1, psso, P1, K2tog, K16 rep fr. *ending last re K12
34th row: P13 *K1, P14 rep fr. * ending last rep P13
35th row: K12 *sl.1, K2tog, psso, K16 rep fr. *ending last rep K12
36th row: P (59 sts.)

For a detachable peplum, cast off the remaining 59 sts. and finish as from ****below.

For an integral peplum, proceed as follows:

Integral peplum (fronts)

For an integral peplum with no line of eyelets for a cord continue working the left and right front pieces from **in the main instructions.

For an integral peplum with a row of eyelets through which to thread a cord tie at the waist, proceed as follows:
Next row: K1, w.f., K2tog
Next row: P (59 sts.)
Now work from **in the main pattern as above to complete left and right fronts respectively.

****Finishing the detachable peplum

Sew the 3 pieces together at the sides to form the complete peplum.

With a 3 mm (3.5 mm) crochet hook, and right side of work facing, join M to bottom corner of side edge of right front and work a row of dc. all across (keep note of the number to repeat on the left side edge).

Ch.1 and turn, repeat to complete 4 rows.

Repeat on left front side edge with the same number of sts. (The contrast edge is worked after completing the top edge for threading the cord at the waist.) Sew in all ends.

Join M (or C if preferred) to first st. on top corner of right front edge of peplum. Now work a row of Trb sts into the cast-off sts. of the top edge, including the ends of the 4 crochet rows just completed down each side.

Ch.3, 1 trb. in next st., *ch.3, skip 3, now work 3 tr. (i.e one in each of next 3 sts.) rep fr. * all across top edge and fasten off.

With C, complete an additional row of dc. down each front edge and including the trb. sts. just worked across the top to make a neat edge.

For the tie cord

With 2 strands of C or M used together, and 3.5 mm crochet hook, leave ends of around 7.5 cm/3″ (for attaching tassels/pompoms) and make a chain of sc. of around 122 cm/48″ in length (or desired length). Leave 7.5 cm at the end before cutting.

For knitting the peplum integrally, a row of eyelets is created through which to thread the tie cord.

Making Up

Embroidery

You may wish to add embroidered details to the separate pieces before sewing together as this can make them easier to handle.

If desired, add lines of chain stitch (one worked into each knitted st.) to emphasize the edges of textured areas, such as the pattern panels and the godets of the peplum, as in the original design.

A line of chain stitch in a contrast colour defines the godets of the peplum where the textures change, adding to the effect.

In the waistcoat option of the Flowers for Laura design, the armholes are finished with a crochet or knitted edge, adding a contrast colour to complete.

For the Waistcoat

Crochet finish: With 3 mm (3.5 mm) crochet hook and M work a row of dc. all around armhole maintaining stretch by picking up more sts. if necessary (you may wish to use a slightly larger crochet hook for this). Ch.1, turn and repeat until 4 rows are completed. Change to C and with right side facing, dc. another row.

Knitted finish: With right side facing using 2.75 mm (3 mm) needles and M, pick up and K 130 sts. all around armhole. K1 P1 rib for 8 rows (or to width desired) and change to C. Cast off in C.

For the Cardigan

If you like the effect of the coloured edging at the armhole edge with the sleeves set in:

Work the armhole edge as above for the waistcoat before setting the sleeves in.

Mark the centre top of the sleeve and match to the shoulder seam, attaching the sleeves to the armholes by pinning the right side of the sleeve to the underneath (wrong side) of the body armhole edge. Stitch this down invisibly through the rows of crochet, leaving the last coloured row free as a 'ridge'.

The Flowers for Laura cardigan.

Set in the sleeves before sewing the side and sleeve seams together in one seam.
If not adding the crochet edging to the armhole:

Gathered sleeve: Mark centre of top cast-off edge and, with wrong sides together, pin this to match the shoulder seam and pin remaining sleeve top to armhole edge, adjusting the top of the sleeve with extra gathers if necessary to fit. Sew together.

Pleated sleeve: Join sides of central extension at sleeve top to the 15 st. cast-off edges to form darts.
Set in the sleeves as with gathered sleeves.

Waistcoat and Cardigan styles

Sew side and sleeve seams.
Sew on buttons.
If choosing a cord for the waistband, thread this through the holes of the detachable or integral peplum before finishing the ends of the cord.
Finish as preferred by sewing in the ends, or adding tassels or pompoms, using the ends to attach these firmly (*see* separate instructions for tassels in Chapter 3 section 'Finishing touches for drawstrings').

ENDNOTE

The last word rightfully goes to Baron Georg Franckenstein, whose preface to the charming book *Original Tyrolean Costumes* of 1937 foretold the timeless appeal of Tyrolean style into the future:

> The Tyrolean vogue … is the fashion of to-morrow as well as today… these will not quickly go out of fashion … and the wearer will assume their feeling of lightheartedness and have a happy smile for everyone she meets.

APPENDIX 1

Crochet Stitch Guide

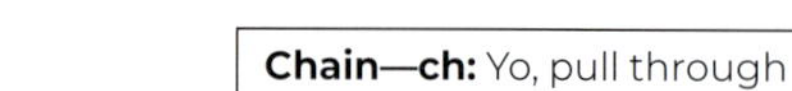

Chain—ch: Yo, pull through lp on hook.

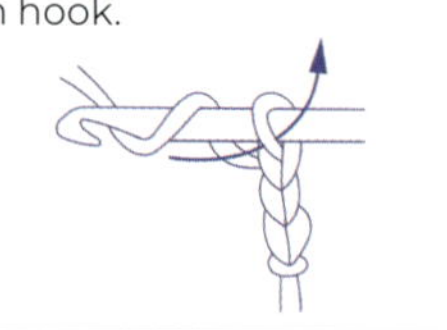

Slip stitch—sl st: Insert hook in st, yo, pull through both lps on hook.

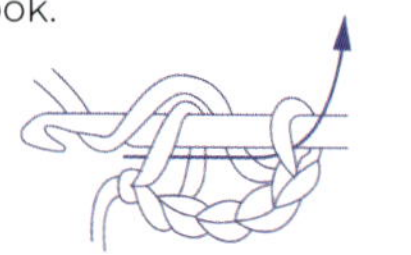

Single crochet—sc: Insert hook in st, yo, pull through st, yo, pull through both lps on hook.

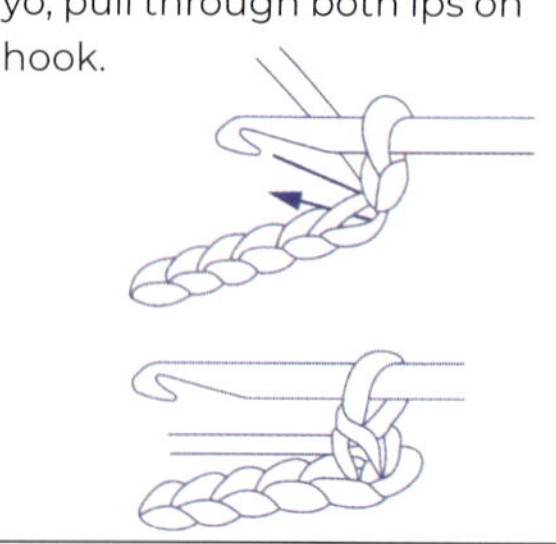

Front loop—front lp
Back loop—back lp

Front Loop Back Loop

Front post stitch—fp:
Back post stitch—bp: When working post st, insert hook from right to left around post st on previous row.

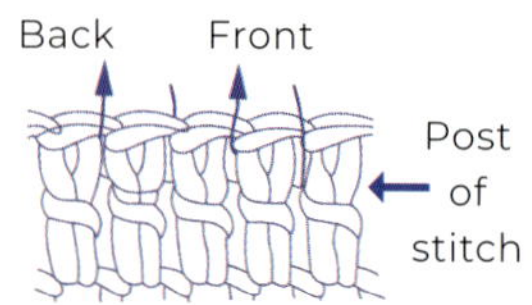

Half double crochet—hdc:
Yo, insert hook in st, yo, pull through st, yo, pull through all 3 lps on hook.

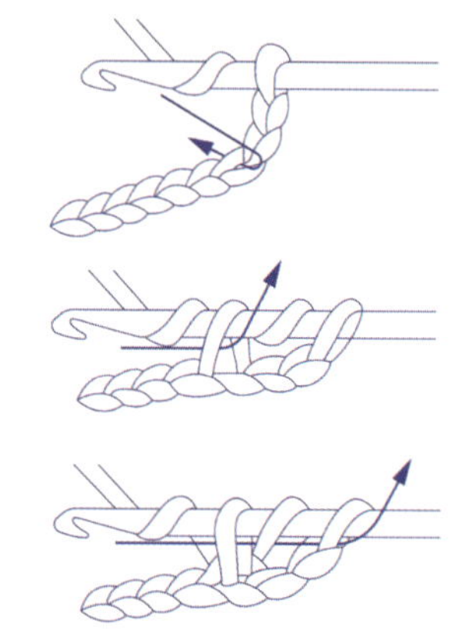

Double crochet—dc:
Yo, insert hook in st, yo, pull through st, [Yo, pull through 2 lps] twice.

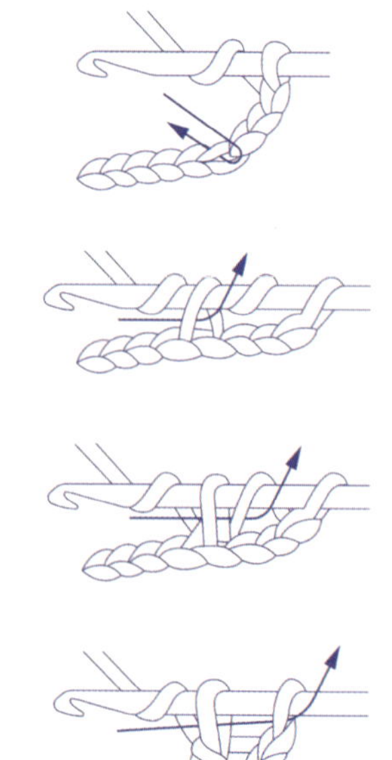

Change colours: Drop first colour; with 2nd colour, pull through last 2 lps of st.

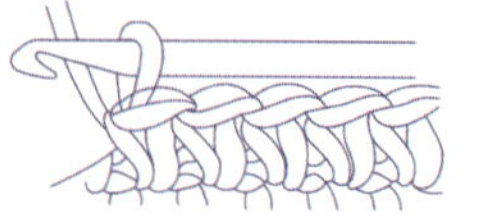

Triple crochet—tr: Yo 2 times, insert hook in st, yo, pull through st, [Yo, pull through 2 lps] 3 times.

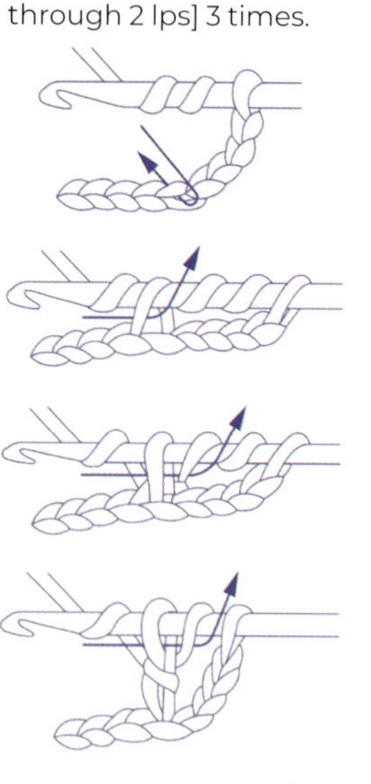

Double triple crochet—dtr:
Yo 3 times, insert hook in st, yo, pull through st, [Yo, pull through 2 lps] 4 times.

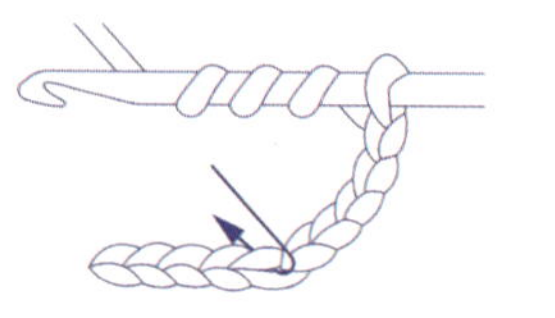

APPENDIX 2

Knitting Needle Size Conversion Chart

Metric (mm)	Old UK	US
2	14	00
2.25	13	0
2.75	12	1
3	11	2
3.25	10	3
3.75	9	4
4	8	5
4.5	7	6
5	6	7
5.5	5	8
6	4	9
6.5	3	10
7	2	10.5
7.5	1	11
8	0	12
9	00	13
10	000	15

REFERENCES

Chapter 1

1. 'Reboux Tyrolean Hat', *Vogue*, December 1924, by Porter Woodruff.
2. *Going Tyrolian, Vogue*, November 1931, by William E. Powell.
3. *Vogue*, October 1933, *Miss Whitney Bourne in the shadow of the Tyrol.*
4. Cherie Burns, *Searching for Beauty, the Life of Millicent Rogers, the American heiress who taught the world about style*, St Martin's Press, 2011.
5. As above, p.130.
6. Baron Georg Franckenstein (Preface), *Original Tyrolean Costumes*, Herbert Reichner, 1937.
7. Article on Lanz, FIDM Museum and Galleries, 2012. https://blog.fidmmuseum.org/museum/2012/03/lanz-original-late-1940s.html#more.
8. Virginia Pope, 'High Style Knitting'. *The New York Times,* 19 July 1936.
9. Jonathan Walford, *Forties Fashion: From Siren Suits to the New Look*, Thames and Hudson, 2008.
10. Trudi Kanter, *Some Girls, Some Hats and Hitler*, Virago Press, 2012.
11. Edina Ronay, *The Edina Ronay Collection*, Sidgwick and Jackson Limited, 1988.
12. Debbie Bliss and Fiona McTague, *Country Knits*, Ebury Press, 1990.
13. Rowan Yarns, *Vintage*, Rowan Yarns Ltd, 2004. Original design by Sarah Dallas.
14. Martin Storey for Rowan Classic, *Alpine*, Rowan Yarns Ltd, 2008.
15. Tamsin Blanchard, Telegraph.co.uk article on the Chanel fashion show, 2 December 2014. http://fashion.telegraph.co.uk/article/TMG11268361/Chanel-Metiers-Dart-Paris-Salzburg-2015-show.html.
16. Nicole Phelps, Vogue Runway article on the Givenchy SS 2015 fashion show, 29 September 2014. https://www.vogue.com/fashion-shows/spring-2015-ready-to-wear/givenchy.
17. Style.com for *Vogue*, article on the influence of Tyrolean style on haute couture. https://en.vogue.me/archive/legacy/chanel-salzburg-tyrolean-style-trends/.

Image of Millicent Rogers provided courtesy of the Millicent Rogers Museum, El Prado, New Mexico.

Chapter 4

1. Original Copley's 636 Knitting Leaflet reproduced by kind permission of Teresa Young.
2. Jane Waller, *Knitting Fashions* of the 1940s, The Crowood Press Ltd., 2006.

Chapter 5

1. Baron Georg Franckenstein (Preface), *Original Tyrolean Costumes*, Herbert Reichner, 1937.

SUPPLIERS

Wool and Yarns

Cygnet Yarns Ltd.
www.cygnetyarns.com

King Cole wool
www.kingcole.com

West Yorkshire Spinners wools
www.wyspinners.com

Stylecraft Yarns
www.stylecraft-yarns.co.uk

Original Vintage Hats, Clothes and Accessories

Maggie Mae's Vintage
www.maggiemaesvintage.co.uk

Past Caring
www.etsy.com/shop/PastCaringVintage

INDEX

RELATED TITLES FROM CROWOOD

978 1 78500 802 3

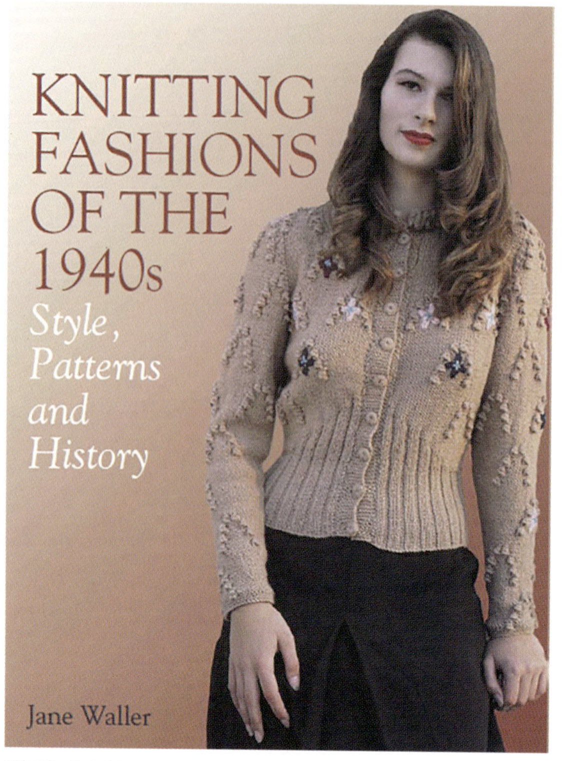

978 1 78500 789 7

978 1 78500 549 7

978 1 78500 569 5